Regulation and Tax in Space

Series on International Taxation

VOLUME 78

Series Editors

Prof. Ruth Mason, University of Virginia School of Law
Prof. Dr Ekkehart Reimer, University of Heidelberg

Introduction & Contents

The Series on International Taxation deals with a wide variety of topics in the global tax arena. The authors include many of the field's leading experts as well as talented newcomers. Their expert views and incisive commentary have proven highly useful to practitioners and academics alike.

Objective

The volumes published in this series are aimed at offering high-quality analytical information and practical solutions to international tax practitioners.

Readership

Practitioners, academics and policy makers in international tax law.

Frequency of Publication

2-3 new volumes published each year.

The titles published in this series are listed at the end of this volume.

Regulation and Tax in Space

Galya Savir

Wolters Kluwer

Published by:
Kluwer Law International B.V.
PO Box 316
2400 AH Alphen aan den Rijn
The Netherlands
E-mail: international-sales@wolterskluwer.com
Website: lrus.wolterskluwer.com

Sold and distributed by:
Wolters Kluwer Legal & Regulatory U.S.
7201 McKinney Circle
Frederick, MD 21704
United States of America
Email: customer.service@wolterskluwer.com

ISBN 978-94-035-3393-3

e-Book: ISBN 978-94-035-3394-0
web-PDF: ISBN 978-94-035-3395-7

As always, for Ohad, Oriel, Hila, Ofir, Noyah, Ronen and Ben

About the Author

Dr. Galya Savir wrote *Tax Infinity & Beyond* as a research scholar at the University of Michigan in 2016. A pioneer in the field of space taxation in the era of the Second Space Age, Dr. Savir researched the tax regime of space source incomes, at both the U.S. federal and the international levels, to which emerging entrepreneurs will be subjected after risking very high up-front capital, while addressing the importance of reshaping tax rules for the rapidly advancing space industry.

Dr. Savir received her doctoral degree from the University of Virginia School of Law. She holds an LL.M. in Tax from the University of Michigan Law School and a B.A. in Economics.

Dr. Savir practices tax law at a BigLaw firm in New York City. She also has experience as a lawyer at a major aerospace company.

Table of Contents

Preface

The emerging space mining industry brings many of today's global governance challenges. The legal issues that arose with the development of the deep-sea mining industry are also likely to appear in the context of the commercialization and privatization of outer space. This book lays out an analysis of what the similarities and differences of the legal challenges in space and deep-sea mining might suggest about the appropriate resource management regime and the tax system for the space mining industry. Due to the fragile and complex nature of extraterritorial resources in both realms and the external costs, environmental concerns, and hazards associated with the commercial exploitation of their resources—all leading to the difficult issues surrounding the assignment of ownership rights to these resources—a unique tax methodology is necessary to ensure that costs and profits of space mining are equitably and efficiently shared on a global basis. Ultimately, the most efficient resource management regime, alongside a predictable tax system, will provide the emerging space industry with the certainty and stability required for its evolution.

Consequently, any resolution to this problem requires that domestic laws be coordinated through an international framework. I propose that the space mining regime should incorporate regulation schemes that protect common world resources and ensure that the costs and benefits of using and conserving them are distributed in a productive and equitable manner. I conclude that a system along the lines of the international royalty regime, provided by the United Nations Convention on the Law of the Sea (UNCLOS), can be a fair and efficient mechanism for allocating the benefits of space resources. This unique tax measure will support a sustainable and equitable socioeconomic development of the space industry through an optimal resource management regime. However, in order not to be perceived as a preliminary trial to monopolize/colonialize the futuristic and looming ecosystem in space, by imposing taxes without nexus to the ecosystem on Earth, the royalty regime in space may need to be reevaluated and mitigated due to other factors when dealing with space, such as the liability risk of the launching state. This book explores how this regime would need to be tailored to meet the specific demands of space mining while ensuring the sustainability and competitiveness of this industry.

Acknowledgments

I would like to take this opportunity and express my deepest gratitude to Professor Andrew Hayashi for his invaluable support and comments at every step along this journey. I am also grateful to Professor Ruth Mason for her input and support, without which this book would not have seen the light of the day. Further, I would like to thank Professor Reuven Avi-Yonah for providing insightful comments and advice. Finally, special thanks to the University of Virginia School of Law.

CHAPTER 1

Introduction

In Old English and Dutch law, the term "commons" represented property or resources that were jointly exploited and subject to common management, which included, for example, shared grazing grounds or village squares.[1] However, when thought of in the field of property law, "commons" denotes resource domains in which "common-pool resources" are perceived to be free for all—particularly regarding access to these domains, or the exploitation thereof, as these cannot be efficiently limited to a "pool" of users.[2] As a result, no single decision-making unit holds exclusive title to these resources; they belong to everyone (*res communis*) and yet are of no one (*res nullius*).[3] As a result, their burdens and profits are jointly shared, a situs which can have a direct effect on the tax ownership test.

For thousands of years, it has been known that space is likely physically infinite. Practically, however, it is not. The resources embedded in asteroids and on the moon that are near enough for exploitation by humanity are finite and nonrenewable. This is especially true given our currently limited ability to traverse even small areas of our solar system. These resources are exhaustible, and so some set of legal rules or principles is necessary to coordinate the exploitation of those resources in an efficient way.[4] The allocation regime of space resources involves fundamental issues, such as the exploitation of global commons, optimal timing, and the inevitable trade-offs between revenue collection and economic efficiency. As a result, the mechanisms for the allocation of space resources, and thus, the tax base derived from the utilization of

1. Per Magnus Wijkman, *Managing the Global Commons*, 36.3 INT'L ORG. 511-36 (1982).
2. T.L. Anderson et al., *Property Rights as a Common Pool Resource*, in BUREAUCRACY VERSUS ENVIRONMENT: THE ENVIRONMENTAL COSTS OF BUREAUCRATIC GOVERNANCE (J. Baden & R.L. Stroup ed., 1981).
3. Nico Schrijver, *Managing the Global Commons: Common Good or Common Sink?*, 37 THIRD WORLD QUARTERLY, 1252, 1253-54 (2016) (hereinafter "Schrijver").
4. Stephan Hobe ed., *Does International Space Law Either Permit or Prohibit the Taking of Resources in Outer Space and on Celestial Bodies, and How Is This Relevant for National Actors? What Is the Context, and What Are the Contours and Limits of This Permission or Prohibition?* INT'L INST. OF SPACE L. 32 (IILS Directorate of Studies 2016) (hereinafter "IILS Directorate of Studies").

these resources, must be defined and created in a way that will ensure efficient use of space resources that is accompanied with a fair and stable tax system. After all, both the regulatory and tax frameworks will have a direct effect on the development of a sustainable space industry.

This book focuses on the possibilities of optimal resource management regimes in space and ways for distributing space resource revenues subject to the common property problems. For doing so, I shall list some of the objectives of the taxation of space resources. Given the uncertainty of this resource allocation regime, I am going to propose a tax system for space resources beyond the conventional tax forms as an international royalty regime, which will help achieve important goals for this industry such as efficiency, administrative convenience and equity.

The management of the various international commons—the oceans, outer space, and Antarctica—is still evolving, as is the very "commonality" of these areas. For example, although the oceans were thought to contain limitless resources, changes in the last century have altered our notions regarding their infinite resources, and now, we have come to realize the need to protect them as scarce resources while drawing boundaries for these global commons. In the case of the oceans, the high seas are governed by the UN Convention on the Law of the Sea (UNCLOS).[5] The high seas are the oceans beyond the Exclusive Economic Zone (EEZ) of each state, which extends seaward up to 200 nautical miles (nm) from its borders. Within the EEZ of each state is its territorial sea, the area which extends seaward up to 12 nm from its baselines borders.[6] No state may subject any part of the high seas to its sovereignty.[7] All states, including landlocked states, have an equal right to the high seas, although, of course, some states have much greater access to the high seas than others. These equal rights are not absolute and must be operationalized when paying heed to the interests of other states.[8]

The Law of the Sea is an ambitious and advanced set of international conventions for regulating the seas, the seabed, and its resources,[9] which attempts to provide a great

5. The United Nations Convention on the Law of the Sea (UNCLOS), also called the Law of the Sea Convention or the Law of the Sea Treaty, is the international agreement that resulted from the third United Nations Conference on the Law of the Sea (UNCLOS III), which took place between 1973 and 1982, United Nations Convention on the Law of the Sea, Nov. 16, 1994, U.N.T.S. 397 (hereinafter "UNCLOS").
6. Anthony Aust, Handbook of International Law 290 (Cambridge University Press 2d ed. 2010) (hereinafter "Aust"); *see also* Nat. Oceanic & Atmosphere Admin., Office of General Counsel, *Maritime Zones and Boundaries* (hereinafter "Maritime Zones and Boundaries"); UNCLOS, *supra* note 5, under Art. 86.
7. UNCLOS, *supra* note 5, under Art. 89.
8. UNCLOS, *supra* note 5, under Art. 87.
9. The Law of the Sea formed a comprehensive legal framework for marine and maritime activities governing the rights of nations with respect to the world's oceans by addressing a number of topics, including economic zones of the sea, the continental shelf, rights to the deep seabed, navigational rights in territorial and high seas, conservation and management of the living resources of the sea, protection and preservation of the marine environment, and others. On the international level, the Convention has created three new institutions: the International Tribunal for the Law of the Sea, which is headquartered in Hamburg (Germany), the International Seabed Authority, which is headquartered in Kingston (Jamaica), and the Commission on the Limits of the Continental Shelf, based in the United Nations Headquarters in New York. It now has 162

deal of legal clarity over what would otherwise be contested areas. The Law of the Sea limits both the territorial sea and the outer limits for internal waters and delineates the boundaries to separate the common seas from EEZs, and by so doing creates different economic systems. By contrast, the boundaries in outer space, including how far national airspace extends above the Earth's surface, remain unclear,[10] and the question of which management regime applies for attributing ownership over space resources has yet to be settled under international space law.

In many respects, the nascent asteroid-mining frontier resembles the ocean-mining frontier as it appeared years ago. Similar legal concerns and questions that might arise regarding the commercialization and privatization of outer space are already being debated in the context of the emerging ocean-mining industry, which is engaged in the exploitation of seabed minerals, such as copper, manganese, cobalt, and other rare elements. With the increasing exploitation in the high seas, there are growing concerns about the regulation and protection of marine environments, and similar concerns will likely arise regarding asteroid mining and the debris expected to be generated as a byproduct of this endeavor.

Currently, on the high seas, there are concerns about the conservation of marine life, the impacts of human activity and the levels and limitations of extraction of marine

---

Parties including the European Union. The Convention comprised of 320 articles, together with 9 annexes on different topics. *See* International Union for Conservation of Nature, *Marine and Polar*; Barbara Bean, *Law of the Sea*, AM. SOC'Y OF INT'L L. 1, 4 (Apr. 7, 2015). *See also* Charles Sheppard ed., WORLD SEAS: AN ENVIRONMENTAL EVALUATION: VOLUME III: ECOLOGICAL ISSUES AND ENVIRONMENTAL IMPACTS (2018). "*The United Nations Convention on the Law of the Sea (UNCLOS) sets out an international legal framework governing the oceans, including shipping. UNCLOS codifies the rules underlying the nationality (registry) of ships, the right of innocent passage for merchant vessels through other nations' territorial waters.*" The legal instruments that are part of the Law of the Sea: *Convention on the Territorial Sea and Contiguous Zone*, entry into force: Sept. 10, 1964; *Convention on the Continental Shelf*, entry into force: Jun. 10, 1964; *Convention on the High Seas*, entry into force: Sept. 30, 1962; *Convention on Fishing and Conservation of Living Resources of the High Seas*, entry into force: Mar. 20, 1966.

10. The altitude from which outer space begins is controversial, and many scholars suggest different altitudes should serve as demarcation points and definitions for non-tax purposes. The developing countries are more likely to adopt the definition which states that space begins at the highest possible point, since they do not have space capabilities and would like to claim sovereignty on space-based products, such as low geostationary satellite. *See Treaty on Principles Governing the Activities of States in the Exploration and Use of Outer Space, Including the Moon and Other Celestial Bodies*, U.N. Doc. A/AC.105/C.2/SR. 355 (1967); *see also* Hobe Stephan, *Legal Aspects of Space Tourism*, 86 NEB. L. REV. 439, 441-42 (2007). Nonetheless, in 1977, the USSR suggested to the Committee on the Peaceful Uses of Outer Space ("COPUOS") the altitude of 110 km above sea level as the demarcation point. The U.S. argued that there is no real usefulness in establishing a boundary and no practical need because "air space and outer space were separated by a buffer zone of about a hundred miles; whereas aircraft, apart from such experimental craft as the X-15, flew at much lower altitudes. There was therefore no problem of ambiguity for the time being." But it should be noted that today this reality has changed. *See* U.N. Secretary-General, *The Question of the Definition and/or the Delimitation of Outer Space*, at 1-7, 22, 42 and 59, U.N. Doc. A/AC.105/C.2/7 (1970). *See also* Galya Savir, *Tax Infinity & Beyond*, available at SSRN 2812866, at 45-46 (2016) (hereinafter "Savir, *Tax Infinity & Beyond*"); Gbenga Oduntan, *The Never Ending Dispute: Legal Theories on the Spatial Demarcation Boundary Plane Between Airspace and Outer Space*, 1 HERTFORDSHIRE L. J. 67 (2003) (hereinafter "Gbenga Oduntan, *The Never Ending Dispute*"). For the definition of "Space" for tax purposes, *see infra* note 364.

resources that should be permitted.[11] These concerns are evident in the consensus reached by the Commission for the Conservation of Antarctic Marine Living Resources (CCAMLR) when twenty-four countries and the European Union established the biggest marine reserve, almost as large as Alaska, in the Ross Sea in Antarctica as the largest international organization committed to ensuring the protection of marine life in Antarctica.[12] This agreement was only reached following years of negotiations, months of pressure on Moscow, and an intervention from former United States (U.S.) Secretary of State, John F. Kerry. Kerry's intervention led to a consensus regarding the designation of a 600,000 square mile area as a no-fishing zone for thirty-five years (subject to consensus decision by CCAMLR to extend this period), ultimately creating the world's largest marine protected area in the Ross Sea. This accord was preceded by years during which the fishing industry was a multimillion-dollar industry—with the help of generous government subsidies. However, the future of the success of this framework highly depends on maintaining worldwide consensus.[13] Similar concerns regarding the extraction of space resources, which seem to lay open to be ripen, and the threats that space debris hovering over Earth impose, are likely to emerge when dealing with commons in space. These concerns could be addressed and resolved by the international community, but more likely to be resolved with prominent interventions, delegations and pressures from space-faring countries, such as the U.S., that supports the commercialization of space for many years at the expense of its taxpayers.

Although private industry has made billions of dollars of investments in space exploration and seems prepared for commercial exploitation, legal and tax rules have not kept pace.[14] The prospect of large asteroid-mining industries, which could be expected to generate economic profits but are also associated with environmental hazards and damages, lends some urgency to legal development in this area. This book will argue that space should be regulated, and space mining subjected to licensing

11. Pew Charitable Trusts, *Deep Sea Mining: The Basics Fact Sheet* (Feb. 3, 2017). *See also* Olive Heffernan, *U.N. Makes a Bold Move to Protect Marine Life on the High Sea*, Sci. Am (Sept. 7, 2018); Matt McGrath, *UN Treaty Would Protect High Seas from Over Exploitation*, BBC News (Sept. 4, 2018).
12. Commission for the Conservation of Antarctic Marine Living Resources, *About CCAMLR*, CCAMLR (Oct. 15, 2019); Conservation Measure 91-05 (2016) (Commission for the Conservation of Antarctic Marine Living Resources); *see also* Thomas Repstad, *Is Krill Oil Sustainable?*, Superbakrill (Jun. 19, 2019).
13. Somini Sengupta, *Nations Will Start Talks to Protect Fish of the High Seas*, Climate, The N.Y. Times (Aug. 2, 2017) (hereinafter "Sengupta, *Nations Will Start Talks to Protect Fish of the High Seas*"); *see also* Staff Reporter, *Russia Comes to the Party as CCAMLR Reaches Agreement on Marine Protected Area for Ross Sea*, The Antarctic Report (Oct. 28, 2016); Sonia Feng, *Bid to Expand Antarctic Marine Protection Area Fails: Conservationist*, Reuters (Oct. 28, 2017); Michelle Innis, *Coast of Antarctica Will Host World's Largest Marine Reserve*, The N.Y. Times (Oct. 27, 2016); John F. Kerry, *China's Chance to Save Antarctic Sea Life*, Opinion: The N.Y. Times (Oct. 26, 2020).
14. Jeff Greason et al., *The Economics of Space: An Industry Ready to Launch*, Reason Found. (Jun. 5, 2019); *see also* Robin Hanbury-Tenison et al., *Debate: For and against Space Exploration—Is Space Research a Waste of Time?*, Eng'g & Tech. (Jan. 1, 2017); *see also* Kamil Muzayka, *The Problems with an International Legal Framework for Asteroid Mining*, in Deep Space Commodities, Exploration, Production and Trading 123-40 (James Tom ed. 2018); Atossa Araxia Abrahamian, *How a Tax Haven Is Leading the Race to Privatise Space?*, The Guardian (Sept. 15, 2017).

requirements that would allow for the protection of common space resources and ensure that the costs of conservation and utilization of space resources will be financed by a stable fiscal regime to which the tax rules for the mining industry will be tailored.

The need to overcome the difficulties of determining who should own and manage extracted space resources will affect the assignment of tax liabilities. Consequently, the dilemma is: will tax jurisdiction go to the residence country of the miners/mining companies, or of the consumer bases (even if the consumption is conducted in space itself),[15] or to the source country, where the end users and the marketplace are located, or be allocated among the international community by the establishment of collective ownership over mankind's treasures in space.

Tax policymakers are already engaged with the challenges that arise from allocating the tax base for digital businesses,[16] but the jurisdictional boundaries associated with commercial space mining industries are even more uncertain. There are other, perhaps even more daunting, challenges in the space context, including the fact that important business assets from space mining might always stay outside of, and be used outside of, any Earthly jurisdiction. Yet, providing the space industry with clear rules for the allocation of a tax jurisdiction and resolving any legal ambiguities around the ownership and management of space resources are necessary steps to foster the space mining industry. Forging global cooperation on the space economy by creating guidelines and principles to establish shares of interest that would benefit all countries from the world's shared commons would secure a sustainable development of the space economy.

A useful point of comparison is the economy and taxation of industry operating in the high seas. However, even when compared with the complexity of the high seas, outer space poses additional and unique challenges to forming an equitable and efficient tax system. Again, these challenges arise from geographic distance, i.e., geographic proximity of space to all countries, the fact that space is out of immediate reach of any state, and the prospect that a whole new economy severed from Earth shall evolve in space. Although space mining operations will likely maintain some economic contacts with Earth that could create a taxable nexus in the short and medium term, either via tangibles or intangibles, such as intellectual property supporting space technology developed on Earth, in the long term, these connections are likely to be severed when a sustainable and independent space economy evolves in space by itself—along with new human life.

15. Similar proposals regarding the authority to tax out-of-states' transaction even without the vendor's physical nexus, but subject to the existence of other economic nexus criteria was led by the OECD's initiative for taxing digital commerce. Chris Livingston and David Deputy, *Tax: A Critical Element of E-Commerce Business Success*, FEI DAILY (Oct. 29, 2019). *See also* Organisation for Economic Cooperation and Development (OECD), *Public Consultation Document, Addressing the Tax Challenges of the Digitalisation of the Economy*, 1, 9-11 (Feb. 13, 2019) (hereinafter "OECD, *Addressing the Tax Challenges of the Digitalisation of the Economy*").

16. Arthur J. Cockfield, *Designing Tax Policy for the Digital Biosphere: How the Internet Is Changing Tax Laws* 34 CONN. L. REV. 333 (2001); *see also* OECD, *Addressing the Tax Challenges of the Digitalisation of the Economy*, *supra* note 15, at 6-22; OECD, *Programme of Work to Develop a Consensus Solution to the Tax Challenges Arising from the Digitalisation of the Economy, OECD/G20 Inclusive Framework on BEPS* (2019).

For these reasons, this book proposes an international royalty regime as one component of a system for sharing and splitting the profits and risks from space mining. The royalty tax may not be a permanent feature of the tax regime applicable to all space activities, particularly when emancipated space colonies have evolved, but it solves a number of problems in the short and medium term, so long as economic activities in space remain connected to Earth. In the long term, the proper taxation of space mining will likely need to be reevaluated in light of the new hazards and other factors that the space mining industry might involve while dealing with its commons. Since the taxation of economic activity in space must be complementary with the allocation of economic rights, I begin by discussing ways in which resources from space should be owned and managed.

CHAPTER 2

Exploitation: Allocating Resources from Outer Space

A. INTRODUCTION

Since 1957, when Sputnik 1 was launched, space has been considered as a commons for all humanity, as was later reflected in the Outer Space Treaty. This treaty was designed with the intention of providing governing principles for outer space in the geopolitical environment of the Cold War, a time when the main participants going into space were nations, not private corporations.[17] Space activities and technologies have since shifted, from being mainly concerned with military applications, which have been regulated by the United Nations (U.N.) Committee on the Peaceful Uses of Outer

17. Treaty on Principles Governing the Activities of States in the Exploration and Use of Outer Space, including the Moon and Other Celestial Bodies, U.K.-Russ.-U.S., Arts. I, II, U.N.T.S. 205 (Jan. 27, 1967) (hereinafter "Outer Space Treaty"); *see* also Jennifer Frakes, *The Common Heritage of Mankind Principle and the Deep Seabed, Outer Space, and Antarctica: Will Developed and Developing Nations Reach a Compromise?*, 21 WIS. INT'L L. J. 409 (2003) (hereinafter "Frakes"); Steven Freeland, *Common Heritage, Not Common Law: How International Law Will Regulate Proposals to Exploit Space Resources*, 35 QILJ 19-33, 32 (2017) (hereinafter "Freeland, *Common Heritage*").

Space[18] (COPUOS) since 1959,[19] to being predominantly focused on commercial interests.[20]

This new development raises economic questions, such as who should cover the costs of space exploration and exploitation, and consequently, who should profit from developing these operations. All these must be considered when designing a tax regime that encourages entrepreneurship and a sustainable investment climate for space operations.[21] The way that investments will be made in space depends on both international and domestic economic policies, as well as the legal obligations of states reflected in trade, investment and tax treaties and agreements.

An overarching concern that must guide investments in exploitation of space is that international covenants on economic, human, social and environmental rights should be preserved, especially when dealing with resources that are commons.[22] Just as in the case of terrestrial mining, which is required to comply with laws protecting local community values including environmental protection,[23] the regulation of economic activity in space, specifically mining, should address similar concerns. Although several of these concerns have already been enshrined under international space law principles, they must continue to be respected. Broad international cooperation and agreement as to how to safeguard the interests of every stakeholder in the space industry are required. Happily, there is reason to think that this is possible in light of the successful negotiations for the exploitation of natural resources in other nonterritorial areas, such as the cooperation achieved by the management of frequency usage

18. G.A. Res. 1472 (XIV), *International Co-operation in the Peaceful Uses of Outer Space* (Dec. 12, 1959) (hereinafter "G.A. Res 1472 (XIV)").
19. United Nations Committee on the Peaceful Uses of Outer (COPUOS) was established by the U.N. General Assembly in 1959, shortly after the advent of the space age brought on by the successful launch of Sputnik 1, in order "to govern the exploration and use of space for the benefit of all humanity: for peace, security and development." *See* United Nations Office for Outer Space Affairs, *United Nations Committee on the Peaceful Uses of Outer Space*: *Membership Evolution*; *see also* G.A. Res 1472 (XIV), *supra* note 18. *See also International Co-operation in the Peaceful Uses of Outer Space*, G.A. Res 1472 (XIV), U.N. GAOR, 14th session, 856th plenary meeting, U.N. Doc. A/RES/1472 (XIV) (Dec. 12, 1959). It currently has 92 Member States, which means that it is "one of the largest Committees in the United Nations."
20. For a list of private commercial spaceflight companies, including space mining companies, please *see* Wikipedia, *List of Private Spaceflight Companies* (last edited Aug. 18, 2019), https://en.wikipedia.org/wiki/List_of_private_spaceflight_companies.
21. Freeland, *Common Heritage*, *supra* note 17.
22. Elisabeth Bürgi Bonanomi, *Trade Law and Responsible Investment*, in INTERNATIONAL INSTRUMENTS INFLUENCING THE RIGHTS OF PEOPLE FACING INVESTMENTS IN AGRICULTURAL LAND, 66-88 (International Land Coalition et al. eds. 2011); *see also* Elisabeth Bürgi Bonanomi, *Sustainable Investment in Land in the Global South: What Would It Require from a Coherence Perspective? The Case of Sierra Leone*, 2 QILJ 434-35, 444 (2015).
23. An example for such legislation can be found under the following statutes: the National Environmental Protection Act, Endangered Species Act, Clean Water Act, Clean Air Act, National Historic Preservation Act and also including environmental standards in the text of the 1872 Mining Law. For criticism of the terrestrial mining industry as being an overregulated and why adding more statutes will not provide additional environmental benefits, *see also* Hal Quinn, the President and Chief Executive of the National Mining Assn., *Readers React: Why Updating the 1872 Mining Act with Environmental Regulations Is Unnecessary*, L.A. TIMES (Apr. 14, 2019).

on the Geostationary Orbit, the governance of orbital slots and associated spectrum,[24] and by the deep-seabed management process agreement incorporated in the Law of the Sea Convention.[25]

The rules for taxation must be complementary to the property rights regime for space. Therefore, before arguing for a particular solution to the taxation question, I will explore potential resource management regimes for space. Aligning the law regulating the exploitation of space resources with the tax regime will provide the certainty and risk reduction necessary to sustain space mining operations and a stable space economy. The foremost concern is the need to consider the potential for a "tragedy of the commons" problem and market failures in relation to space resources, some of which have already arisen with regard to increasing space debris. In the case of common property, there is the tendency to misuse resources, via overuse or underuse, as it is challenging to make decisions for present and future stewardship without private property rights. This can result in resources being overexploited, thereby leaving little for future generations.[26]

There are well-established existing models that could be used in the context of the space resource management regime.[27] In the case of resources that have common-pool properties, competitive private market activities may lead to inefficient resource usage and market failure created by divergences between private and social costs and benefits. While private costs are being borne by a firm or a consumer, production and consumption decisions based on these costs will generate a rate of output that is socially efficient only when there are no external costs (also known as spillover effects) that society needs to bear.[28] Where external costs are associated with a business activity, these should be added to the private costs, to ensure that, in a competitive market, society produces and consumes a socially efficient rate of output, since these costs (both the private and the external costs) together reflect the social costs. These external costs, which typically exist where environmental values are involved, have

24. S. Freeland and R. Jakhu, *Article II of the Outer Space Treaty*, in COLOGNE COMMENTARY ON SPACE LAW, VOLUME I—OUTER SPACE TREATY 44-63 (S Hobe, B Schmidt-Tedd and K Schrogl eds., Carl Heymanns Verlag 2009); *see also* Guilhem Penent, *Governing the Geostationary Orbit Orbital Slots and Spectrum Use in an Era of Interference*, NOTE DE L'IFRI 70 (January 2014). According to Art. 44 of the ITU Constitution "radio frequencies and any associated orbits, including the geostationary-satellite orbit, are limited natural resources and that they must be used rationally, efficiently and economically." "This is a delicate and complex issue, involving political, economic and strategic interests of countries, as well as strong economic interests of existing satellite operators."
25. Frakes, *supra* note 17; UNCLOS, *supra* note 5; *see also* Annex to the Agreement relating to the Implementation of Part XI of the United Nations Convention on the Law of the Sea of Dec. 10, 1982.
26. Carol Rose, *The Comedy of the Commons: Custom, Commerce, and Inherently Public Property*, 53 U. CHI. L. REV. 711-81, 712 (1986) (hereinafter "Carol Ross"). ("[W]hen things are left open to the public, they are thought to be wasted by overuse or underuse. No one wishes to invest in something that may be taken from him tomorrow, and no one knows whom to approach to make exchanges. All resort to snatching up what is available for "capture" today, leaving behind a wasteland.")
27. Freeland, *Common Heritage*, *supra* note 17, at 30-33.
28. BARRY C. FIELD, ENVIRONMENTAL ECONOMICS: AN INTRODUCTION, 52 and 63-73 (McGraw-Hill/Irwin 4th ed. 2006), at (hereinafter "Field, Environmental Economics").

clear impacts on product pricing, levels of output, amount of resources used, and competition.[29] When external costs are internalized, either by the producers/firms or the consumers, the output rate would be lower and at a higher price than when only private costs are considered and would result in a better societal outcome from an efficiency perspective since lower output would generate less negative externality.[30] For example, the private costs associated with mining should include either the costs of purchasing equipment, maintenance, depreciation, and hired labor when viewed from the producers' perspective or the price of minerals when viewed from a consumer's perspective. However, mining activities also carry external costs, as typical with business activities that carry environmental values, such as pollution, environmental degradation, and the clean-up of debris. When the environmental costs are borne by neither the miners nor the consumers, inefficiency occurs, since the whole of society needs to bear these costs. As a result, the extracted goods are likely to end up being sold at an inefficient rate, which means at a lower price and at a higher quantity level than it should be when the market value of the goods correlates with their social value. Furthermore, in the case of mining open-access resources, such as seabed and space resources, the inefficiency can lead to a competitive advantage, even across states and nations, as space and seabed miners can gain an advantage over terrestrial miners if the latter is obligated to bear and internalize the external costs associated with their business operations and productions while the former is not.

An open-access resource is a resource that is open to uncontrolled access by individuals who wish to use the resource. Thus, there is no mechanism to control the level of its usage in order to maximize its overall value and be socially efficient.[31] The differences between the market value (as set in a competitive market by the difference between the willingness to pay/the marginal benefit curve and the marginal cost curve) and the social value (when external costs are added) indicate a market failure and economic inefficiency. Once the social and market values correlate and external costs are internalized, either by the consumers or the producers/firms, the market reaches economic efficiency. At this point, the goods are sold at a higher price and the output rate of production should be lower than in the case where neither the producers/firms nor the consumers pay for the external costs, since in the latter case too much output is being produced and sold at a lower price since no one pays for the external costs.[32]

Such market failures can be resolved by forms of collective agreements among producers or by government actions that can improve competitive market performance.[33] An example of the former is the case of oil and gas extraction, where adjacent surface rights have access to a common underground pool of oil or gas. In these cases,

29. Federal Reserve Bank of San Francisco, *What Is the Difference between Private and Social Costs, and How Do They Relate to Pollution and Production?*, Publications (November 2002).
30. Field, Environmental Economics, *supra* note 28; Federal Reserve Bank of San Francisco, *What Is the Difference between Private and Social Costs, and How Do They Relate to Pollution and Production?*, Publications (November 2002).
31. Field, Environmental Economics, *supra* note 28, at 73-74.
32. *Id.*, at 65 and 69-71.
33. Richard James Sweeney et al., *Market Failure, the Common-Pool Problem, and Ocean Resource Exploitation*, 17 J.L. & Econ. 179, 192, at 180 (1974) (hereinafter "Sweeney").

common resources were found to be successfully managed by the users of the wells under production-sharing solutions and operators' agreements that minimize the common-pool problems without government regulation or privatization.[34] Collective actions were also found more useful and advantageous for solving problems with the commons than actions from centralized agencies and institutions when dealing with small-scale organizations. The prominent explanation for this is that the interactions among a small number of players enable the participants to develop finely drawn practices and organizations by themselves for keeping an eye on and regulating standards for cooperation. Examples of such situations can be seen in the case of alpine pastures and forests communally owned by citizens of Swiss villages, communal meadows and forests in Japanese villages, and local irrigation reservoirs and ditches in Spain, and the Philippine Islands.[35] Additionally, an example of government intervention to solve the common-pool problem is the case of the fishing industry, where early governmental policies tried to control overfishing by restricting the number of fishing vehicles and the equipment that can be used and by assigning catch quotas under regulation of annual individual transferable quota system (ITQ) for setting total allowable catches.[36] Any resource management regime for space must manage the common-pool problem and market failures that exist there, while also providing economic actors with the incentive to make capital investments in space mining and increasing its value for future generations. The remainder of this chapter will discuss alternative management regimes and the advantages and disadvantages of each possibility. Additionally, to accompany the right to resource exploitation and management, an allocation mechanism for a new tax base and a new tax policy needs to be formed as soon as profits are derived from space resources. Therefore, the next chapter will further argue that, while shaping a just and efficient international tax regime for the space mining industry, the significance of exploring a space resource regime, even given its uncertainty, cannot be ignored.

34. T. Heaps and J. Helliwell, *The Taxation of Natural Resources*, in HANDBOOK OF PUBLIC ECONOMICS VOLUME I, 421-72, at 423 (Alan J. Auerbach and Martin Feldstein eds. North Holland 1985) (hereinafter "Heaps").

35. ELINOR OSTROM, GOVERNING THE COMMONS: THE EVOLUTION OF INSTITUTIONS FOR COLLECTIVE ACTION (Cambridge University Press 1990) (hereinafter "Ostrom"). Elinor Ostrom states that: "We can expect many groups to fail to achieve mutually productive benefits due to their lack of trust in one another or to the lack of arenas for low-cost communication, institutional innovation, and the creation of monitoring and sanctioning rules ... Without individuals viewing rules as appropriate ... no police force and court system on earth can monitor and enforce all the needed rules on its own." *See also* Theodore C. Bergstrom, *The Uncommon Insight of Elinor Ostrom*, 112.2 SCAND. J. ECON. 245-61, 246-48 (2010).

36. An example can be found in the success of the British Columbia ITQ system, which yields positive results in the fishery industry as costly monitoring systems are used to help enforce this system. *See* Wilson James, *Fishing for Knowledge*, 66.1 LAND ECON. 12-29 (1990); Daniel H. Cole et al., *The Variety of Property Systems and Rights in Natural Resources*, in 2 ELINOR OSTROM AND THE BLOOMINGTON SCHOOL OF POLITICAL ECONOMY, 134 (Daniel H. Cole and Michael D. McGinnis ed. 2015); CLARK W. COLIN, THE WORLDWIDE CRISIS IN FISHERIES: ECONOMIC MODELS AND HUMAN BEHAVIOR, 238-40 (CAMBRIDGE UNIVERSITY PRESS 2007).

B. EXPLORING AN EXPLOITATION MECHANISM FOR AN OPTIMAL YIELD

Before unleashing mankind to exploit resources in space for commercial purposes, a regulatory regime for securing the best optimal yield of the world's common resources should be explored. In Old English and Dutch law, the term "commons" represented the common management of property or resources that were jointly exploited.[37] However, in the terminology of property law, the term "commons" denotes resource domains to which access is open and free.[38] Theoretically, they could belong to no one (*res nullius*) or to everyone (*res communis*), and hence, only once captured can a legal title to these resources can be obtained.[39] A global commons, without a way of limiting access or exploitation, may be appropriate for resources that are in surplus; thus, their exploitation cannot be efficiently limited to a "pool" of users. On the other hand, property rights tend to be viewed as important for an efficient management of resources when those resources are scarce. The rationale for this distinction stems from the fact that when the supply of a resource is abundant and unlimited, there are no conflicts between claimants over the ownership and exploitation of that resource; individuals' use of the resource does not reduce the availability of the resource to anyone else. Property rights become more important when there is competition over scarce resources and the use by one person affects the use by another. An example where a resource that is abundant became a scarce resource and a market for property rights has been developed can be found in the settlement of plentiful land in the U.S., at a time when pioneers had the right to cultivate uncultivated land and to claim ownership of the developed land after a specific interval had passed without anyone else substantiating claims for the same piece of land. The squatter's ownership rights, once established, were not limited, but the squatter could proceed to deed or divide this property.[40] Once land became a scarce resource and a market for land rights developed, stronger economic incentives to protect their value and invest in their conservation arose.[41] If these principles were extended to the ocean or space arenas, similar

37. Per Magnus Wijkman, *Managing the Global Commons*, 36.3 Int'l Org. 511-36 (1982).
38. Schrijver, *supra* note 3, at 1253-54.
39. *Id. See also* Robert L. Friedheim, *Fishing Negotiations at the Third United Nations Conference on the Law of the Sea*, 22.3 Ocean Dev. and Int'l L. 209, 210 (1991) (hereinafter "Friedheim, *Fishing Negotiations*").
40. Clas G. Wihlborg et al., *Outer Space Resources in Efficient and Equitable Use: New Frontiers for Old Principles*, 24 J.L. & Econ. 23, 44 (1981) (hereinafter "Clas G., *Outer Space Resources*"); *see also* Margherita Colangelo, Creating Property Rights: Law and Regulation of Secondary Trading in the European Union, 15 (Martinus Nijhoff Publishers 2012) (hereinafter "Margherita Colangelo, Creating Property Rights").
41. National Center for Policy Analysis, *Progressive Environmentalism: A Pro-Human, Pro-Science, Pro-Free Enterprise Agenda for Change* (April 1991) (hereinafter "*Progressive Environmentalism*"); *see also* David E. Ault et al., *Land Scarcity, Property Rights and Resource Allocation in Agriculture: Eastern and Southern Africa*, 61.1 S. African J. Econ. 32-44 (1993); *see also* Terry L. Anderson et al., *The Evolution of Property Rights: A Study of the American West*, 18.1 J. L. and Econ. 163, 170 (1975). It is described how "[F]or much of the 1860's and 1870's 'squatter sovereignty' was sufficient for settling land ownership questions. But the growing demand for land by cattlemen, sheepherders, and grangers eventually caused the value of land to increase

incentives would arise among individuals to invest in the protection of their resources, which would otherwise be abandoned to the commons.

At first glance, space appears to be infinite. And while the physical boundaries of space may indeed be infinite, the part of it that is accessible for commercial exploitation is limited. In practice, it cannot absorb all human activities, especially given that, due to our limited ability to traverse even minute fractions of our solar system, the number of resources which are near enough to Earth for exploitation by humanity are finite;[42] moreover, space resources are, in fact, exhaustible, unlike traditional renewable "common-pool resources," such as fish stocks and grazing grounds. An argument can be made that whereas major stocks of common resources, such as the world fisheries, have been overexploited (or overfished) and stressed, their tragedy could be managed and resolved by a type of control management regime (i.e., by managing and rebounding their stocks efficiently).[43] However, in the case of nonrenewable resources, which are expected to be found in space, the threat of imminent tragedy might even exacerbate.[44] Therefore, ensuring an efficient allocation of rights to exploit resources in space will require some method of rationing, and this needs to preferably happen soon, as the space mining industry is in its nascent state.

The allocation of ownership of space resources has political implications, as well as economic implications. There is a common understanding that space is the "province of all mankind," and an inequitable distribution of the benefits of that common resource is apt to cause international conflict and division. This risk of inequities is especially great where legal complexities exist from the uncertain application of law under the international space regime.

Since the law for outer space has evolved as a separate and independent body of law within public international law, it is governed by five U.N. declarations and legal principles that direct conduct of space activities. The international space law is based mainly on five treaties negotiated and drafted in the COPUOS during the 1960s and 1970s.[45] Among these are the Outer Space Treaty[46] and the Moon

---

and hence increased the benefits from definition and enforcement activity." *See also* Walter Prescott Webb, The Great Plains, Vol. 766, 229 (U. of Nebraska Press 1959).

42. IILS Directorate of Studies, *supra* note 4, at 32.
43. Todd Woody, *The Sea Is Running out of Fish, despite Nation's Pledges to Stop It*, National Geographic (Oct. 8, 2019).
44. Friedheim, *Fishing Negotiations*, *supra* note 39, at 214. It should be noted that this argument ignores any variations in quality of the resources or their costliness when comparing space resources to terrestrial ones. However, in practice, it is expected that the exploitation of the first will be costlier (at least in the short or medium term), thus, the tragedy of both resources might be similar when judged in terms of economic values and extent. Additionally, it can be argued, that although the space resources are limited in total supply the prospectus resources contained in space hold huge potential even beyond the consumption capability of the whole mankind.
45. Freeland Steven, *Fly Me to the Moon: How Will International Law Cope with Commercial Space Tourism*, Melb. J. Int'l L. 11 90, 94 (2010).
46. Outer Space Treaty, *supra* note 17. Article I of the Outer Space Treaty declares that states are to explore and use outer space "for the benefit and in the interests of all countries" and that outer space "shall be the province of all mankind." Article II prohibits any means of appropriating outer space. Article III states that the exploration and use of outer space is to be in accordance with international law in order to maintain "international peace and security" and to promote "international cooperation and understanding."

Agreement.[47] Under both of these latter treaties, notions regarding non-appropriation of space resources and space as the "province of all mankind" are deeply enshrined. Reflecting that era, these treaties were joint accordances and mostly had accommodations that took place between the U.S. and the Soviet Union, which were the most important space competitors from that era. However, in the new modern space era, as space mining evolves, it is expected to have more space powers[48] involved at the international level when trying to solve questions that have been left unsettled under the space law, including the resource management regime. To support this vision, similar complexities can be seen in the case of ocean resources, where the political and economic implications and resolutions of seabed minerals' exploitation originated from many discussions and debates about the pros and cons associated with the accession to UNCLOS, which also established the notion that the "common heritage of mankind" should be used to govern the deep seabed.[49] Without agreed upon, equitable and enforceable rules that support the governance of the rights and duties of states with respect to the global commons, the pressure created by the demands for finite resources will have the capacity to destroy their economic value, efficiency and ecological integrity over time. Negative social and political implications will also follow as future generations will be impoverished once these resources are degraded, and furthermore, those individuals who suffer most will be those who live in low-income countries who have the least capacity to stake any claims in a free-for-all system.[50] As the future of the space industry in the new space era becomes mostly dependent on the private sector and the pace of the industry begins to be defined in terms of companies' balance sheets, rather than in terms of long-term policy considerations benefiting

47. Agreement Governing the Activities of States on the Moon and Other Celestial Bodies, Nov. 12, 1979, 18 I.L.M. 1434 (entered into force Jul. 11, 1984) (hereinafter "Moon Treaty"). Article 11 of the Moon Treaty states that "[t]he Moon and its natural resources are the common heritage of mankind." In addition, under Art. 11(2) to the Moon Treaty "[t]he moon is not subject to national appropriation by any claim of sovereignty, by means of use or occupation, or by any other means." The U.S. refrained to sign the Moon Treaty stating that no sovereignty claims of any kinds were made on the moon. *See* Urbano Fuentes, *Understanding the Legal Status of the Moon*, The Space Review (Mar. 2, 2015).
48. For example, although NASA's 2019 budget of USD 22 billion is considered, more and more countries become involved in space exploration. China has allocated USD 10.8 billion to space activities in 2019. Similarly, ESA and Russia have allocated USD 6.3 billion and USD 3.3 billion respectively to space research. Other countries such as Japan, India, and Germany have appropriated roughly USD 2 billion for space. Additionally, satellite technology and resource extraction are also becoming a focus for many Middle Eastern nations. The Middle Eastern oil States, such as Saudi Arabia and the United Arab Emirates, are investing heavily in space mining as they are looking at space as a way to diversify out of the earthly benefits of fossil fuel. Mohamed Al Ahbabi, *The UAE Space Programme*, UAE Space Agency; Lucy Bernard, *UAE to Finalise Space Laws Soon*, The National (Mar. 7, 2016); Kelsey Warner, *UEA Looks to Regulate Asteroid Mining as It Aims to Lure Private Space Sector*, The National (Nov. 26, 2019); Thomas Heath, *Space-Mining May Be only a Decade Away*, Wash. Post (Apr. 28, 2017); Utpal Bhaskar, *ISRO Plans to Mine Energy from Moon by 2030 to Help Meet India Needs*, LiveMint (Apr. 21, 2017); United Space in Europe, *Helium-3 Mining on the Lunar Surface*, ESA; Anurag Kotoky, *The Quest to Find a Trillion Dollar Nuclear Fuel on the Moon*, Bloomberg (Jun. 26, 2018).
49. UNCLOS, *supra* note 5, under Art. 136.
50. *Our Common Future: Report of the World Commission on Environment and Development*, at 11, U.N. Doc. A/42/427, 4 (Aug. 4, 1987), at 258 (aka "Brundtland Report")(hereinafter "Report of the World Commission").

humanity or any patriotic goals, this state of affairs is expected to be exacerbated. When the size, wealth and influence of companies increases, companies start overruling and controlling governments' decisions, as seen, for example, in the oil and coal industries. The excessive concentration of wealth and political and economic influence in the hands of a few, such as the small group of the Emerging Space Entrepreneurs (ESEs), may become a destructive power globally. At this point, vaguely written laws and the influence of corporate lobbies may pose a threat to the political landscape. The notions of public goods and economic efficiency tend to be neglected for corporate profits, their stakeholders' short-term interests and opportunistic causes. Therefore, the question is whether different space powers, including those that participate directly or indirectly in the race to exploit space resources, will come together to rein in the private companies. It is crucially important that this be done in this industry's nascent state.

The international community needs to decide on a broad scale on a resource management and fiscal regime at an early stage, in order to assure that the exploitation of space resources be used for a greater social cause, meaning for an optimal long-term economic yield. This presettled regime will block the possibility that the corporate world will enforce its will on governments, after disassembling and abusing partnerships with the same governments that allowed it to develop. This regime will become a major force that will guide the conduct of commercial activities in space. This set of regulations, in turn, will mitigate any financial "bottom-line" concerns that the corporate world may have.

In general, open-access or common-pool management of natural resources leads to economic inefficiencies and often environmental disasters, because the individual decisions about how to exploit the common resources do not internalize all of the costs and benefits. In fact, the individuals who use the commons bear only a small portion of the social costs of their own actions as the effects of overuse are shared by all.[51] The explanation for this is that, when too many owners have a right to use the commons and no one has the right to exclude the others, the resource is prone to overuse and overexploitation relative to the social optimum, and the outcome is commonly known as "tragedy of the commons."[52] Earthly examples include depleted fisheries, overlogged forests, overgrazed fields and pollution.[53] Since common resources are freely

51. Christopher Costello et al., *Partial Enclosure of the Commons*, 121 J. Pub. Econ. 69-78 (2015). *See also* Edward F. Tverdek, The Moral Weight of Ecology: Public Goods, Cooperative Duties, and Environmental Politics, 41-42 (Lexington Books 2015); *Progressive Environmentalism, supra* note 41, at 14-15.
52. Andrew Herr, Thesis: Appropriation Externalities in the Commons: Theory and Experimental Evidence, Department of Economics, Indiana University (1996); *see also* Garret Hardin, *The Tragedy of the Unmanaged Commons*, 9 Trends in Ecology and Evolution 199 (May 1994); Anthony Scott, *The Fishery: The Objectives of Sole Ownership*, 63.2 J. Political Econ'y 116-24 (1955); Terry L. Anderson et al., Environmental Markets: A Property Rights Approach, 27-30 (Cambridge University Press 2014).
53. Garrett Hardin et al., Managing the Commons (W.H. Freeman & Co. 1977); *see also* Ronald N. Johnson et al., *Contracting Problems and Regulation: The Case of the Fishery*, 72.5 The Am. Econ. Rev. 1005-22 (1982); Frederick W. Bell, *Technological Externalities and Common-Property Resources: An Empirical Study of the U.S. Northern Lobster Fishery*, 80.1 J. Political Econ'y 148-58 (1972).

available to everyone, and no one can limit anyone else's access, individuals have an incentive to take as much of the resource as they can, even at the collective result/price of risking its destruction in the long run.[54]

Since the end of the twentieth century, there has been a growing emphasis on rational and sustainable management of common natural resources and ecosystems, which aims to protect biological diversity and fresh-water sources while combating climate change, overfishing and pollution.[55] Efforts have been made to replace traditional, open-access regimes by developing and using government regulations. This growing attention to balancing resource exploitation rights and conservation duties have resulted in a collection of multilateral treaties. These include, most notably,

---

54. G. Hardin, *The Tragedy of the Commons*, 162 Sci. Magazine 1243 (1968) (hereinafter "Hardin, *The Tragedy of the Commons*"). According to Hardin: "As a rational being, each herdsman seeks to maximize his gain. Explicitly or implicitly, more or less consciously, he asks, 'What is the utility to me of adding one more animal to my herd?' This utility has one negative and one positive component.

    1) The positive component is a function of the increment of one animal. Since the herdsman receives all the proceeds from the sale of the additional animal, the positive utility is nearly +1.
    2) The negative component is a function of the additional overgrazing created by one more animal. Since, however, the effects of overgrazing are shared by all the herdsmen, the negative utility for any particular decision making herdsman is only a fraction of -1.

    Adding together the component partial utilities, the rational herdsman concludes that the only sensible course for him to pursue is to add another animal to his herd. And another; and another ... But this is the conclusion reached by each and every rational herdsman sharing a commons. Therein is the tragedy. Each man is locked into a system that compels him to increase his herd without limit-in a world that is limited. Ruin is the destination toward which all men rush, each pursuing his own best interest in a society that believes in the freedom of the commons. Freedom in a commons brings ruin to all."

    See also Margherita Colangelo, Creating Property Rights, *supra* note 40, at 14-15; Richard L. Stroup and Jane S. Shaw, *Ending the Environmental Tragedy of the Commons*, in The Commons: Its Tragedies and Other Follies 59-88, at 59-62 (Tibor R. Machan ed., Hoover Institution Press, Stanford University, 2001) (hereinafter "Tibor R. Machan, The Commons").
55. Report of the World Commission, *supra* note 50, at 11. Under this report the World Commission on Environment and Development was asked to formulate "a global agenda for change," which was described as "an urgent call by the General Assembly of the United Nations:

    - to propose long-term environmental strategies for achieving sustainable development by the year 2000 and beyond;
    - to recommend ways concern for the environment may be translated into greater co-operation among developing countries and between countries at different stages of economical and social development and lead to the achievement of common and mutually supportive objectives that take account of the interrelationships between people, resources, environment, and development;
    - to consider ways and means by which the international community can deal more effectively with environment concerns; and
    - to help define shared perceptions of long-term environmental issues and the appropriate efforts needed to deal successfully with the problems of protecting and enhancing the environment, a long term agenda for action during the coming decades, and aspirational goals for the world community."

the UNCLOS, the Convention on Conservation of Biological Diversity (CBD),[56] and the United Nations Framework Convention on Climate Change (UNFCCC).[57] However, no similar conventions for space have yet been ratified.[58]

This state of affairs is likely to change as soon as a legal battle over the future management and exploitation of space and its resources begins in earnest, especially, since predictions have already been made that space extraction activities could become a multibillion-dollar industry, with the first trillionaire expected to be made in space.[59]

As private commercial entities rapidly progress their efforts to harvest space resources,[60] the need to establish a legal and tax regime for mineral exploitation is growing stronger, but so are obstacles to developing such a regime. Economic, technological and environmental forces and conflicts will necessarily require global cooperation to resolve in the space context, just as the same forces required international agreement in the case of the high seas.

B.1. Comparing Resource Management Regimes for Various "Global Commons"

The management of the international commons (the oceans, space, and Antarctica) is still evolving, as is the definition and determination of the "commonality" of these areas.[61] For example, many members of the international community (excluding, notably, the U.S.) have collaborated to develop the Law of the Sea to regulate the seas

56. Andrew Balmford et al., *The Convention on Biological Diversity's 2010 Target*, 307. 5707 SCIENCE 212-13 (2005); Zedan Hamdallah, *Convention on Biological Diversity*, 2 DEVELOPMENT 3 (2005).
57. United Nations Framework Convention on Climate Change (UNFCCC) (Effective Mar. 21, 1994).
58. Schrijver, *supra* note 3, at 1259-60.
59. Soon after a bill was signed increasing the 2018 budget for NASA, Senator Ted Cruz said, "I'll make a prediction right now—the first trillionaire will be made in space." Politico, Ted Cruz: *The First Trillionaire Will Be Made in Space*, U.S. Senator for Texas (Jun. 1, 2018). *See also* Emily Ketterer, *Cruz Calls for "Bold Vision" for Future Space Exploration at Senate Hearing*, THE WASHINGTON TIMES (Jul. 10, 2019).
60. The Morgan Stanley's report on the global space economy estimates that the space economy could generate revenue of more than USD 1 trillion by 2040, up from USD 350 billion, currently, while the share of governments in the global space economy will decrease from 25% (which is evaluated at approximately USD 84 billion) to 17%. The predictions concerning the growth of the space economy into a trillion-dollar economy highly depend on the possibility that besides the Earth-focused space activities (like telecommunication, consumer TV and surveillance), new industries, such as space mining, will emerge. Similarly, Goldman Sachs' 2017 report argues that "whereas the psychological barriers to asteroid mining are high, the actual financial and technological barriers are far lower."
    Brittany De Lea, *Space Race: The Next Trillion-Dollar Economy?*, FOX BUSINESS (Dec. 3, 2019); *see also* Morgan Stanley, *Space: Investment Implications of the Final Frontier* 13-14 (October 2017); Morgan Stanley, *Space: Investing in the Final Frontier* (Jul. 24, 2020); Morgan Stanley, *The Space Economy's Next Giant Leap* (February 2021), https://www.morganstanley.com/Themes/global-space-economy; *see also* Andrew Zaleski, *How the Space Industry Came Down to Earth?*, FORTUNE MAGAZINE (Nov. 24, 2018); Jim Edwards, *Goldman Sachs: Space-Mining for Platinum Is "More Realistic than Perceived,"* THE BUSINESS INSIDER (U.K.), 6 (2017); Turksoy Emen, *The Global Space Economy: A Short Overview of the New Space Race*, TPQ (Dec. 6, 2019). In the latter, it is stated that "[i]n 2017 the largest share in global space economy was belonged to ground equipment with 113 billion dollars, followed by consumer TV, with 98 billion dollars."
61. Report of the World Commission, *supra* note 50, at 258.

and manage the seabed and its resources by setting clear boundaries in the oceans and different ecological and economic systems. By contrast, the boundaries in outer space and the legal landscape for space resource management remain unclear and have yet to be settled under international space law.[62]

A U.N. Working Group on the Definition and Delimitation of Outer Space from the COPUOS is currently addressing the question of whether there is a need, in light of the pace of technological development in space and the aviation industry, for nations to demarcate the boundary between airspace and outer space.[63] Some nations argue that the absence of clear rules in this area is creating problems that might lead to disputes among sovereign countries.[64]

Looking down the road to the development of an international regime for taxing space exploitation, this jurisdictional uncertainty is a serious impediment.[65] As commercial uses for space develop, investors will require certainty about legal ownership and the allocation of taxing rights to different countries so they can avoid taxation by multiple tax authorities; for example, by being bound under the territorial airspace rules of one nation, and at the same time perceived as owing taxes based on their corporation's country of residence, and in every country where space commercial services and sales are conducted. Tax certainty is important for encouraging private investment in a fledgling industry. To establish a sound environment for investments, investors need the ability to make an accurate assessment of the tax and compliance costs associated with their investments or a continuation of an investment in a country over the lifecycle of said investment.[66] A recent report by the Organisation for Economic Co-operation and Development (OECD) and International Monetary Fund

62. Gbenga Oduntan, *The Never Ending Dispute*, *supra* note 10.
63. United Nations Office for Outer Space Affairs, *Working Group on the Definition and Delimitation of Outer Space of the Legal Subcommittee*, https://www.unoosa.org/oosa/en/ourwork/copuos/lsc/ddos/index.html.
64. In December 2014, the Government of Ukraine shared in COPUOS this kind of view. *See* Comm. on the Peaceful Uses of Outer Space, *Questions on the Definition and Delimitation of Outer Space*, U.N. A/AC.105/889/Add.15 (2015) (hereinafter "Delimitation of Outer Space"). *See also infra* note 358.
65. Bin Cheng, *Commercial Development of Space: The Need for New Treaties*, 19 J. Space L. 17-44, 21-24 (1991) (hereinafter "Bin Cheng, *Commercial Development of Space*").
66. Jeffrey Owens, *The Role of Tax Certainty in Promoting Sustainable and Inclusive Growth*, Iins. for Austrian and Int'l Tax L. (Oct. 26, 2018). In the theoretical literature, it has been asserted that the effect of tax uncertainty on business operations is difficult to assess, although investors are assumed to be risk-neutral, whereas if they were risk averse, uncertainty would be inherently harmful to them. In Kevin A. Hassett et al., *Investment with Uncertain Tax Policy: Does Random Tax Policy Discourage Investment*, 109.457 The Econ. J. 372-93 (1999), for instance, it has been argued that the direction of the effect depends on whether the random tax rates move smoothly or in jumps. *See also* IMF, *Tax Certainty*, Report for G20 Ministers 2017, at 13 (March 2017) (hereinafter "IMF 2017"); George Bittlingmayer, *Regulatory Uncertainty and Investment: Evidence from Antitrust Enforcement*, 20 CATO J. 295 (2001); Roger Buckland et al., *Political and Regulatory Risk: Beta Sensitivity in U.K. Electricity Distribution*, 19 J. Reg. Econ. 5 (2001); E.R. Larsen et al., *Deregulation in Electricity: Understanding Strategic and Regulatory Risk*, 50 J. Operational Res. Soc'y 337 (1999); Claudio Morana et al., *Regulatory Uncertainty and Share Price Volatility: The English and Welsh Water Industry's Periodic Price Review*, 17 J. Reg. Econ. 87 (2000); Andrew B. Whitford, *The Reduction of Regulatory Uncertainty: Evidence from Transfer Pricing Policy*, 55 Louis ULJ 269 (2010).

(IMF) found that tax certainty is necessary to create an attractive business environment and economic growth.[67] The report states that:

> [a]lthough no empirical evidence is available, there are good reasons to suppose that large multinationals, undertaking diversified projects and being held by diversified shareholders, should act in a risk neutral fashion. For smaller operations, risk aversion may be a reasonable premise and adverse effects on investment consequently more likely. One consequence, moreover, is that variation of risk preferences across enterprises means that tax uncertainties can imply both inequities and inefficiencies in the allocation of resources between them.[68]

A stable and clear tax system is needed to encourage investment in space. When dealing with space operations and exploration, there are already a number of unique and inherent business uncertainties, and so it is important to avoid adding even more uncertainties in space tax policy and administration. Therefore, the legal and economic framework for managing space exploitation must balance at least three competing objectives: (1) the collection of tax revenues from space activities; (2) ensuring that the resources are used in ways that maximize long-term social product, welfare and equity; and (3) capturing as large a proportion as possible from the benefits generated for the public and the private investors. In order to achieve these goals, tax certainty must be a part of the regime.[69]

Since the formation of the Outer Space Treaty, the international community—including the most important space powers of the late 1960s, the U.S. and former Soviet Union—has lived up to its commitment to not colonize space and to maintain space as a peaceful environment for the benefit of all, acknowledging that orbital space cannot be effectively managed by any single country.[70] This commitment has already been enshrined under the 1958 National Aeronautics and Space Act's policy and purpose, where it is articulated that "[t]he Congress hereby declares that it is the policy of the United States that activities in space should be devoted to peaceful purposes for the benefit of all mankind."[71] This declaration has also been reinstated when the first astronaut to land on the moon, Neil Armstrong, held a plaque stating

67. OECD, *2019 Progress Report on Tax Certainty*, IMF/OECD Report for the G20 Finance Ministers and Central Bank Governors IMF, at 8 (June 2019) (hereinafter "OECD, *2019 Progress Report on Tax Certainty*"). In the latest report, it is stated that that "the need to ensure a predictable and stable investment environment and international rules that facilitate global trade remains a fundamental component of the international tax architecture ... tax certainty for taxpayers is an important influence on investment and other commercial decisions and can have significant impacts on economic growth. Improving tax certainty also cuts both ways, benefiting both taxpayers and tax administrations." *See also* Ross Garnaut and Anthony Clunies Ross, *Uncertainty, Risk Aversion and the Taxing of Natural Resource Projects*, 85.338 The Econ J. 272-87, at 275 (1975) (hereinafter "Garnaut").
68. IMF 2017, *supra* note 66, at 5-6 and 13-14. In this report it is stated that "[i]nvestment will clearly be discouraged, for instance, if the rate at which rents are taxed if they turn out to be positive is higher than the rate at which loss offset is provided if they are negative ... Differences in uncertainty across countries could affect the location of investment." *See also* OECD, *2019 Progress Report on Tax Certainty*, *supra* note 67.
69. Garnaut, *supra* note 67, at 272.
70. Report of the World Commission, *supra* note 50, at 274. *See also* Art. II under the Outer Space Treaty, *supra* note 17.
71. The National Aeronautics and Space Act of 1958 (unamended), Public Law 85-568, 72 Stat., 426.

"[w]e came in peace for all mankind." This assertion was contradictory to the perception that planting national flags on the lunar surface can serve as an act of territorial conquest by any single nation. Nevertheless, deploying the U.S. flag on the moon was as an honor attributed to the American nation—its taxpayers, engineers, astronauts, hard-working scientists, philanthropists and entrepreneurs—who to this day make the space dream and "the other things" in space feasible, as President John F. Kennedy famously stated. Nevertheless, in December 2020, the Chinese Chang'e 5 moon lander deployed a small version of China's five-star red flag on the moon during China's mission to collect lunar's rock samples and bring them back to Earth. And although the flag was not planted in the lunar surface like all six U.S. flags planted during Apollo missions between 1969 and 1972, questions and suspicions were raised on whether this act by China, which became the second nation to plant flag on the moon, was merely intended as an honorary attribute for China's achievements or does it imply any other intentions.[72]

These concerns may stem from the fact that the resource management regime in space has not been settled yet. This fact may not only reflect political factors, but also indicates the significant timing-issue during the promulgation of legal rules to regulate space. Since outer space is essentially unlimited, it comprises different spectrums that have been and will continue to be explored and regulated at differing rates. On an institutional level, the World Commission on Environment and Development has suggested that a "fine balance must be struck between regulating activities too late and regulating non-existent activities too soon."[73] The striking of the appropriate balance is a moving target and depends on the pace of advancements in space technology. These new technologies may require new principles beyond, yet consistent with, the ones laid out in the Outer Space Treaty. As technology evolves, so must the law, and this law needs to pose and resolve new challenges, including those with respect to legal ownership, as well as a resource-management system, just as it had to grapple with commercial exploitation of the high seas.

In the context of the high seas, developing countries were successful in negotiating an alternative to a "first-come, first-served" regime that would have greatly preferred advanced industrialized economies on a "most favored nations" basis. Instead, access to the high seas is regulated by and for the international community.

The high seas were not always subject to the common ownership framework reflected in UNCLOS, and to understand the nature of the transition, I focus on the

72. *John F. Kennedy Moon Speech–Rice Stadium*, NASA, Sept. 12, 1962 (retrieved Mar. 19, 2018). *See also* Savir, *Tax Infinity & Beyond*, *supra* note 10, at 10-17 and 35. *See also* Donald R. Rothwell and Imogen Saunders, *Does a US Flag on the Moon Amount to a Claim of Sovereignty under Law?*, the INTERPRETER (Jul. 25, 2019); Leonard David, *China Plants Its Flag on the Moon with Chang'e 5 Lunar Lander*, SPACE.com (Dec. 8, 2020); Bill Harwood, *China Releases Image of Its Flag on the Moon as Spacecraft Carrying Lunar Rocks Lifts Off*, CBS NEWS (Dec. 6, 2020); Dustin Jones, *Chinese Chang'e-5 Is Returning from Moon with Rocks, Left a Flag to Celebrate*, NPR (Dec. 4, 2020); Harry Pettit, *FLYING THE FLAG China Taunts West by Flying Flag on the Moon in Chang'e 5 Probe Mission as Space Race with US Heats Up*, THE U.S. SUN (Dec. 4, 2020).

73. Report of the World Commission, *supra* note 50, at 274.

Maltese Ambassador, Arvid Pardo,[74] who inaugurated the official discussion regarding the exploitation of the seabed beyond national jurisdiction and originated the "*Common Heritage of Mankind*" descriptor for the high seas that was eventually embedded in the UNCLOS,[75] while warning against "intolerable injustice" or any other solution which:

> would reserve the plurality of the world's resources for the exclusive benefit of less than a handful of nations. The strong would get stronger, the rich richer, and among the rich themselves there would arise an increasing and insuperable differentiation between two or three and the remainder.[76]

This belief led Pardo to argue for a more just and equitable international framework and for an effective international regime, asserting that it is:

> the only alternative that gives assurance that the immense resources on and under the sea will be exploited with harm to none and benefit to all.[77]

Although the U.S. has refrained from ratifying the UNCLOS and, hence, from codifying its notion regarding the "common heritage,"[78] Pardo's warning resonates an assertion that was made in 1966, prior to his speech to the General Assembly at the U.N., by the then-U.S. president, President Lyndon B. Johnson, who declared at the launch of research vessel "Oceanographer" that:

> Under no circumstances, must we ever allow the prospects of rich harvest and mineral wealth to create a new form of colonial competition among the maritime nations. We must be careful to avoid a race to grab and to hold the lands under the high seas. We must ensure that the deep seas and the ocean bottoms are, and remain, the legacy of all human beings.[79]

---

74. Address by Arvid Pardo to the 22nd session of the General Assembly of the United Nations (1967), U.N. GAOR, 22nd sess., U.N. Doc. A/6695 (1967) (Address by Arvid Pardo); U.N. GAOR, 25th Sess., at 24, U.N. Doc. A/8028 (1928) (reflects Pardo's proposal); *see also* Jasper A. Bovenberg, *Mining the Common Heritage of Our DNA: Lessons Learned from Grotius and Pardo*, 5.1 DUKE L. & TECH. REV. 1, 12 (2006).
75. Ambassador Pardo's well-known speech extended for two meetings of the Committee. *See* U.N. GAOR, 22nd Sess. First Committee, 1515th and 1516th meetings, U.N. Docs. A/C.1/PV 1515 and A/C.1/PV 1516 (1967) (hereinafter: "1515th meeting" and "1516th meeting" respectively); *see* 1516th meeting at ¶ 3; *see also* Martin Harry, *The Deep Seabed: The Common Heritage of Mankind or Arena for Unilateral Exploitation?*, 40 NAVAL L. REV. 207, 210 (1992); Dire Tladi, *The Common Heritage of Mankind in the Proposed Implementing Agreement*, in LEGAL ORDER IN THE WORLD'S OCEANS: UN CONVENTION ON THE LAW OF THE SEA, Ch. 2, 80-90 (Myron H. Nordquist et al. eds, Brill 2017).
76. 1515th meeting, at para. 91.
77. 1516th meeting, at para. 3.
78. Markus G. Schmidt, *Common Heritage or Common Burden? The United States Position on the Development of a Regime for Deep Seabed Mining in the Law of the Sea Convention* (OUP 1989).
79. U.S. Government Printing Office, United States Congress, Senate, Interior and Insular Affairs, Mineral Resources of the Deep Seabed: Hearings Before the Subcommittee on Minerals, Materials, and Fuels of the Committee on Interior and Insular Affairs United States Senate, 23rd Congress, 2nd Session on Legalization to Revise the Laws Governing Mineral Development of Federal Lands 440 (1973). *See also* PHILIP E. STEINBERG, THE SOCIAL CONSTRUCTION OF THE OCEAN, CAMBRIDGE, 181 (Cambridge University Press 2001).

Shortly after this, Pardo argued during the UNCLOS negotiations that the phrase of "*Common Heritage of Mankind*" should be adopted as a guiding principle of a new regime to replace the customary rule of the freedom of the high seas. That customary rule, built upon the Grotian notion of *mare liberum*, which served to justify the law of prize[80] (which essentially resembles the law of capture)—that is, that whoever catches the resources/fish owns them—and the "natural" right to trade, tended to benefit powerful nations that were able to exploit ocean resources faster than other countries.[81] In his critical review of the law of the sea negotiations, Ambassador Pardo wrote:

> The objective of the Maltese proposal was to replace the principle of freedom of the seas by the principle of common heritage of mankind in order to preserve the greater part of ocean space as a commons accessible to the international community. The commons of the high seas, however, would be no longer open to the whims of the users and exploiters; it would be internationally administered. International administration of the commons and management of its resources for the common good distinguished the principle of common heritage from the traditional principle of the high seas as res communis.[82]

Furthermore, Ambassador Pardo explained that:

> [I]n the Maltese view the common heritage concept has five basic implications. First, the common heritage of mankind could not be appropriated; it was open to use by the international community but was not owned by the international community. Second, it required a system of management in which all users have a right to share. Third, it implied an active sharing of benefits, not only financial but also benefits derived from shared management and transfer of technology, thus radically transforming the conventional relationships between states and traditional concepts of development aid. Fourth, the concept of common heritage implied reservation for peaceful purposes, insofar as politically achievable, and, fifth, it implied reservation for further generations, and thus had environmental implications. For Malta, the principle of common heritage was conceptually joined with the idea of functional sovereignty, as distinguished from the traditional concept of territorial sovereignty.[83]

Nevertheless, even before Arvid Pardo promoted the concept of the deep seabeds as the "common heritage of all mankind," Prince Wan Waithayakon of Thailand, while serving as the President of the 1958 Conference for the Law of the Sea, worked to

80. As Grotius' resulting work named *De Jure Praedae*, which means in Dutch "*On the Law of Prize and Booty.*" *See* GROTIUS HUGO, DE JURE PRAEDAE COMMENTARIUS. I: COMMENTARY ON THE LAW OF PRIZE AND BOOTY (Translated by Gwladys L. et al., 1950); HAAKONSSEN KNUD ED., NATURAL LAW AND ENLIGHTENMENT CLASSICS, xii-xiv (LIBERTY FUND 2006).
81. L.F.E. Goldie, *A Note on Some Diverse Meanings of "The Common Heritage of Mankind,"* 10 SYRACUSE J. INT'L L. AND COM. 69, 86-87 (1983); *see also* KEMAL BASLAR, THE CONCEPT OF THE COMMON HERITAGE OF MANKIND IN INTERNATIONAL LAW 30-31 (1998) (hereinafter "BASLAR, THE CONCEPT OF THE COMMON HERITAGE").
82. Arvid Pardo, *Law of the Sea Conference—What Went Wrong*, in MANAGING OCEAN RESOURCES: A PRIMER 137, 139 (1979). *See also* 1516th meeting, *supra* note 75 at paras. 8, 13, 15 and 57.
83. Arvid Pardo, *supra* note 82, at 141.

preserve the sea as "the common heritage of mankind" while calling for the "preservation of that heritage for the benefit of all."[84]

Eventually, these principles became the foundation for the regime implemented by the UNCLOS, and prompted the creation of the International Seabed Authority (ISA) in order to protect the resources within this international arena, and to promote marine scientific research.[85] There was a broad level of support among the U.N.'s delegations for the Maltese proposal that the continental shelf should be exploited for the benefit of and in the interests of mankind as a whole and, consequently, the concept of the "common heritage" was implemented in the international treaty law.[86]

The historic outcome of the surprising involvement of such a small European country as Malta in the negotiations over the drafting of the UNCLOS resembles and can be compared to the case of another small nation, Luxembourg, which became a leader in the satellite communications industry in the 1980s (after the crisis and recession in its thriving steel economy following the 1973 oil crisis) in order to diversify and to not impede the wealth of its economy.[87] Luxembourg is also currently aiming to become a hub for space mining companies by shaping an attractive space policy for this emerging industry.[88] This policy, as history shows, even when made by a small country, might have significant implications on the global policy discourse regarding the space mining industry, similar to how Malta managed to effect and shape the policy toward the exploitation of seabed resources.

However, unlike the Law of the Sea regime, outer space, including the Moon and other celestial bodies, is described in the Outer Space Treaty as "the province of all mankind" that is "not subject to national appropriation by claim of sovereignty, by means of use or occupation, or by any other means."[89]

Comparing the histories of the phrases "*the province of all mankind*"—used in the space treaties—and the "*Common Heritage of Mankind*"[90]—used in the ocean

84. U.N. GAOR, 13th Sess., 1st plen. Mtg. at 3 U.N. Doc. A/CONF.13/SR. 1 (Feb. 4, 1958).
85. Schrijver, *supra* note 3, at 1257.
86. The Law of the Sea, Concept of the Common Heritage of Mankind, Legislative History of Articles 133 to 150 and 311(6) of the United Nations Convention on the Law of the Sea, United Nations, New York (1996), p. 1. *See also* U.N. Secretary-General, Working Paper submitted to the Sea-Beds Committee, *Proposals and Views Relating to the Adoption of Principles*, U.N. Doc. A/AC.138/7 (Mar. 6, 1969); U.N. Doc., Malta: Draft Resolution, A/AC.138/11 (Mar. 18, 1969); Satya N. Nandan, Michael W. Lodge and Shabtai Rosenne, *The Development of the Regime for Deep Seabed Mining* (Kluwer Law International and Center for Oceans Law and Policy, University of Virginia, 2002).
87. OECD, OECD Economic Surveys 1985/1986: Belgium-Luxembourg 61-6 (1986); *see also* David G. Tarr, *The Steel Crisis in the United States and the European Community: Causes and Adjustments*, in Issues in US-EC Trade Relation (Robert E. Baldwin et al. eds. University of Chicago Press, 1988).
88. Robert Mackenzie, *Why Luxembourg, of All Places, Is a Global Leader in Asteroid Mining*, Motherboard Vice (Dec. 26, 2016). In May 2016, Luxembourg's Prime Minister Xavier Bettel explained that they "realized it wouldn't be forever, the steel," so they, "decided to do other things."
89. Outer Space Treaty, *supra* note 17.
90. Although the definition of the common heritage concept is controversial, the common heritage principle generally recognizes five basic implications that "(1) the area under consideration cannot be subject to appropriation; (2) all countries must share in management of the resources; (3) there must be an active sharing of the benefits derived from exploitation of the resources; (4)

treaties—reveals a number of differences in definitions, arguments, and legal interpretations of the two provisions. These differences resulted from the intensity of the conflict between spacefaring and non-spacefaring nations during the negotiation of the space treaty, and illustrate political challenges in arriving at agreement on these provisions and their applications.[91] The global commons developed from Hugo Grotius' concept of *mare liberum*.[92] The concept of *mare liberum* aimed to preserve the freedom of access to a shared resource for the benefit of all; however, by providing resource rights to the first actor to exploit the resource, the approach advantages industrialized nations.[93] This approach has been gradually replaced by a new law of international cooperation that protects the natural wealth and resources beyond the boundaries of national jurisdictions. This new approach is reflected in the Law of the Sea and in other areas of international environmental law.[94] Examples of this contemporary approach include the ban on whaling,[95] sanctions on emissions of ozone-depleting substances,[96] and the stagnation of claims of territorial sovereignty over Antarctica, which for over a generation has been governed by an environmental management regime promoting multilateral conservation efforts and the preservation of Antarctic resources.[97] In accordance with the Antarctic Treaty,[98] Antarctica has been maintained solely for peaceful uses, prohibiting all military activities, weapons testing, nuclear explosions and the disposal of radioactive wastes. In addition, the treaty promotes freedom for scientific investigation in Antarctica and international cooperation to reach this end.[99]

---

the area must be dedicated exclusively to peaceful purpose; and (5) the area must be preserved for future generations." *See* N. Jasentuliyana, *The U.N. Space Treaties and the Common Heritage Principle*, 2 Space Pol'y 296 (1986); Barbara Ellen Heim, *Exploring the Last Frontiers for Mineral Resources: A Comparison of International Law Regarding the Deep Seabed, Outer Space, and Antarctica*, 23 Vand. J. Transnat'l L. 819, 827 (1990).

91. Second Conference on Lunar Bases & Space Activities, J.I. Gabrynowicz, *The Province and Heritage of Mankind Reconsidered: A New Beginning* 691, 691-93 (Sept. 1, 1992).
92. Hugo Grotius, Mare Liberum (1609).
93. Schrijver, *supra* note 3, at 1263. *See also* Baslar, The Concept of the Common Heritage, *supra* note 81, at 31. It should be noted that although the Grotian freedom of the high seas argued that nature has given all things to all people, the main thought was to provide protectionism for the economic and military superiority of the Netherland as a powerful nation. Therefore, it can be argued that the notion of "freedom of the high sea" was a mere cover for the depredations of the developed states' fishing efforts of their coasts. Similarly, the freedom of access into outer space given to all can turn into a useful tool by technological and spacefaring powers to monopolize space.
94. PAME International Secretariat 1-76 (April 2015); Kamrul Hossain et al., *Protecting Arctic Ocean Marine Biodiversity in the Area Beyond National Jurisdiction*, in The Future of the Law of the Sea, 105, 115 (Andreone G. (ed.) 2017).
95. International Convention on the Regulation of Whaling 1946; *see also* International Whaling Commission; International Pacific Halibut Commission; Inter-American Tropical Tuna Commission.
96. Ozone Protection under Title VI of the Clean Air Act 1990, 42 U.S.C. §601 (1990). *See also* Christopher C. Joyner, *Governing the Frozen Commons: The Antarctic Regime and Environmental Protection*, U. of South Carolina 369 (1998).
97. Schrijver, *supra* note 3, at 1263.
98. Antarctic Treaty System of 1959.
99. Report of the World Commission, *supra* note 50, at 274-75.

Another example of successful multilateral cooperation for resource management, which may be instructive for devising a space regime, is the case of fisheries. Since many fish stocks are present in the maritime zone of more than one coastal state or in both coastal state and the high seas, an effective management requires taking into account the stock as a whole. This need led to two opposing stances as was addressed at the 1955 International Technical Conference on the Conservation of the Living Resources of the Sea, a conference in Rome sponsored by the U.N. and the Food and Agricultural Organization and attended by representatives and observers of more than fifty states and intergovernmental fishery organizations. During this conference two opposing stands were taken regarding the role of the shore state. One stance was that, since the coastal state holds a special interest, it should be entrusted to regulate alone its fishing activities and conservation measures subject to technological and ecological limitations, while the other stance was that the coastal shore is not necessarily better qualified to regulate its fishing activities since these should be based on scientific and technical information which all states can gain, thus, equal rights with respect to the control and conservation measures over fisheries should be granted to all participating fishing states.[100] As a result, the problem of overfishing by one country, and its effects on other countries, was resolved by a cooperation between the coastal states and the participants in fishing on the high seas, which led to the establishment of successful and stable fisheries, coastal communities, and coalitions of multiple fishing states coordinating through the regional fisheries management organizations. An example of such global resolution can be seen in the 1958 Convention on Fishing and Conservation of the Living Resources of the High Seas.[101] Another way that a solution for the overfishing problem was achieved was through bans implemented under UNCLOS and the Fish Stock agreement,[102] which successfully prohibited exploitation. Additionally, the International Whaling Commission (IWC) put into place a moratorium on commercial whaling beginning in 1986. Moreover, in the case of the exploitation of high sea resources, another efficiency argument for joint-cooperation for exploitation of global resources across international jurisdiction can be based on the formation of regulatory framework laid out in the 2011 International Tribunal for the Law of the Sea, which was aimed to provide environmental protections for the current and future explorations of deep seabed mining (DSM) by fixing the liabilities for those states that sponsor DSM.[103]

---

100. Report of the International Technical Conference on the Conservation of the Living Resources of the Sea, U.N. Doc. A/CONF. 10/6, s. VI, paras. 45, 47, 48 and s. II, para. 18 (1955). *See also* Weissberg Guenter, *The Convention on Fishing and Conservation of the Living Resources of the High Seas*, in RECENT DEVELOPMENTS IN THE LAW OF THE SEA AND THE JAPANESE-KOREAN FISHERY DISPUTE, 31-43, at 31-32 (Springer 1966).
101. Convention on Fishing and Conservation of the Living Resources of the High Seas, U.N. Doc. A/CONF, 13/L, 54, 52, AJIL 851.
102. Agreement for the Implementation of the Provisions of the United Nations Convention on the Law of the Sea of 10 December 1982 relating to the Conservation and Management of Straddling Fish Stocks and Highly Migratory Fish Stocks.
103. Schrijver, *supra* note 3, at 1256-60; *see also* Responsibilities and Obligations of States Sponsoring Persons and Entities with Respect to Activities in the Area, Advisory Opinion, International Tribunal for the Law of the Sea [ITLOS] Case No. 17, [2011] ITLOS Rep. 10, ICGJ 449 (ITLOS 2011), 1 February 2011.

Nonetheless, 58% of the waters constituting the high seas is effectively open access; the remainder is delineated to individual states in exclusive economic zones, where a classic "partial enclosure of the commons" system has been established. This system provides partial property rights that are fully delineated within these exclusive economic zones. However, since migrating fish traverse these jurisdictions, they are subject to harvest on the high seas in the open-access fringes.[104]

In thinking about the optimal resource management regime for common resources, economic theory does not generally favor the adoption of the first possession rule.[105] For example, most economists who have considered the question agree that the various forms of settlement used in the nineteenth-century American West likely encouraged people to enter the land earlier than they would have under a system of competitive bidding. Under the first possession rule, the race to possess free (or nearly free) land leads to the total dissipation of the value of the new useful resources, as individuals and corporations are usually expected to occupy or extract resources at a faster rate than may be optimal, in order to secure possession.[106] The premature occupation of land, induced by the first possession rule, is usually associated with foregoing returns on investment elsewhere. For example, when competing on occupying two gold mines, where one mine is terrestrial and the other in space, and where the terrestrial gold mine output is constant but the other mine's output in space is equal to the first mine at *t* time and lowers at 10% for each time unit before *t* time and yields a surplus at 10% at each time unit from *t + 1* time onward, then the incentive to occupy the latter mine in space at an earlier point of time (i.e., at *t-1* until *t-10*) is higher, even at the cost of pulling out resources for investment in the terrestrial parcel, in order to obtain priority rights (and profits). This scenario will result in premature occupation of the mine in space, instead of at the time when it becomes profitable. As a consequence, the first possession rule can lead to total dissipation of the value of the useful asset and its potential surplus, since the present value of the expected returns from the newly acquired asset equals to the stream of output generated during the time of the preoccupation of the asset on the account of investments in a more productive one.[107] In the case of space, it can also be contended that premature possession of space resources, under the first possession rule, may lead the private space sector to export space resources of precious and rare elements back to Earth, especially when their terrestrial stocks degrade, although their future use in space itself might be more economically efficient. Considering the described model above, this result might only exacerbate the extent of the rapid dissipation of the expected profits from space resources and escalate the problem of preoccupation. However, this result depends on

104. Crow White et al., *Close the High Seas to Fishing?*, PLOS (Mar. 25, 2014); *see also* Christopher Costello, *supra* note 51, at 70.

105. Dean Lueck, *The Rule of First Possession and the Design of the Law*, 38 J.L. & Econ. 393 (1995) (hereinafter "Dean Lueck").

106. *Id.*, at 117. *See also* David D. Haddock, *First Possession Versus Optimal Timing: Limiting the Dissipation of Economic Value*, 64 Wash. U. L. Q. 775, 792 (1986) (hereinafter "Haddock").

107. Yoram Barzel, *Optimal Timing of Innovations*, 50 Rev. Econ. & Statistics 348 (1968); *see also* Haddock, *supra* note 106, at 783-91. For a simple numerical example for illustrating how the first possession rule dissipates the asset's entire net worth, please *see* the table at *id.*, Haddock, at 784.

other factors, such as the resources value on Earth once imported from space and the volume of the minerals extracted and imported. If the costs of mining and shipping space resources to Earth will be so high that they will be traded at an uncompetitive price in the market when compared to similar terrestrial resources their efficiency will be harmed. Alternatively, if the predictions for finding abundant rare minerals become reality, the stocks of these resources might pick-up on Earth, thus causing their prices to significantly drop as their supply soars. This result will also escalate the economic efficiency problem associated with preoccupation of asteroids in space.

On the other hand, the economists who advocate for property rights and otherwise unregulated markets, which are typically associated with the first possession rule, tend to believe that the economy thrives when left alone and that government intervention and management of common property is associated with costly regulations, wasteful management, ecological deterioration, and a focus on short-term interests.[108] A classic example of wasteful and costly governmental regulation of the commons is the U.S. legislative framework for regulating air and water pollution that expanded dramatically in the 1970s but has generally been ineffective in many respects,[109] and apparent evidence of its beneficial effects may be overstated. For example, by the time the Clean Air Act Amendments of 1970 were passed, ambient levels of the key pollutants targeted by the legislation (sulfur dioxide, ozone and carbon monoxide) had already been declining.[110] The Clean Air Act has also been criticized as having a negative impact on nonattainment areas—designated geographical areas that are above the permitted levels of pollution—which caused more than USD 100 billion in lost productivity, including declining employment for blue-collar workers.[111] Criticism against governmental control also appeared in the field of energy regulations where the Energy Policy Act of 2005 (EPAct) was enacted to increase and diversify domestic energy production, encourage energy conservation, and boost investments in

108. YORAM BARZEL, ECONOMIC ANALYSIS OF PROPERTY RIGHTS 1-161, 128 (1997) (hereinafter "BARZEL, ECONOMIC ANALYSIS").

109. Kay M. Crider, *Interstate Air Pollution: Over a Decade of Ineffective Regulation*, 64 CHI.-KENT L. REV. 619 (1988); *see also* Lisa Heinzerling, *Do Environmental Regulations Do More Harm or Good? Presidential candidates disagree*, THE CONVERSATION (Apr. 20, 2016); ROBERT W. CRANDALL, POLLUTION CONTROLS (The Library of Economics and Liberty); Robert W. Han et al., *Where Did All the Markets Go?*, 6.1 YALE J. ON REGULATION 109-53 (1989); U.S. Office of Management and Budget, 2005 Report to Congress on the Costs and Benefits of Federal Regulations, 1-72, 8-10, and 21-22 (2005); Clyde Wayne Crews Jr., *Trump Administration Releases Updated Regulatory Cost-Benefit Report*, FORBES (Mar. 6, 2018); David A. Keiser et al., *The Low but Uncertain Measured Benefits of US Water Quality*, 116.12 PNAS 5262-69 (Mar. 19, 2019). In the latter research, scholars debate regarding the question whether the costs of current U.S. water and air quality regulations actually exceed their benefits, or do existing analyses understate true benefits or overstate true costs. According to their research, there is no sufficient evidence to answer this question. Therefore, the results of cost-benefit and cost-effectiveness analyses of environmental regulations implying on negative net benefits (meaning that the regulations' benefits are much smaller than their costs) are uncertain.

110. Brian Wang, *History of Carbon and Air Pollution in Charts*, NEXT BIG FUTURE (2016); National Ambient Air Quality Standards (NAAQS) Table (last updated Dec. 20, 2016).

111. TIBOR R. MACHAN, THE COMMONS, *supra* note 54, at 59-88, 62-64. *See also* Jordan K. Lofthouse, *How Good Intentions Backfire: Failures and Negative Consequences of Federal Environment Policies* 24-25 (2016) (hereinafter "Lofthouse").

new energy technologies.[112] The EPAct has been criticized as a political grab bag for dozens of special interests and well-connected industrial groups who could benefit at the taxpayers' expense.[113] The EPAct provided special privileges and billions in subsidies to nearly all energy industries while costing taxpayers billions of dollars with limited benefits.[114] Many of the most adverse consequences stem from the Renewable Fuel Standard, which caused economic and environmental damages from the incentives it created for large-scale monocropping and carbon emissions.[115] In addition, exemptions from environmental protection policies for the fossil fuel industry provide an unfair and likely inefficient advantage to oil and natural gas companies.[116]

Differing views about the usefulness of governmental regulation stem, in part, from the belief that the prices mechanism in the market tends to direct resources to their highest-value uses, but that in areas, such as national defense, police and the courts, government intervention is required for facilitating the functioning of markets.[117] Therefore, in the case of space, the question is whether government regulation would complement and enhance the activities of the private sector in exploiting its resources, or would it hinder the development of the industry instead. Additionally, non-market allocation of common goods based on non-price allocation can hold important objectives other than efficiency. An example can be seen when allocating scarce medical resources. The medical profession disallows allocation of resources to the highest bidder, but instead uses different criteria, such as the highest chances of survival from receiving the resources where the goal set for allocation is to save the

---

112. Act, Energy Policy, "Energy Policy Act of 2005," in U.S. Congress (2005).
113. *Bush Signs Energy Bill, Cheers Steps Toward Self-Sufficiency*, WASH. POST (Aug. 9, 2005); *Bush Signs Sweeping Energy Bill*, CBS NEWS (Aug. 8, 2005).*See* Peter L. Kahn. *Politics of Unregulation: Public Choice and Limits on Government*, 75 CORNELL L. REV. 279, 280 (1989), who states:

> Many economists and economically-minded lawyers in recent years have come to view much governmental regulation of business as the unfortunate result of a perverse quirk in our political system. In this view, representative democracy gives unwarranted weight to the interests of small and discrete pressure groups, whose interests may be directly opposed to the interests of the larger public.

114. For more criticism of the act since many political and group interests are involved, *see* Martha Marks, the President of the National Republicans for Environmental Protection, who said, "It really gives a short shrift to conservation and it still continues to subsidize the well-established oil and gas industries that really don't need subsidizing especially when (crude) oil is $60 a barrel." Representative Nancy Pelosi (D-California) also said, "This energy policy is yet another example of Republicans catering to corporate special interests at the expense of the public interest."
115. M. Grunwald and J. Eilperin, *Energy, Bill Raises Fears About Pollution, Fraud*, WASH. POST (Jul. 30, 2005).
116. Lofthouse, *supra* note 111, at 41-42.
117. BARZEL, ECONOMIC ANALYSIS, *supra* note 108, at 128. *See also* Thomas Hobbes, LEVIATHAN OR THE MATTER, FORME AND POWER OF A COMMONWEALTH ECCLESIASTICALL AND CIVIL (Michael Oakeshott ed. 1960); WILSON WOODROW, CONGRESSIONAL GOVERNMENT: A STUDY IN AMERICAN POLITICS (Houghton Miffin 1885); Elinor Ostrom, *Beyond Markets and States: Polycentric Governance of Complex Economic Systems*, 100(3) AM. ECON. REV. 641-672(June 2010). The argument is that "[w]ithout a hierarchical government to induce compliance, self-seeking citizens and officials would fail to generate efficient levels of public goods, such as peace and security, at multiple scales."

highest number of lives. This example describes situations where non-market allocation can generate higher values than under private ownership, or might even be considered more efficient when efficiency is defined in terms of the number of live saves. The mechanism for resource allocation from space must reflect the different objectives that society has for those resources, meaning that if the goal is to foster a new independent life in space, a type of regulatory framework might be required, different from when the only goal is economic in nature.[118] Another example for inefficient market allocation of resources in the hands of private ownership can be seen when comparing private and public ownership of roads. It should be noted that public roads are not managed as "common property," although these are free-access roads and typically held in the public sector, since they are subject to restrictions, such as the safety and the size of the vehicles, and to various registration/licensing fees and taxes, such as a purchase tax for owning vehicles and the gasoline tax, which is being used as a device for rationing the road use. The higher the tax, the lower the level of traffic congestion (and maybe even of the pollution from carbon dioxide omission). Nevertheless, this gas tax, while being proportional to the number of gallons purchased, hence, of the miles driven, fails to distinguish between peak and off-peak hours, and consequently, fails to distinguish between more and less fuel-efficient cars. However, even in terms of congestion (which results in delays to all) or pollution costs, it is unlikely that there will be an increase in the value of roads, even if they are privatized. It is unlikely that private ownership of roads would yield a perfectly competitive market structure because alternative routes are generally not perfect substitutes. Therefore, those road owners might exploit their locational attributes and monopolistic prerogatives by raising charges above marginal cost. In addition, even where lumpiness of roads is found, the competition would be at best imperfect. Consequently, the relevant comparison, based on efficiency considerations, can be the welfare cost associated with government intervention vis-à-vis the dead-weight loss associated with the monopolistic or oligopolistic pricing practices of private ownership, including the costs of policing the use of the roads. In addition, there can be other reasonable grounds—such as inequity and even constitutional rights for travel—for opposing the landowners' supernormal profits as undesirable. Hence, in this situation, it is likely that effectively decentralized ownership will always be required to produce the proper resource allocation.[119] Similarly, when using space for transportation or once occupying land on the Moon or Mars, the same arguments can arise.[120] It might, as well, be uncertain if non-market allocation in the case of space mining will be more efficient and

118. A discussion of the factors behind these ethical judgments is beyond the scope of this book.
119. James M. Buchanan, *Private Ownership and Common Usage: The Road Case Re-Examined*, 22.3 SOUTHERN ECON. J. 305-16 (January 1956), published by Southern Economic Association Stable; *see also* TIMOTHY D. HAU, ECONOMIC FUNDAMENTALS OF ROAD PRICING: A DIAGRAMMATIC ANALYSIS, at 4-8 (Transport Division Infrastructure and Urban Development Department, The World Bank, December 1992); BARZEL, ECONOMIC ANALYSIS, *supra* note 108, at 100; Daniele Condorelli, *Market and Non-market Mechanisms for the Optimal Allocation of Scarce Resources*, Technical Report (2012).
120. Michael Sheetz, *New Virgin Galactic Chairman Chamath Palihapitiya Says Tourism Spaceflights within a Year*, CNBC (Jul. 9, 2019).

yield the best outcome, unlike market allocation of space resources, or if a decentralized ownership will be a more efficient method for resource allocation.

Enforcing the first possession rule is also less appropriate where title is given over resources that are undefinable and are not yet ready to be exploited, but are merely anticipated to have value in the future, such as those expected to be found on asteroids. In such situations, the first possession rule can result in losses caused by overly rapid depletion of the resource and reduction of its present value. For example, this problem occurs when wells containing petroleum are drilled too closely together and pumped too rapidly, as it is only by capturing petroleum that a first possession entitlement over the petroleum is granted. Where the number of participants competing over freely accessible resource is high relative to the amount of resource too much efforts are invested in capture activities. This result, also known as the problem of rent dissipation, is typical under the first rule possession and might only exacerbate due to additional problem of premature resource development.[121]

In general, in a competitive market, it is expected that the marginal benefit of capturing a unit of a resource will equal the opportunity cost of the resources required to capture it. In the context of natural resource, the benefit of capturing resources greatly depends on the abundancy of the resources found relative to the amount of participants, who are contesting and racing for property rights.[122] The more abundant the resources relative to the number of racing contestants, the less likely that the problems of rent dissipation and externalities result from both the premature and the first possession rules. This problem amplifies when the number of claimants for property rights increases relative to the amount of resources, since too much efforts are invested in capturing resources in such case. In an environment where the amount of resources is fixed, then under both the first possession rule and open-access methods, the equilibrium level of harvest (number of harvesters) is determined by the rent dissipation condition.[123] This situation can be explained by the fact that higher returns will lure additional input (e.g., more fishing nets or hooks) to be invested in, in order to claim first possession, so that expenditures will increase and essentially again equal the marginal reward per unit.[124] These affairs can be demonstrated in the case of the fishery industry, where the common-pool problem has been enhanced due to overfishing under an open-access fishery regime, as will be further discussed under section 2.D. Only a monopoly owner that controls both the rate and the technique of capture can preclude this result. Indeed, by limiting and optimizing the number of units of a resource exploited, the rewards per unit can increase. However, this transformation into a single ownership is not only costly, but in the context of space, the notion of full ownership—over asteroids, the moon and other celestial bodies—can also create

121. Mark F. Grady & Jay I. Alexander, *Patent Law and Rent Dissipation*, 78 VA. L. REV. 305 (1992).
122. Dean Lueck, *supra* note 105, at 395-403.
123. Haddock, *supra* note 106, at 779-80; *see also* Jason Scott Johnston, *The Rule of Capture and the Economic Dynamics of Natural Resource Use and Survival Under Open Access Management Regimes* ENVTL. L. 855 (2005), at 859-61.
124. Haddock, *supra* note 106, at 779-80.

severe and adverse international repercussions, especially since space is perceived as a domain that is not subject to appropriation.[125]

Furthermore, the view of first possession as a solution for granting full ownership appears to be more of an "all-or-nothing" view of well-defined property rights, which, as shown in the case of open access to common property, has been proven to be not useful (as was demonstrated in the case of fishing in international, public domain, waters and "the tragedy of the commons," in H. Scott Gordon's critical analysis (1954)).[126] This perspective is fitting when commodities are characterized as homogenous entities, and one-dimensional property uses have only one attribute. Therefore, these commodities can be either owned or not owned, and thus, the economic rights associated with them equal the legal rights. However, since most assets have many attributes (i.e., characteristics and possible uses of assets), of which some are defined and some unspecified, the notion of ownership can become vague. This is why the focus on the ownership of attributes rather than assets can help resolve this vagueness and the distinction between legal and economic ownership rights makes important contributions to this process.[127] The legal rights of ownership hold the legal rights to future—yet undiscovered—attributes and usages of the asset, whereas the economic importance of ownership rights derives from the owner's ability to exercise residual control over the asset. This ability is "concerned not with what people are legally entitled to do but with what they believe they can do."[128] Therefore, the rethinking of the possibility of intermediate states of ownership, in which rights are imperfectly defined, should be addressed.[129]

In the case of space, rights must be created in a near vacuum environment, outside of any state's jurisdiction, where there is no single authority for allocating resources. In order to lure private commercial activities into this environment, and ensure peaceful economic development in space, an individual's "economic rights" over an asset need to be defined. These economic rights should include "*the individual's ability to consume the good (or the services of the asset) directly, or to consume it indirectly through exchange.*"[130] However, the process of defining and enforcing those rights can be costly. As a result, property rights are never perfectly delineated, and

125. *Id.*, at 780-81; *see also* U.N. GAOR, 16th Sess., U.N. Doc. A/Res/1721 (1961). "The General Assembly, ... 1. Commends to States for their guidance in the exploration and use of outer space the following principles: ... ; (b) Outer space and celestial bodies are free for exploration and use by all States in conformity with international law and are not subject to national appropriation."
126. Gordon, H. Scott, *The Economic Theory of a Common Property Resource: The Fishery*, 62 J. POLITICAL ECON'Y 124-42 (1954) (hereinafter "Gordon").
127. Note that, in economic analysis, the asset maintains importance, as it is the asset that is being priced and not its attributes due to measurement costs. *See also* BARZEL, ECONOMIC ANALYSIS, *supra* note 108, at 92-93 and 100.
128. Yoram Barzel, *The Capture of Wealth by Monopolists and the Protection of Property Rights*, 14.4 INT'L REV OF L. AND ECON. 393-409, at 394 (1994).
129. Kirsten Foss and Nicolai Foss, *Assets, Attributes, and Ownership*, 8(1) INTERNATIONAL JOURNAL OF THE ECONOMICS OF BUSINESS, at 8-10 (2001). *See also* BARZEL, ECONOMIC ANALYSIS, *supra* note 108, at 3-4 and 89.
130. BARZEL, ECONOMIC ANALYSIS, *supra* note 108, at 3; *see also* YORAM BARZEL, A THEORY OF THE STATE: ECONOMIC RIGHTS, LEGAL RIGHTS, AND THE SCOPE OF THE STATE, 15 (Cambridge University Press 2002).

people's equilibrium with respect to a satisfying level of the delineation of rights over their assets can change concurrently with a change in economic conditions. In addition, while "economic (property) rights" are the end goal people ultimately seek, "legal rights" are the means to achieve this end, their major function being to accommodate third-party adjudication and enforcement.[131] The legal rights hold not merely the right to use the assets, but also the right to prevent others from using it. "*Legal rights are the rights recognized and enforced, in part, by the government. These rights, as a rule, enhance economic rights, but the former are neither necessary nor sufficient for the existence of the latter.*"[132] A classic example to demonstrate this is of a thief who has economic, rather than legal, rights over the stolen goods. Another example is of a person who does not acquire a right to coconuts merely because he alone is physically capable of climbing the tree. Otherwise, how could a tree cutter dispossess them, without consent or compensation, simply by cutting down the tree? Neither the tree cutter nor the tree climber possesses legal right to the coconuts, but rather a lesser interest, such as a liberty or privilege, or mere right for use. Similarly, there is no legal right for a fisherman to stake claims on the fish nor the right to demand that others be excluded from the fish, simply because the fisherman knows where to catch them. In fact, what he has is an advantage of superior access to information, which will be lost once this information is spread.[133]

In the context of common property, whenever an asset is valuable, unclaimed, and available to the first possessor, it is a common-pool asset.[134] As the economic value of common property resources increase, individuals (or more accurately, private forces) are considerably more prone to delineate rights over them and convert them into private property. Although in terms of legal rights, space is not owned by any state, yet in terms of economic rights, this does not mean that space is deprived of any value. However, common assets, which in economic terms (rather than legal) are owned by no one, are deprived of value.[135] Thus, as space-based markets, in particular markets

131. BARZEL, ECONOMIC ANALYSIS, *supra* note 108, at 3-4 and 103-04.
132. *Id.*, at 4.
133. Daniel H. Cole & Peter Z. Grossman, *The Meaning of Property Rights: Law Versus Economics?*, 78 LAND ECON. 317-30, at 318-19 and 323-26 (2002). In the article, it is explained that economists' definitions of property rights do not reflect legal reality, although this state of affairs can last only as long as transacting is costless. However, in the real world since transaction costs are typically positive there is significance who possesses the legal rights and what that means. In coherence with the "Coase Theorem" (*see also* Ronald H. Coase, *The Problem of Social Costs*, 3 J. L. AND ECON. 1-44 (1960)), however, in a world of positive transaction costs, the meaning of property rights is important. And a realistic analysis of the transactions costs effectively involved actually requires using the expression in its legal meaning.
134. Haddock, *supra* note 106, at 778.
135. Harold Demsetz (1967), in his study of the Montagnais Indians of Labrador, argued that as the value of a common-property resource increases, people are more likely to establish rights over it. Specifically, he pointed out that prior to the Europeans' arrival in Labrador, when the value of beaver pelts was low, beaver habitats were held as common property. However, when the European market became accessible and the value of beaver pelts increased, then beaver habitats were converted to private property. In the same article Demsetz seems to oscillate between the positive view that property rights are established in response to economic conditions once resource values increase and the normative view that government should enhance private rights. A similar idea was utilized by Libecap (1996) in his analysis of the

in space minerals, become accessible and profitable in terms of economic value, especially as soon as the minerals' marginal value increases and exceeds their marginal costs (including transaction costs and the costs for measuring, policing and enforcing rights), the pressure to delineate rights will accordingly rise. Unless the gains which private entities achieve from owning rights over space minerals exceed their costs, these minerals are deemed to be left to the public domain.[136] The reason is that "*[w]hen the costs of metering and policing assets or assets' attributes exceed the valuations, such assets or attributes will be relinquished into the public domain and become common property.*"[137] In the case of space, for example, if the private space sector deems certain rights too expensive to exercise, they may choose to relinquish them to the public domain. Conversely, as the benefits and, more precisely, the possibility of profits associated with the rights to commodities found within the public domain rises, people will expend more resources to seize them and adopt accommodating property rights to turn these into private property. This change in the equilibrium property rights delineation can be affected by individuals, or occasionally by the state.[138]

Hence, the question remains if there is a method for demonstrating that private ownership in space is necessarily more efficient than and superior to government ownership, and that designating properties as private, such as those in mid-ocean, will yield net benefits. An example in support of the transfer of rights from the public domain can be found in the case of the conversion of the North Sea into an owned property; this sea was divided among countries bordering it under the 1958 Convention on the Continental Shelf, which was held in Geneva. This convention was preceded by a decline in underwater drilling costs, and by pressure from oil companies to secure legal and economic ownership over drilling in the North Sea, before they began to invest in the search for oil. As the value of the North Sea oil resources increased, so did the forces to delineate rights over it. These ownership rights over segments of the sea allowed countries to exploit their sea rights, either directly or indirectly, by granting these rights to private parties. In the case of the North Sea, the formal agreements and the delineation of borders proved to be of special significance. At that time, when the countries conferred to determine what rights to the sea should exist, there was not enough information on the precise locations where oil might be found. Thus, a simple method for establishing a formula was used, which gave each country the territory nearest to it, thereby avoiding creating disputes over setting borders.[139]

---

miners prospecting for gold in late nineteenth in California. *See* Harold Demsetz, *Toward a Theory of Property Rights*, 57.2 Am. Econ. Rev. 347-59 (May 1967), Papers and Proceedings of the Seventy-Ninth Annual Meeting of the American Economic Association (hereinafter "Demsetz, *Toward a Theory of Property Rights*"); Krishna Gupta, The Political Economy of Forest Management, 1-197, at 38 (2005); Barzel, Economic Analysis, *supra* note 108, at 92-93 and 100.

136. Libecap 1989 analyzes common-pool problems in a similar way by focusing on conditions under which political institutions evolve in order to overcome open-access problems and where political bargaining leads to the legal delineation of rights. *See* Barzel, Economic Analysis, *supra* note 108, at 5-6, 92 and 100; Gary D. Libecap, Contracting for Property Rights (Cambridge University Press 1989) (hereinafter "Libecap, Contracting for Property Rights").

137. Barzel, Economic Analysis, *supra* note 108.

138. *Id.*, at 103-04. *See also* Libecap, Contracting for Property Rights, *supra* note 136, at 1-2.

139. Peter D. Cameron, Property Rights and Sovereign Rights: The Case of North Sea Oil, Vol. 12, 210 (Academic Press 1983); *see also* Barzel, Economic Analysis, *supra* note 108, at 100-02.

In the case of space mining, similar to that of the high seas, it is best to assume that private companies will not invest without agreement among all countries on how to establish ownership segments in space, or with regard to specific operations. However, as the distance between specific celestial bodies and any state on Earth (which also rotates with the Earth's cycles) is equal, rights in space cannot be delineated in the same way as in the case of the North Sea. Another formula is needed.

As simple views of "owning" asteroids and the moon are not applicable, another analogy to cases from wildlife can be made. The Supreme Court declared that "owning" wildlife is an oxymoron, and that although no one owns wildlife, the sovereign has an obligation to assert rights over a public good. In international law, the sovereign in the context of space is "all mankind," and the international community is the representative of the people in their common ownership holding it in trust for the benefit of all mankind.[140] Additionally, if metering, pricing and policing are costly, as can be expected in the case of space, then private ownership, even in a scenario where there are zero-transaction costs, is never going to avoid creating inefficiencies. Nevertheless, if neither restrictions on the use of space resources nor limitations on the exploitation of its resources are enforced, it might be possible that the delineation of private property rights is still a better solution than the application of public ownership rights.[141] Therefore, the question remains whether efficiency motivates placing assets in the public or the private sector.

In general, when the government provides commodities at a zero pecuniary price and makes them available on a first-come, first-served basis, commodities are strictly allocated according to the order in which individuals join the queue, as is typical when "first-in-time first-in-right" is brought to bear. Although orderly queues typically would be kept, the competition for getting the first spot in line might arise from using one's power and might, if the line is not policed and those who are not able to compete effectively will not try to compete or even join the line.[142] Turning to the case of mining in space, those who own the technology and economic resources for achieving the "first right" might deter those who lack both of these from joining the space race, thus causing an unjustifiable distortion of the global wealth distribution. Consequently, similar debates between the developed and developing countries associated with concerns about the misuse of political and economic influence, as, for example, in the high seas, could resonate with the case of space.

When dealing with competition for free goods, the nature of restrictions delineates the margins of the competition. For example, the restrictions could be first-come, first-served and have no policing. Theoretically, therefore, everyone may join the race to space. However, the real margins of the competition in space could be decided

---

140. *Missouri v. Holland*, 252 U.S. 416 (1920). *See also* Richard Cahoon, *The Relation of Patent Law and Wildlife Conservation Law in the United States*, Cornell Theses and Dissertations (2007).

141. Barzel, Economic Analysis, *supra* note 108, at 100-01. Note that Lueck (1989) in his study demonstrated in the context of the evolution of property-wildlife regime that state action was consistent with the hypothesis that its objective was to maximize the value of wildlife. *See* Barzel, Economic Analysis, *supra* note 108, at 100-01; *see also* Lueck Dean, *The Economic Nature of Wildlife Law*, 18.2 The J. Legal Studies 291-324, at 317 (June 1989).

142. Barzel, Economic Analysis, *supra* note 108, at 16-17.

ultimately by power or technological advancement rather than time.[143] This will ultimately bar many from participating in the emerging space mining industry.

Indeed, it can be argued that allocating zero-priced resources through the market can be considered economically efficient when allocated without assigning property rights or enforcing any regulatory systems, since in the latter cases, the costs will outweigh the benefits. Take, for example, the assignment of free parking spaces at certain shopping centers, where the cost of employing resources to charge for parking services and to exclude drivers who park, but do not shop, exceeds the value of these resources for other uses.[144] Instead of policing the use of a large parking lot, it is more economically efficient to let it be rationed among users, free of charge, by queuing rather than by price. However, it can be argued that space resources are not genuinely "free" goods, due to the research and exploitation costs associated with their mining.[145] Even though space is speculated to contain "free" resources greater than those Earth would ever need (since the universe is infinite), when considering the number of asteroids that are near Earth and accessible for exploitation, space cannot absorb all human activities, since these resources are, in fact, much more finite. The limitation associated with access to space resources by itself increases the costs of space resources and creates doubt regarding the efficiency of allocation by the market.[146]

Moreover, based on the theorem of the second best,[147] it can be argued that even when the exploitation of space resources is not handed over to the most efficient user (or extractor of space minerals), if there are positive externalities from these activities, there still might be a trade-off for the sake of developing an efficient market in the future, even though this is the second most optimal situation, and is clearly an alternative solution to sole ownership of the entire resource domain.[148] Additionally, even if, as in isolated cases, such as the allocation of space resources through regulatory regimes, or through the assignment of property rights in place of market competition, there are other inefficiencies in the system (like the negative externality stemming from the cost of space debris as a negative byproduct of space mining), all of these inefficiencies eventually create a zero-sum for each other. In effect, these inefficiencies balance each other out, since less output with negative externalities can create second-best options and a better solution, when compared to market competition. For example, when industrial plants pollute the air, the formation of a monopoly, which is usually perceived as a socially inefficient system (creating lower output at

143. *Id.*
144. Jürgen G. Backhaus ed., *The Elgar Companion to Law and Economics*, 41-42 (Edward Elgar Publishing 2nd ed. 2005.); *see also* BARZEL, ECONOMIC ANALYSIS, *supra* note 108, at 92-96.
145. Ross D. Eckert, *Exploitation of Deep Ocean Minerals: Regulatory Mechanisms and United States Policy*, 17 J.L. & ECON. 143, 178, 152-53 (1974) (hereinafter "Ross, *Exploitation of Deep Ocean Minerals*").
146. IISL Directorate of Studies, *supra* note 4, at 32.
147. Note that "*The general theorem of the second best states that if one of the Paretian optimum conditions cannot be fulfilled a second best optimum situation is achieved only by departing from all other optimum conditions.*" *See* Wiens David, *Assessing Ideal Theories: Lessons from the Theory of Second Best*, 15.2 POLIT. PHILOS. ECON. 132-49, at 132 (2016).
148. Richard Lipsey et al., *General Theory of the Second Best*, 24.1 REV. ECON. STUDIES 11-32 (1956-1957); *see also* Richard Lipsey, *Reflections on the General Theory of Second Best at Its Golden Jubilee*, 14 INT. TAX PUB. FIN. 349, 352 (2007).

higher prices), could be the second best solution and a better one compared to a perfectly competitive market, where conditions allow for more manufacturers to create more inefficiency and, thereby, generate even higher amounts of pollution than the single monopolistic producer.[149]

However, when rights are initially in the public domain, these rights could become well defined only when the ultimate owner is determined, a process that can lead to anarchy and even violence along the way. This is the reason why the Gold Rush in California was exceptionally costly, and was characterized as a time of uncertainty about who would win the rights to the deposits found in mines, even though the U.S. and Mexico had signed a peace treaty finalizing the transfer of the gold-bearing land to the U.S.[150] In the case of space, it is unclear what costs will be associated with allocating the rights over resources from the "province of all mankind" into private hands.

Nevertheless, even when private users leave property to the public domain, they are still able to extract value from it, which cannot be aggregated without incurring costs. The owners, who relinquish properties into the public domain, are sometimes able to reduce their losses by restricting access to these properties. For example, the state may restrict access to "free" goods by requiring licenses or imposing catch limits for recreational fishing and hunting. In other cases, the state may find that imposing restrictions is not to their benefit, allowing for open access in the public domain, as in, for example, allowing fishing when it is beyond states' territorial waters or in the consumption of air.[151] To better understand the development and movement from community rights to open-access regimes and back to collective action, as in the case of the seas, and the potential effects and efficiency of joint exploitation of resource stock in the case of space resources, please *see* section 2.C. Ultimately, the most efficient ownership regime, for which its advantages will outweigh its disadvantages, should reshape the future of the eco-political regime in space. It should also be sustained and encouraged through an appropriate tax policy for the commercial space industry, and vice versa.

B.2. The First Possession Rule as an Allocation Method in the Context of Space

While first possession is a poor allocation method, there are several advantages to applying this mechanism in space, such as: (1) it is a simple mechanism that requires little government involvement, aside from a recording system that will most likely have to be developed in order to allocate rights to the first possessors (once established, this ease of administration swill lower the transaction costs of property rights in the future);

149. On the other hand, it should be noted that among the criticism against the second-best theory, the concern was "*that second best theory would be used to justify all kinds of misguided government interventions.*" Richard G. Lipsey, *Successes and Failures in the Transformation of Economics*, 8.2 J. Econ. Methodology 169, 191-92 (2001).
150. Barzel, Economic Analysis, *supra* note 108, at 16-17 and 85-86.
151. *Id.*, at 95-96.

(2) this system might reduce government protection and policing costs and encourage space entrepreneurs to develop self-protection mechanisms against raids in their mine operations (this assumption is supported by the same rationale for inducing self-protection that led the U.S. Government, in its process of settling the West, to enact the Homestead Act of 1862, which set an underpricing policy for land at below-market prices, or, at times, even free, as happened when settlers gained property rights on a "first-come, first-served" basis, albeit these rights had various constraints and restrictions subjected on the use of the land);[152] (3) the rapid development that the first possession rule attracts might be advantageous as space development also serves noneconomic goals, especially when these are associated with high investment risks (e.g., to deepen our journey into the cosmos or to enhance efficient cultivation on Mars); (4) this allocation method might ultimately hold significant spillover benefits for the space community and for the entire international community, such as increasing technological progress and science education,[153] even though it could create more inefficiencies in the space race (note that advances in space technology, now almost exclusively the domain of industrialized countries, also hold a promise for the Third World, including agricultural-based economies. Examples of this include satellites and communications networks that offer weather forecasting services relied upon by farmers for making decisions about when to plant, water, fertilize, and harvest their crops; or when remote sensing and satellite imagery are used to help monitor and assess long-term trends in climate change, marine pollution, or soil erosion to help support the best uses of resources).[154] In addition to these advantages, a "first possession" rule is less likely to create a situation where the lowest valued celestial bodies will be left unclaimed, and, thus, adversely impact the value of rights over future mining operations when comparing the infinite territories of space with the finite ones on Earth.[155]

Nevertheless, the first possession can lead to adverse repercussions at the international level, especially when imposed on a nonrenewable asset—for example, water or rare metals—that can be exploited only once. However, these repercussions can be precluded by establishing a strong common interest among all countries, including those who want to participate in space activities, in order to maximize the

152. According to the Homesteading Act of 1862, homesteaders before gaining full ownership of the land had, first, to occupy the homestead for at least five years and, second, to improve the land before acquiring the right to sell it. These restrictions aimed to turn leaving of the land costly. BARZEL, ECONOMIC ANALYSIS, *supra* note 108, at 121-23. *See also* Megan E. Jenkins, Rendy T. Simmons, and Camila H. Wardle, *The Environmental Optimism of Elinor Ostrom*, 1-265, 10-17 (Center for Growth and Opportunity at Utah State University 2020).
153. Robert P. Merges et al., *Space Resources, Common Property, and the Collective Action Problem*, 6 N.Y.U. ENVTL. L.J. 107, 119-21 (1997) (hereinafter "Merges").
154. Report of the World Commission, *supra* note 50, at 218.
155. Note that according to the Homesteading Act of 1862 the "first-come, first-served" basis allowed the earliest arriver to claim the best homestead. As a result, the lowest-value homesteads remained unclaimed. However, the Graduation Act of 1854 provided for progressive price reductions for such unclaimed land. Blumm Michael and Kara Tebeau, *Antimonopoly in Public Land Law*, 28 GEO. ENVTL. L. REV. 20 (2015); *see also* BARZEL, ECONOMIC ANALYSIS, *supra* note 108, at 122.

new tax base in space, as long as they can ensure an equitable socio-economic share from the new space undertakings.

When dealing with mining in extraterritorial areas, as in the cases of both outer space and the high seas, the international community, as the resource owner, possesses a valuable asset. Toward the goal of transforming this asset into financial resources, the international community must attract capital on terms that ensure that it obtains the greatest possible value for its resources—even given the uncertainty as to the value of these resources—while aligning with the private investors' objectives.[156] This goal can only be achieved under a stable global commons regime that carefully balances optional value of the resources that account for the uncertainty around markets, technology, the environmental and social costs of the world's shared resources, and the private interests of the DSM investors and of the ESEs. An international royalty regime can serve as a tool for creating just such a stable global commons regime that creates this needed balance, as will be further discussed under section 2.F.

C. TILTING BETWEEN COMMUNITY RIGHTS AND OPEN ACCESS

In both realms, the oceans and the space, efforts to apply similar doctrines and notions to these global resources, while also promoting economic development, need a strong international consensus and approach on how to treat these commons. For example, the common heritage principle and the *res communis* and *res nullius* notions, which result in enforcing non-appropriation rules to resources that are not subject to national sovereignty but are said to belong to all nations, have all been legally adopted at the international level as a means for promoting political goals and economic growth. These attempts to compare the commons in both the oceans and space can lead to similar approaches with respect to resource allocation management, although a different outcome is possible given the prospects of economic efficiency, dependency, and nexus of the evolving ecosystem in space to Earth, a system quite different from that of the ocean. Therefore, several legitimate approaches for management regimes in space can be created, particularly, regarding how the oceans have been managed and their transition and evolution in recent history. In particular, there has been a transition from community rights to open access, and vice versa. The reasons for this maritime eco-political and economic development, and the movement between different management regimes, can provide and lead to a new perspective about a management regime for space resources.

C.1. The Development of State Property Rights and Unregulated Open-Access Regimes in the Maritime Case

Since ancient times, millions of humans, both those living along ocean shores and further inland, have thrived off of the oceans' food and resources. The coastal

156. Emil M. Sunley et al., *Revenue from the Oil and Gas Sector: Issues and Country Experience*, Post-Conference Draft (Jun. 8, 2002).

communities formed along the shores gained control over these natural resources and began to create and develop rights and claims to the living resources there. These rights were localized customary rights that were formed to grant the coastal communities the freedom to control the utilization of their resources, including the ways and types of technologies to be used, and the responsibility for preserving the fauna.

However, several significant events have impacted these legal rights to these communities' marine resources, including: the growth of international trade and the development of market channels for the food supply, especially as a result of new technologies (as can be reflected in the efforts to organize exports of fish and fishery products to Europe and Japan in the first half of the twentieth century); the establishment of modern nation-states; and the formation of the League of Nations, arising from the controversy around ownership and control over the oceans and their resources. These geopolitical controversies between nations began only at the beginning of the twentieth century. With the world's recognition of the economic value of oil and the mineral resources lying deep below the seabeds, nations opened discussions about the standardization of maritime boundaries, hoping to enter into more formalized agreements and to pass statutory laws regarding rights to use these living resources in the oceans.[157]

Before this process began, most countries established their territorial jurisdictional limits at sea independent of one another. Based on the seventeenth-century concept of the "freedom of the seas," a country's territorial waters were typically developed and limited to from 3 nm up to 12 nm from the nation's coastlines,[158] leaving all waters beyond that to be treated as international waters open to all nations but belonging to none (the *mare liberum* principle promulgated by Hugo Grotius).[159]

However, as pressure on fish stocks increased, partly due to new technologies, such as the satellite capabilities developed by the Soviet Union, which allowed distant nations to roam all over the world's oceans and track fish stock movements, it became clear that the 12-mile fishing limits were no longer useful. These hardly mattered to coastal countries anymore but were particularly important for the developing countries that had previously been colonies, and who had become more concerned about protecting their natural resources and the incomes these provided.[160]

During the 1930 League of Nations Conference for the Codification of International Law in the Hague, the issue of delimiting maritime boundaries and the territorial seas was discussed. Nations were aiming to exercise sovereign claims and rights over both the living and non-living resources of the high seas, as well as the seabed and subsoil underlying thereof, and within their exclusive economic zone and continental

157. John Kurien, The Blessing of Commons: Small Scale Fisheries, Community Property Rights, and Coastal Natural Assets at 3-4 and 8-10 (2004) (hereinafter "Kurien").

158. At the UNCLOS III (1973-1982) Conference, that came into force on 1994, it was agreed that 12 nm is a country's territorial water.

159. Hugo Grotius, *supra* note 92.

160. Rögnvaldur Hannesson, *The Exclusive Economic Zone and Economic Development in the Pacific Islands Countries,* ScienceDirect 886, 897, at 888 (2008), published by Center for Fisheries Economics, The Norwegian School of Economics and Business Administration (hereinafter "Rögnvaldur Hannesson").

shelf, and over the benefits resulting from their economic development. As the 1930 Conference resulted in a dearth of agreements, the U.S., under the Truman Administration in 1945, in a unilateral decision, was the first to claim rights on resources found within the continental shelf off the coast of the U.S.—extending the ocean floor almost 200 nm from the shoreline of the Atlantic coast. Following this action, more nations, such as Argentina first, followed by Brazil, Nicaragua, Panama, Peru, Salvador, Uruguay, Chile, Ecuador and Iceland proclaimed exclusive sovereignty over their continental shelf areas or over a maritime zone extending 200 miles from their baselines of their coast, as well as the fish stocks, the soil and the subsoil thereof.[161]

With an increased understanding of the potential for anarchy in ocean governance, the U.N. General Assembly instructed the International Law Commission to prepare draft articles and conventions for a law of the sea. The first United Nations Conference on the Law of the Sea (UNCLOS I) met in 1958 to begin discussions. In 1960, UNCLOS II was held, and the third convention, UNCLOS III, took place between 1973 and 1982.[162] During the debates in the first conferences, UNCLOS I and UNCLOS II, two important concepts were addressed. The first was the concept of the "special interest" of a coastal state, with regard to the maintenance of the productivity of living resources in coastal waters. The second concept was the "preferential right" of coastal states, as advanced by countries such as Vietnam, Philippines and Iceland, all of whose economies greatly depend on their fishing industries, and where fishing methods were limited to local fishing from small boats, vis-à-vis other states whose allocation of fishery resources were considered to be larger, commercial industries. Within the first coastal states, there was a greater opportunity for success in terms of resource conservation and management.[163]

However, only during UNCLOS III was a treaty developed that attempted to specify the boundaries of all coastal countries, treating the first 12 nm as territorial seas, and the next 200 nm as EEZs, within which each country would maintain the sole exploitation and property rights over all natural resources, and be expected to control both the economic exploitation and environmental quality. When countries lay closer than 24 nm apart or their EEZs were closer than 400 nm apart, a median line boundary between each country would need to be drawn. Though the treaty has not yet been ratified by all countries, this 200-nm limit has gained widespread support. Most countries adhere to the 1982 treaty guidelines by considering themselves as in control

161. Matt Rosenberg, *Political Geography of the Oceans, Who Owns the Oceans?*, ThoughtCo. (Jul. 30, 2018); *see also* Rögnvaldur Hannesson, *supra* note 160, at 887; Kurien, *supra* note 157, at 9 and 18-20; Chinese Society of International Law, *The South China Sea Arbitration Awards: A Critical Study*, 17(2) Chinese J. Int'l L. 207-748 (June 2018); United Nations, *Ocean & Law of the Sea (A Historical Perspective)*, Division for Ocean Affairs and the Law of the Sea; Adi Mazen, *The Application of the Law of the Sea and the Convention on the Mediterranean Sea*, Division for Ocean Affairs and the Law of the Sea Office of Legal Affairs, The United Nations New York (2009).

162. United Nation, Ocean & Law of the Sea, Division for Ocean Affairs and the Law of the Sea.

163. Dolliver Nelson, *The Development of the Legal Regime of High Seas Fisheries*, in International Law and Sustainable Development: Past Achievements and Future Challenges Ch. 6, 118-24 (Alan E. Boyle and David Freestone eds. Oxford University Press 1999). *See also* William W. Bishop, Jr., *The 1958 Geneva Convention on Fishing and Conservation of the Living Resources of the High Seas*, 62.7 Columbia L. Rev. 1206, 1229 at 1217-24 (November 1962).

of this 200-nm domain, with respect to the natural resources of these zones, including living resources and minerals on and underneath the sea bottom, but not over navigation rights.[164]

As a result of the standardization of the maritime boundaries set under the UNCLOS treaty, the wealth of the territorial seas and EEZs, which account for approximately one-third of the world's oceans and contain 85% of the living natural assets of the oceans, was transferred to coastal countries, essentially becoming their property rights, while just two-thirds of the ocean's total area and wealth remain within the realm of the common heritage of humanity as open-access domains. These deeper parts of the ocean beyond the EEZs are regarded as the "high seas" and are international waters. They contain 15% of the living resources, where possession rights can only be established by capture and harvest. This fact provides countries with more financial capital and better technology an advantage in asserting such rights.[165]

The national ownership regime over resources established in the EEZ gave the coastal countries the right to rent out their access to these resources. The advantages from such an arrangement depend on the ability of the coastal countries to extract rents from the exploiters by appropriately setting access fees and the productive use of the access fee revenues to boost their economic development. Often, the coastal states, through joint ventures with foreign companies, have succeeded in developing their own fishing industries.[166]

However, the sovereignty given to coastal countries to exploit their proximate sea resources has not always led to economic growth and development, nor has it been used as an engine of economic development. Inadequate policies and the lack of an appropriate regulatory and political framework make these unattractive to private interests who might have wanted to become involved in the exploitation of resources, as has been the case with the fishing industries in many Pacific Island states. Moreover, aside from close proximity to these resources, the lack of other comparative advantages for the development of successful extraction industries may also preclude the evolution of successfully integrated logistical operations, such as those needed in the fishing industry, where the lack of transportation infrastructure and distribution systems can lead to delays in handling the perishable products.[167]

Additionally, the collection of rents by coastal countries has led to increasing competition for licenses among new entrants in the fishing industry, exacerbating the overexploitation problem of the commons by the fishery industry, and hence dissipating all rents or pure profits generated by the licensees and, as a result, the access fees, as well. Consequently, an intervention through intergovernmental agreements among

---

164. UNCLOS, *supra* note 5, Part V, Arts. 55-75. *See also* Rögnvaldur Hannesson, *supra* note 160, at 888 and 891; Maritime Zones and Boundaries, *supra* note 6.
165. Kurien, *supra* note 157, at 10.
166. Rögnvaldur Hannesson, *supra* note 160, at 888 and 891-92.
167. *Id.*, at 896.

the coastal countries was required, and in order to coordinate their actions and maximize their aggregate benefits, licenses have been limited.[168]

Unsurprisingly, fishery management was nevertheless criticized as a solution of "political economy" that was not based on the economics of the fishery resource utilization, but contested as management *"for the benefit of man, not fish,"* and, *"therefore the effect of management upon fish-stocks cannot be regarded as beneficial per se."*[169] This result can impact economic growth in international realms, both in the case of the oceans and space, despite the need for setting licensing schemes to limit access and user rights to the global commons, which are also needed to meet certain conservation requirements so that an inefficient and harmful degradation of resources can be avoided.

An argument about the distinction between the right to use and management rights can be made. When dealing with the commons, management rights and the benefits derived from these, including licensing restrictions, should be held by both the users and non-users of these commons and set into a Code of Conduct,[170] so that the right to use and gain ownership of these resources can be distinctly regulated. As such, a stable global management regime that provides ecological and economic protections and offers benefits to both the users and non-users of the commons using a distinct ownership rights system can be formed in both the oceans and the space, especially in the latter case where the amount of users is much more limited and so is the imminent potential for the exploitation of near-earth asteroids, factors which only increase the threat of space resources being looted by a small elitist group of entrepreneurs and reduce benefits for non-users. However, differing from the case of the oceans, the limited scale of use—right holders and participants—in the race for space resources can merely mitigate and undermine the concerns regarding potential problems created by an open-access regime while supporting free access for all who use it. This can be the case as long as the cost of extracting resources is large relative to the value of the resource itself. However, once space technology capabilities mature, so that space minerals can be used or produced in space itself and, thereby, space technology can support the value of space resources while decreasing the extracting costs, the concerns regarding the negative spillovers from an open-access regime may enhance, similar to what had happened in the case of the fisheries which were not threatened by overexploitation until the emergence of sophisticated fishing equipment.[171] However, an argument can be made that, when dealing with exhaustible and nonrenewable

---

168. For example, the Palau Arrangement among the Pacific Island states, which was concluded in 1992, set a limit for the number of purse seine vessels that could be licensed in the region. *Id.*, at 890-91 and 894.
169. Martin D. Burkenroad, *Theory and Practice of Marine Fishery Management*, 18 J. DU CONSEIL PERMANENT INT'L POUR L'EXPLORATION DE LA MER 300-10 (January 1953); *see also* Gordon, *supra* note 126, at 124-42.
170. A.T. Charles, *Use Rights and Responsible Fisheries: Limiting Access and Harvesting through Rights-Based Management*, in A FISHERY MANAGER'S GUIDEBOOK: MANAGEMENT MEASURES AND THEIR APPLICATION, Ch. 6, at 131-57, FAO Fisheries Technical Paper, No. 424 (K. Cochrane ed., Food and Agriculture Organization of the United Nations 2002).
171. P. Dasgupta, *The Control of Resources*, 17-18 (Delhi: Oxford University Press and Cambridge, MA: Harvard University Press 1982).

resources in space, the impact of overexploitation should be noticeable at the beginning stages of resource extraction regardless of the costs and technological means of the extraction.

C.2. Transition of the Marine Ecosystem Back to a Regime of Collective Action and Norms

From the problems and the arguments described above, the creation of state property regimes did not resolve the problems associated with the management of the natural resources in coastal waters, neither in the developed maritime countries nor in the developing countries where the possession rights of those who own the capital and political power degenerated the state into an unregulated "open-access" regime. This failure in the management regime led to an ecological, economic and social crisis. In contrast to the open-access regime, it has been contended that a small-scale fishery controlled by municipal fisherfolk communities would be a much more beneficial and viable solution, for economic, ecological, technical, organizational, and social reasons.[172]

Therefore, a community property rights regime was recommended as a replacement for the unbridled freedom regime, allowing the accumulation of excessive private capital investments, including by outsiders, while reducing private risks owning to communal ownership.[173] By definition, this regime requires co-owners to hold community consultations and reach a common process for approval of actions that are mutually agreed upon, and which they may, thereafter, undertake individually, including decisions on the nature and the quantity of capital to be invested in fishing, norms regarding the extent of the effort to be expended, and the manner in which the products of one's labor are disposed. This community property rights regime does not usurp the crucial role played by individuals, but only circumscribes it within collective norms in a way that ensures the redistribution of resources and the wealth of the coastal waters to a larger number of persons who greatly rely on these for their sustenance. This redistribution also promotes the conservation of the resources and the socioeconomic well-being of the community and helps in preventing tensions and struggles over the appropriation of resources. Additionally, the reinstitution of a community property rights regime requires collaboration between the community and the state, which is also needed for supporting an effective and sustainable redistribution of the resources between them, whereas the one who bears the greater risk gains a meaningful appropriation from it.[174]

172. Ostrom, *supra* note 35. *See also* Svein Jentoft, *Fisheries Co-management Delegating Government Responsibility to Fishermen's Organizations*, 13.2 MARINE POLICY 137-54; Robert S. Pomeroy et al., *Fisheries Co-management and Small-Scale Fisheries: A Policy Brief* (International Center of Living Aquatic Resources Management (ICLARM), PHILIPPINES 1994) (hereinafter "Pomeroy"); K.K. Viswanathan et al., *Fisheries Co-management Policy Brief: Findings from a Worldwide Study*, WORLD FISH CENTER POLICY BRIEF 2 (2003).
173. Partha Dasgupta, *Common Property Resources: Economic Analytics*, 40 ECON. AND POLITICAL WEEKLY 1610-22 (2005).
174. Kurien, *supra* note 157, at 16-19.

C.3. Connecting the Use of Resources in the Oceans to Space

This movement, from community rights to open-access regimes and on to collective action, can shed light on various facets of issues that are to be encountered in space. Despite the legitimacy of nations' concerns regarding the future of their wealth from natural resources, the geographical proximity principle does not support granting exclusive property rights to any state, nor would it justify the delineation of territorial jurisdiction. Additionally, the solutions offered by community property rights and collective management of space resources might not lead to proper management of resources for several reasons. As long as the controlling community, supposedly the one with the property rights, exists on Earth and has not evolved into a space-based community, disagreements among those who hold the rights over how the resources are to be used are likely to arise and turn the management and enforcement rules more complex than in the case of the oceans.[175]

Furthermore, in the case of the oceans, coastal communities have been able to gain access to information about potential fish stocks, especially as their livelihood was highly dependent upon these, and, hence, also able to make the exploitation of these resources cost-efficient while representing adequately all users' interests.[176] However, in the case of space, no Earth-based community can fully determine the opportunities hidden in space resources or become highly dependent upon these, at least as long as Earth's resources are sustainable. Therefore, no effective communication and decision-making regarding efficient exploitation can be made, especially as differences and gaps in information and technological capabilities among the space mining participants exist, and provide obstacles to reaching agreement on the allocation rules for sharing the net benefits generated by collective action.[177] As the space economy evolves and becomes more dependent upon space-based resources, especially as these resources become highly beneficial in outer space (e.g., refueling satellites with water pumped from asteroids), the holistic and homogenous understanding and reliance on space-based resources are likely to increase, and, thus, change and tip the balance toward a hybrid ownership management, if not toward a communal management system.[178]

Nevertheless, corrupt practices in the use of resources and a lack of understanding of how to restore degraded ecosystem functions, associated with high financial and technological barriers and gaps, might undermine an international collective management regime (unlike the case in coastal resources), and is, therefore, less likely to occur with space resources.[179] In such a situation, a community movement that elects the poor (the developing countries, for example) as the guardians of natural resources, and empowers them with significant decision-making role (even though they are not

175. Pomeroy, *supra* note 172, at 11-12.
176. *Id.*
177. Gary D. Libecap, *The Conditions for Successful Collective Action*, in *Local Commons and Global Interdependence: Heterogeneity and Co-operation in Two Domains*, at 187-88 (R.O. Keohane and E. Ostrom eds. Sage Publications Ltd. 1995) (hereinafter "Libecap, *The Conditions for Successful Collective Action*").
178. *Id.*, at 165-69 and 187-89.
179. *Id.*, at 20-21.

equipped to understand efficiency considerations regarding space utilization and would, thereby, be expected to make decisions based only on self-interest) could adversely impact this type of collective ownership.

All these considerations and implications should be taken into account when structuring the not-so-distant future of the space mining regime. This regime should be able to provide further clarity with regard to the differences between the states-parties rights which have already been legally accepted at the international level—that is, by the Member States to the Outer Space Treaty,[180] or even the Moon Treaty[181]—such as to collect, remove and use samples, minerals and other substances in a manner that maintains space resources for the benefit and interests of all countries, as well as other targeted commercial transactions and exploitation activities in those areas that will continue to be perceived as *res communis*.[182] Furthermore, this exploitation regime should be capable of resolving the common-pool and externalities problems associated with space mining activities, as will be discussed below in sections 2.D and 2.E.

D. APPROACHES TO EXTERNALITY PROBLEMS IN "NONTERRITORIAL" ARENAS

Where resources are common to all parties and open to competitive, unrestricted entry and production, excessive rapid exploitation and resource rent dissipation can result.[183] The viability of the common-pool problem has been proven in the case of the fishery industry, particularly when dealing with fisheries that are not restricted to a single nation. It has been demonstrated that due to the unrestricted entrance of private powers to this unregulated industry, many species have been overfished. Therefore, regulating the fisheries market, except via monopoly power, can yield economically efficient outcomes and help to maximize the economic rent,[184] which is the *"return in*

180. Outer Space Treaty, *supra* note 17, at Arts. I and II.
181. Moon Treaty, *supra* n. 47. Under Art. 11(2) to the Moon Treaty, while "The moon is not subject to national appropriation by any claim of sovereignty, by means of use or occupation, or by any other means," it is provided under its Art. 6 that:

    1. There shall be freedom of scientific investigation on the moon by all States Parties without discrimination of any kind, on the basis of equality and in accordance with international law.
    2. In carrying out scientific investigations and in furtherance of the provisions of this Agreement, the States Parties shall have the right to collect on and remove from the moon samples of its mineral and other substances. Such samples shall remain at the disposal of those States Parties which caused them to be collected and may be used by them for scientific purposes. States Parties shall have regard to the desirability of making a portion of such samples available to other interested States Parties and the international scientific community for scientific investigation. States Parties may in the course of scientific investigations also use mineral and other substances of the moon in quantities appropriate for the support of their missions.

182. Freeland, *Common Heritage*, *supra* note 17.
183. Libecap, *The Conditions for Successful Collective Action*, *supra* note 177, at 162-63.
184. Note that for extraction, economic rent is due to a scarcity (uneven distribution) of natural resources (e.g., land, oil, or minerals). Henry George describes "economic rent" as, *"[I]n the economic meaning of rent, payments for the use of any of the products of human exertion are*

excess of the resource owner's opportunity cost," or can also be defined as the extra money or payments in excess of the amount expected.[185]

Leaving aside a dispute over the meaning of the concept of rent[186] and the appropriate goal of exploitation—if it is the maximization of the present value of resources rather than rent maximization—when turning to space resources, an analysis regarding how rents could be maximized from space mining is needed so that unrestricted entry will not dissipate rent in this industry, similar to what occurs in the fisheries. Furthermore, since the supply of space minerals in the solar system, in particular, those observed in the low Earth orbit (LEO), can and should be treated as a scarce resource, the depletion of the mineral stocks embedded in asteroids in LEOs due to overexploitation and overcapitalization by the private sector can and would be considered as a negative externality. Similarly, as has happened in the case of other common property resources, such as the fishing grounds, space might become vulnerable to "the tragedy of the commons" if appropriate environmental governance is not enacted.

In the case of the high seas, where ample resources, including food and minerals, lay unowned in a "common pool," it has been found that these resources suffer from inefficient exploitation as a result of externality problems associated with the creation of property rights. Similarly, as with ocean resources, and unlike fixed subsurface mineral resources, the migratory and fugitive nature of subterranean oil and gas does not allow for the assignment of property rights to surface land owners over oil and natural deposits that lay under private lands in the U.S. and are, thereby, considered open-access resources. As a result, property rights are granted only upon extraction or capture of these resources.[187]

Additionally, unlike in the fishing industry, for resolving the externality problem in the oil production industry, the unitization method has developed as the common-pool difficulties extended only over each particular pool of oil. Under this method, each member contributes a share of her profit to a general pool that is ultimately redistributed across members in a particular way. Thus, unlike fisheries, no regulation of the overall rate of exploitation of oil is required for efficient exploitation. Instead, either

---

excluded, and of the lumped payments for the use of houses, farms, etc., only that part is rent which constitutes the consideration for the use of the land. The part that is paid for the use of buildings or other improvements is properly interest, as it is a consideration for the use of capital." See https://www.henrygeorgefoundation.org/the-science-of-economics/economic-rent.html?jjj = 1578174927959.

185. Sweeney, *supra* note 33, at 180.
186. Note that there are economists who claim that the total surplus or economic rent attributable to the limited factor is the rectangle p*q (i.e., entire price*unit of quantity), as in the case of limited natural resources (because of their limited availability and inelasticity and fixed supply). Rents can also be defined as "the excess payment (imputed or otherwise) to a factor in fixed supply." *See* Ragnar Arnason, *Fisheries Rents: Theoretical Basis and an Example,* U. of Iceland and European Comm. Joint Research Ctr. (2006).
187. Gary D. Libecap et al., *The Economic Evolution of Petroleum Property Rights in the United States,* 31 J. Legal Studies 204, 209, 208-20 (2002); *see also* Richard T. Miller, *A Mineral Owner's Implied Rights to Use Surface Property Owned by Others,* 32 Energy & Min. L. Inst. 204, 249, at 208-20 (2011); A. Soliman, *Duty of Stewardship and Fisheries Governance: A Proposed Framework,* 13 Maritime Studies 11 (2014).

single ownership or specific collective agreements concerning each individual pool of oil is sufficient for free market activity to yield efficient outcomes.[188] Similarly, in the case of ocean-bed nodule mining, it has been demonstrated that no common-pool problem exists. Thus, it was concluded that an unregulated regime would be economically efficient.

Turning to space resources, analyses are needed on whether international regulation is necessary or whether rents might be maximized from space mining without a unique regulatory regime, so that unrestricted entry to this industry will not dissipate rents, as occurred with fisheries. The more similarities space mining bears to offshore oil exploitation, the less the likelihood that this industry would suffer from common-pool problems, and, thus, the higher the likelihood that an unregulated regime for space resources exploitation would yield an economically efficient outcome. However, this could be accomplished by maintaining single ownership of each mine. As a result, the first possession rule is not deleterious in this situation as it is with other common-pool resources subject to the first possession rule.[189] Nevertheless, when comparing space mining to these industries, e.g., fisheries or oil, other unique characteristics and overreaching principles should be considered and addressed when establishing risk-sharing and allocation rules that deal with the division of externality costs associated with space mining activities, as, for example, the risks associated with the liabilities of the spacefaring state (which is discussed in detail below). This important factor might tip the balance toward a type of hybrid ownership mechanism, between the first possession rule (as adopted under the unitization solution for oil exploitation) and the community property regime (as adopted in the fisheries case), since the significant costs of externalities associated with space objects are, by necessity, internalized by the launching states.

Indeed, there are more unique characteristics to be added to the debate regarding an appropriate resource management system in space and that can support different arguments, such as that unregulated market activity will result in a rapid depletion of space resources when dealing with nonrenewable resources. However, these arguments "must rely on a belief in the general failure of a market system to lead to correct investments and production decisions because of a failure of private decision-makers to use socially appropriate discount rates."[190]

In traditional economic theory regarding property rights, it has been argued that all environmental and natural resource problems associated with overexploitation stem from incompletely defined and unenforced property rights, whether informal or formal, group or individual, while an unregulated resource management regime is subject to the whims of private decision-makers, who have no incentive to internalize social benefits and costs associated with their business model when deciding on production or investment activities.[191] This situation leads to a gap between private

188. Sweeney, *supra* note 33, at 181.
189. *Id.*, at 181-82.
190. *Id.*
191. Demsetz, *Toward a Theory of Property Rights*, *supra* note 135, at 350-51; *see also* Antonio Nicita, Matteo Rizzolli and Maria Alessandra Rossi, *Towards a Theory of Incomplete Property Rights*, ISNIE Conference, Universidad Pompeu Fabra, Barcelona (2005).

and social net returns and results in externalities—harmful effects to third parties, such as costly technological or pecuniary externalities. Examples of these externality problems can be seen in the case of overfishing, which depletes the aggregate stock, overgrazing of village grounds, air pollution that reduces overall air quality, and exhaustion of oil and gas reserves that lead to lowering of overall production and raising costs. These situations are all examples of "*the Tragedy of the Commons.*"[192]

This tragedy occurs through short-term aggregate production or use levels that are too high accompanied by long-term investment in the stock that is too low. In other words, it is overinvestment in the short term and optimizing the benefit for the self in the short term which leads to a suboptimal benefit for everyone over the long term. These anticipated spillovers lead to a damaging rush to exploit resources. In addition to the tragedy, according to the Coase Theorem—which correlates between well-defined property rights and negligible bargaining costs, as classic terms for finding efficient solutions to externalities, as will be further explained in section 2.E.—in the absence of recognized property rights, an exchange is not possible, and so there is no efficient allocation of resources by the market itself, but instead a waste of resources due to the diversion of valuable labor and capital inputs from alternate productive uses that could be inflicted. Moreover, damaging conflicts and violence may follow.[193] All these justify an adequate policy response, as further discussed below.

E. POLICY INSTRUMENTS FOR ELIMINATING THE TRAGEDY OF THE COMMONS AND EXTERNALITIES

The waste associated with common-pool resources can be large, especially when the value of assets rises (perhaps due to greater depletion). As a result, the social savings from avoiding this waste and mitigating the cost of externalities might justify a collective action in order to: establish informal property rights (individual or group), or, if these are not achievable, regulate the access and resource use, or delineate formal property rights.[194] Each of these areas will be specifically addressed in the next three subsections.

E.1. Informal Property Rights

This first solution allows for group solutions or common property that provides effective resource allocation management for the number of parties involved—provided these should be comparatively low, while somewhat similar in terms of costs, discount rates and production goals.[195] An example of the success of this solution is found among coastal communities that have developed small-scale fishery

192. Gary D. Libecap, *The Tragedy of the Commons: Property Rights and Markets as Solutions to Resource and Environmental Problems*, 53.1 AUST. J. AGRICULTURAL AND RES. ECON. 129-44, at 129-30 (2009) (hereinafter "Libecap, *The Tragedy of the Commons*").
193. *Id.*, at 130.
194. *Id.*
195. Ostrom, *supra* note 35.

industries instead of the large-scale fisheries driven by open access (*see* section 2.C.). However, exogenous factors such as price increases or new production technologies can make common property less effective. These exogenous factors can attract new and more heterogeneous entrants to exploit the same resources, a scenario which is more realistic in the case of space as new scientific and technological developments make a greater leap. These new entrants might also be reluctant to commit to the constraints and cooperative internal rules of the group, and could undermine its localized arrangements, which may be highly dependent upon the group's political influence on the state, compared to that of the new entrants.[196] This solution requires highly centralized control over the common property resources, and can result in one of two undesirable outcomes: (1) destruction of the commons since no one can be excluded or (2) excessive cost of negotiating allocations.[197] Therefore, in the case of space, this solution is less likely to withstand the test of time.

E.2. Standardized Regulations

The second option is government regulation—in the case of space, this may even be an international central regulation—to maintain control and enforcement, which involves restrictions on inputs or outputs to achieve optimal levels of production, and/or the implementation of tax schemes (i.e., as measures for imposing constraints on access to the resources) in order to better align between private and social-use costs and, as a result, to eliminate externalities.[198] An example consistent with the hypothesis that state action objectives maximize the value of property can be found in the case of property rights to wildlife. In the U.S. and Canada, where much wildlife is treated as common property, a great regulatory power by the states with restrictive regimes and laws regarding rights to wildlife—such as restrictions on the length of the hunting season and limits on the trade in wildlife products—have, in effect, helped reduce the overexploitation of wildlife and, consequently, increased its value to individuals. However, in England, where individual land holdings conform quite closely to wildlife habitats (and, thereby, should mostly not be treated as a commons), there is a more lenient regulatory regime, leaving the bulk of the rights to wildlife to be assigned to private individuals, rather than to the state.[199]

It should be noted that in many cases, the empirical history of government regulation options has not particularly satisfied the common-pool problem.[200] One reason is that when imposing effective regulations and taxes, the regulators need adequate information, which is difficult to collect, about all associated social costs, private production costs, and compliance costs by individual users (many times, these costs vary between users) and the optimal level of production. In addition, the lack of information about opportunity costs (the value of alternative resource uses) in the

196. Libecap, *The Tragedy of the Commons*, *supra* note 192, at 130-31.
197. Ostrom, *supra* note 35, at 9 and 60-61.
198. Libecap, *The Tragedy of the Commons*, *supra* note 192, at 131.
199. Barzel, Economic Analysis, *supra* note 108, at 145-47.
200. Libecap, *The Tragedy of the Commons*, *supra* note 192, at 131.

market could lead to waste and misallocation of resources. To overcome this requirement and to reduce demands on information, government regulation typically relies upon uniform standards, such as centralized controls on access, fixed tax levels, similar prescriptive limitations on schedules for utilization and/or limitations on capital for technology or production investments. This standardization and uniformity make the regulation appear equitable and more politically resilient. However, since uniform regulations and taxes ignore differences in production or compliance costs, they are less likely to align with both the efficiency, or optimal use, of the resource and with the incentives of users of the resource to maintain the social objectives of reduced harvest and environmental conservation of the stock.[201]

Additionally, under regulation and tax policies, users, the regulated and taxed parties, by definition, are not "owners" of the resources. Hence, they typically do not gain increased social returns from eliminating externalities by protecting or investing in the resource's stock through conservation. As such, they are lured to evade profits, and attempt to maximize private returns through manipulation. Similar ills alleged against government regulations and tax policies, in general, can be used to contest against the regulation solutions in the context of open access to resources, including increases in enforcement costs, inflexibility and ineffectiveness. All these have resulted in an undue burden on the resources and their actual end users, and in the dissipation of any social gains for the users, the government and the politicians, without maximizing the economic value of the resources or conserving them.[202]

Despite the shortcomings associated with regulations and tax policies, this does not necessarily mean that these policies cannot be considered as solutions for open-access problems. In fact, when viewed in comparison to market-based pricing approaches (such as emission taxes, as in the case of air pollution) or other eco-taxes, addressing the failures of the market when considering environmental impacts and how the private sector might bear the costs of externalities and social burdens caused by its actions, the uniformly enforced measures and command-and-control regulations are considered to be less costly to administer. They are also less costly to comply with by polluters (since in addition to the cost of reducing pollution that the latter would incur under a command-and-control regime, they must pay, in the case of pollution taxes, for the harm caused by the pollution remaining after compliance with the standard), and are, therefore, more politically acceptable.[203]

---

201. *Id. See also* Gary D. Libecap, *Open-Access Losses and Delay in the Assignment of Property Rights*, NBER Working Paper No. W13642 (November 2007), at 388 (hereinafter "Libecap, *Open-Access Losses and Delay*").
202. Libecap, *The Tragedy of the Commons*, *supra* note 192, at 131-32.
203. Libecap, *Open-Access Losses and Delay*, *supra* note 201, at 398. *See also* Jason Scott Johnston, *Tradable Pollution Permits and the Regulatory Game*, Faculty Scholarship at Penn Law, 1-43 (2005), at 7. It can be explained that "*[I]ndeed, from a traditional law and economics perspective, the difference between pollution taxes and a readjustment in pollution entitlements through command and control may be usefully understood as the difference between a property rights approach under command and control versus a liability rule approach under pollution taxes. The property rights approach taken by command and control regulation cut back on what had been a relatively clear entitlement to pollute, limiting polluters' rights to that level of pollution consistent with statutorily required abatement efforts. By giving polluters the right to pollute as much as they wish, but charging them a tax equal to the harm caused by their*

In order for market-based pricing methods to solve the open-access problem, the economic value of pollution taxes needs to equal the real damage caused by pollution, which is challenging to evaluate with any degree of precision. Moreover, in terms of property rights, the imposition of pollution taxes is a means to give polluters a conditional right to pollute, to the extent that they can compensate for the damage caused by their actions, rather than a way of giving the public the right to be free from pollution; and, as such, it is inconsistent with the preferred political and environmental goals.[204]

Moreover, when the value of the resource or the cost of the externality is relatively low, prescriptive and standardized regulations to limit exploitation through uniform restrictions can be cost-effective and politically acceptable.[205] For example, the externality costs of space debris are uncertain, and in the case that this it is not a costly regulating activity that produces debris, it could be efficient. However, this efficiency also depends on the value of space resources. The higher the cost of an externality and the more significant the value of resources, the less efficient the standardized regulation regime would likely be.

In many cases, except for centralized regulation solutions, there may be no feasible alternative, as in the case when the delineation of rights-based arrangements is cost-prohibitive or due to the high political and social costs of "privatizing" assets.[206] This state of affairs might sound, on the one hand, quite realistic when considering the exploitation of space resources, where the global share of the social gain derived from "the province of all mankind" is at high risk and may lead to political disputes if handed over to unbridled management by the private sector, meaning that, eventually, a uniform regulatory regime could help avoid these costs. On the other hand, the externality and political costs might be merely speculative. For example, the transaction costs associated with a bilateral agreement between a U.S. company to refuel a Japanese satellite in space are uncertain. In doing so, would the U.S. company have to negotiate with every country in the world and have all countries agree? It might be that, over time, the externality costs of the removal of debris in space will become cost-prohibitive, whereas the delineation of property rights in space and their enforcement costs will not be so high. By considering all the above-mentioned costs, it might be possible to decide in advance whether an allocation of property rights is justified, or if it is more efficient to have an international body approving and regulating space to facilitate economic activities there, such as mining.

Nevertheless, since standard and uniform rules enforced by government regulations ignore many real costs, these have often proven to be costly with limited effectiveness, such as in the case of fisheries and air pollution regulations.[207] This is

pollution, taxes give the public a right to be free of pollution, but do not allow them to demand reductions in pollution below the levels induced by pollution taxes. They may thus be understood as recognizing a public right to be free of pollution, but allowing polluters to infringe that right so long as they pay the required price."

204. *Id.*, at 8.
205. Libecap, *Open-Access Losses and Delay, supra* note 201, at 381.
206. Libecap, *The Tragedy of the Commons, supra* note 192, at 132.
207. *Id.*

why, instead of command-and-control policies, other solutions using the "invisible hand" of the market for resource allocation have been adopted, such as tradable pollution permits.[208] Under the Clean Air Act Amendments of 1990, two policies were tried, including the first—the command-and-control policy—which mandated that each power plant reduce its pollution by a determined amount while ignoring each plant's compliance costs for doing so. A second policy—the tradable pollution permits (TPPs)—empowered firms to use knowledge of their cost curves to lower their own polluting emissions and to sell and buy pollution "allowances" as needed. This policy was found to be more economically efficient. When comparing these two policies, the latter policy, enabling the regulated parties to decide how, where and when to reduce pollution, was preferred; it allowed the parties to achieve the same social good of clean air in a more efficient way, without wasting resources at the expense of more productive alternative uses.[209]

In a similar fashion, in the case of the fisheries, in order to alleviate the losses of open-access, tradable harvest rights to fish have been adopted. These are commonly known as ITQs and set the annual total allowable catch and the distribution of tradable harvest rights and shares to fishers and other stockholders. Unlike under the open-access regime, since these ITQs impact the value of fishery stocks, they also reduce overcapitalization, change incentives for fishing and, hence, promote conservation incentives by aligning private investment in the fish stock with stock restoration objectives (through avoiding a harvest of juvenile fish, slowing the "race to fish," and

208. Tom Tietenberg, *Tradable Permits in Principle and Practice*, 14 PENN ST. ENVTL. L. REV. 251 (2005).

209. In order to overcome the common-pool problem in the case of air pollution by plants and with consistent to the Coase Theorem (providing that, when cost transactions are low and property rights are clear, private bargain will ensure that the market equilibrium is efficient even if there are externalities) an alternative approach was found by the state imposing tradable permits as a solution. Through the use of these permits, the government controls pollution by commanding that all factories install certain technologies in order to reduce pollution to a certain amount. When one of the factories can reduce pollution at a lower cost (because of its newer technology or use of another type of coal, or there is another use of cheaper technology for reducing pollution that the government did not consider) comparing to another factory (older for example), it would be more economic efficient to reduce pollution of the factory with the lower costs than where reducing pollution has higher cost. The usage of tradable permits enables to reduce the total pollution to the same certain amount imposed by the government, but at a lower cost, thus wasting fewer resources. Without the need for the state to know which factory pollutes more or less, since it is hard and costly to collect this dispersed information, each factory is being assigned a limited and same certain amount of pollution permits—rights to omit pollution—by the government, and factories start trading between themselves to purchase or sell these permits depending on how much these pollutions are worth and are economic efficient for them. As a result, the owner of the plant with lower cost for reducing pollution will be willing to sell his unused pollution permits for making profits. By selling its permits to the plant with higher costs for reducing pollution, the "old" plant in the end pollutes more than the first, but in a more economic efficient way, because it is cheaper to buy permits than reducing pollution at high cost. As result, less resources are wasted (spending less on pollution allow spending resources on other products), and both plants increase their profits, while at the same time the desired result of increase in social good, the clean air, is achieved. When the government can gain commanding control for defining property rights and reducing transaction costs, markets can be used to control externality problems. Video: Alex Tabarrok, *Trading Pollution* (MRU), https://www.mruniversity.com/courses/principles-economics-microeconomics/clean-air-act-pollution-control.

limiting pollution and other damages to habitats and biodiversity). These ITQs may be cost-effective and can maximize the economic rents from resources when compared to open-access fishery, due to the cost savings from closing externality problems, or when compared to full ownership of the stock or part of the ocean. This is especially true when migratory species are involved, when the cost of enforcement is great, and when political resistance to sole proprietorship and wealth/resource distribution pressures are intense.[210]

Similar to the case of the oceans, in space mining, the adoption of TPPs or ITQs can mitigate political opposition to sole ownership, while concurrently taking into consideration the anticipated externality damages from space debris associated with mining activities. However, as a general rule, defining quotas and entitlements to extract and catch can be challenging, in particular when unknown environmental problems can arise, or if there is a lack of scientific information about the extent and volume of space resources, all of which can lead to mis-entitlements and over-allocation issues, and to a wide array of inefficient investment decisions.[211]

Additionally, since it is likely to be challenging and expensive to monetize the harm caused by space debris in order to determine how to set an allowable quota of space minerals, and since space commercial activities (unlike the case of high seas activities) are associated with an exceptional risk of liability under the space law—the Space Liability Convention[212]—a third alternative should be considered.

Under the Convention, the liability for space debris could be assigned to a specific state. The potential of constituted absolute liability (for damages that occur on the surface of Earth or in the air) or fault-based liability (for space-based damages) for damages caused by space debris should be taken into consideration when output quotas need to be set, since both measures—a limited quota and the liability risk factor—are intended to resolve the same externality and mitigate the social and environmental damages it has caused. In order to set a balanced quota, liability risk must be taken into consideration. However, reaching consent on such a balanced quota can be a long and complex process.

It should be noted that, under the Space Liability Convention, in order to establish the groundwork for liability with regard to damages caused by a space object, three important elements need to be established: "damage," "space object," and

210. Libecap, *Open-Access Losses and Delay*, *supra* note 201, at 391. *See also* Libecap, *The Tragedy of the Commons*, *supra* note 192, at 134; Eugene H. Buck, *Individual Transferable Quotas in Fishery Management*, CRS Report for Congress (1995).

211. An example for a case of mis-entitlements can be seen in the case of water sharing plans/regimes designed put in place in a manner that lacks hydrological integrity in the sense that entitlements are not defined in a manner that is consistent with the ways that water arrives, flows across and flows through land and can be intercepted. See in general, Michael D. Young et al., *Double Trouble: The Importance of Accounting for and Defining Water Entitlements Consistent with Hydrological Realities*, 53 Australian J. Agricultural and Res. Econ. (2009).

212. Convention on International Liability for Damage Caused by Space Objects Arts. II, III, IV, 24 Sept. 1972, 961 U.N.T.S. 187; TIAS 7762; 24 UST 2389; UKTS 1974 No. 16; Cmnd. 5068; ATS 1975 No. 5; 10 ILM 965 (1971) (hereinafter "Space Liability Convention"), which imposes strict/absolute liability (meaning liability without fault while denoting the only factors as causation and damage, but not fault) or fault-based liability in certain circumstances.

"caused by." Damage is defined as: "loss of life, personal injury or other impairment of health; or loss of or damage to property of States or of persons, natural or juridical, or property of international intergovernmental organizations."[213] However, it is doubtful if the definition of "*damage*" includes "unpredicted future damages," or "unforeseeable risks" as adverse environmental effects, and if the causation test can be met if these sorts of damages exist, in order to establish liability. Moreover, since "*space object*" is defined as "include[s] component parts of a space object as well as its launch vehicle and parts thereof,"[214] it is unclear if "space debris" adequately falls within this definition of a space object, since there is no legal definition of space debris.[215]

This incomplete definition leaves the question open as to whether the Liability Convention regime is applicable to additional potential damages caused by the new emerging space industry, as in mining, which were neither contemplated by the Space Liability Convention drafters nor fit the traditional definition of "space object." For example, space debris caused by asteroids towed into Earth's orbit by a mining firm, which collides with a spacecraft, or any other damages caused by human activities in outer space—not component parts—such as back contamination of Earth by extraterrestrial materials "do not fall squarely within the language of the treaty, but in equity, should be protected, include man-made objects that are constructed completely in space from raw materials (and were therefore never launched), and damage caused by the intentional interference with outer space, the moon, or a celestial body that causes direct harm on earth."[216]

It should be noted that the Scientific and Technical Subcommittee of the United Nations Committee on the Peaceful Uses of Outer Space (UNCOPOUS) adopted a draft set of "high-level qualitative guidelines" in 2007.[217] Endorsed by the U.N. General Assembly, "*space debris*" is defined as: "all man made objects including fragments and elements thereof, in Earth orbit or re-entering the atmosphere, that are non functional."[218] Although this definition is not legally binding, it "reflect[s] the existing practices as developed by a number of national and international organizations, and invites Member States to implement those guidelines through relevant national mechanisms."[219] As the risk of and concern about space debris increases, it is likely that a broader definition of "*space object*" and "*space debris*" than is found in the set of guidelines would be desirable among both developed and developing countries. In particular, these guidelines would form the basis of part of their commitment to utilize

213. *Id.*, Space Liability Convention, at Art. I(a).
214. *Id.*, at Art. I(d).
215. Scott Kerr, *Liability for Space Debris Collisions and the Kessler Syndrome (Part 1)*, THE SPACE REVIEW (Dec. 11, 2017) (hereinafter "Kerr").
216. Elena Carpanelli et al., *Interpreting "Damage Caused by Space Objects" under the 1972 Liability Convention*, INT'L INST. OF SPACE L. 2-3 (2013).
217. Comm. on the Peaceful Uses of Outer Space, Rep. on its Fifteen Session, U.N. Doc. A/62/20 (2007), Annex at 47-48; *see also* Scott Kerr, *supra* note 215.
218. Inter-Agency Space Debris Coordination Committee, *Space Debris Mitigation Guidelines* (Sept. 1, 2007).
219. G.A. Res. 62/217 (Feb. 1, 2008).

outer space for peaceful purposes and their goal of promoting the best practices for sustainable use of space.[220]

As a result of the controversial liability definition and its legal applicability—for example, if it is applicable merely to damages caused by space objects or if it could encompass other advanced activities in space, as well—higher compliance and externality costs in the case of space should be added to any complementary regulatory regimes, such as the TPP or ITQ, if adopted. It should be mentioned that the purchase of allowances—as in TTP or ITQ—enables the internalization of the costs of externalities in the overall economy. It is an efficient system whereby the allowances impose costs on the companies and their customers who have previously benefited from the externalities. However, in the case of space, the additional costs derived from liability might undermine the economic efficiency and the legal rationale of this type of regulatory regime, in the sense that it is a sort of "double accounting." Moreover, since the liability risk factor can, in some sense, be compared to the imposition of a pollution tax, it can be considered a preassignment of rights to the actual users of space to produce debris. Thus, by itself, this risk factor can contradict the rationale for adopting an additional quota regime as an alternative solution to the open-access problems anticipated in space. Therefore, this indicates the need for an alternative regime.

E.3. Formal Property Rights

After exploring the two solutions above, a third alternative should be analyzed. Returning to the list of social wastes and savings associated with common-pool resources, which justify collective action, this alternative is defined as assigning "formal property rights for private restrictions on behavior."[221] This alternative deals with the choice of formal property rights as a solution to the problems of the commons, and, in particular, externalities. Formal property rights would ensure better alignment of individual incentives with both social objectives for resource use and environmental conservation, and toward investment in the resources (such as investments in technologies that lower releases into the atmosphere), and in complying with and policing one owner by another. The reason for this is that when operators are owners of a certain part of greater resource rents, resulting from reducing an externality and losses to the common-pool resources (as the depletion of open-access resources as an asteroid), they have greater incentives to comply with each other, police one another, and invest in the stocks. Although the considerations with respect to the benefits associated with reducing the externalities may vary and depend on the type of the resources exploited, such as whether these resources are limited, renewable, or nonrenewable, ultimately, it has already been suggested "that property rights arise when it becomes economic for those affected by externalities to internalize benefits and costs."[222]

220. Outer Space Benefits Must Not Be Allowed to Widen Global Gap between Economic, Social Inequality, Fourth Committee Told, Concluding Debate on Item, GA/SPD/562 (Oct. 17, 2014).
221. Libecap, *The Tragedy of the Commons*, *supra* note 192, at 132.
222. *Id.*, at 134. *See also* Demsetz, *Toward a Theory of Property Rights*, *supra* note 135, at 354.

Property rights generate data on the costs and benefits associated with constraining common-pool extraction, as applied to emissions, fishing and other forms of common resources. As a result of this data and information generated by property rights, efficiency subsequently increases. These rights help provide cost saving due to the gains from closing externalities (such as the reduction of overuse of open access) and allocating the resources into the hands of the owners who most highly value the uses of these resources.[223]

Rights-based solutions to open access, however, are costly and complex to design, allocate, and enforce, due to the high resource and political costs used in allocating, delineating, policing, and settling entitlements. All these costs are functions of the extent of the impact which these property rights have on the distribution of wealth and political influence. They all must be offset by the benefits derived from fixing rights.[224]

The main question is whether the benefits from defining and enforcing property rights for mitigating open-access losses and problems offset the losses from resource rents and the political costs involved, thereby justifying the adoption of the solution of rights-based management regimes as the socio-politically desirable and optimal solution to the "Tragedy of the Commons." In the case of space, as "the province of all mankind," where the competition for resource profits is driven by economic and political powers, and could impact global inequality, it is reasonable to believe that distributional pressures would play an important role in the political economy of rights-based arrangements. Hence, these would affect the design, extent and types of property rights granted.[225]

However, it should be noted that there have been cases where it was decided that there would be no taking of property rights, but instead the allocation would be determined under the public trust doctrine, a doctrine traceable to a Roman legal principle governing the public's right to use certain resources as commons. This doctrine limits the power of the legislature to alienate natural resources for private use, where some resources are so inherently public in their nature, and important to the public welfare, that permanent assignment to exclusive, private ownership is inappropriate.[226] This doctrine created a method of reassigning use of public resources and a tool for "effective judicial intervention," on behalf of environmental protection and natural resource conservation, for resolving resource management problems.[227] However, this doctrine has been found to be limited by its "historic shackles," as courts have declined to actively intervene in resource management; the courts have been

223. Libecap, *The Tragedy of the Commons*, *supra* note 192, at 132-35; *see also* Libecap, *Open-Access Losses and Delay*, *supra* note 198; Demsetz, *Toward a Theory of Property Rights*, *supra* note 135.

224. Libecap, *The Tragedy of the Commons*, *supra* note 192, at 132-36.

225. *Id.*, at 133.

226. *Id.*, at 140; *see also* William D. Araiza, *Democracy, Distrust, and the Public Trust: Process Based Constitutional Theory, the Public Trust Doctrine, and the Search for a Substantive Environmental Value*, 45 UCLA L. REV. 385, 386-87 (1997) (hereinafter "Araiza").

227. Joseph L. Sax, *The Public Trust Doctrine in Natural Resource Law: Effective Judicial Intervention*, 68 MICH. L. REV. 471, 474 (1970) (hereinafter "Sax"); *see also* J. Brewer et al., *Property Rights and the Public Trust Doctrine in Environmental Protection and Natural Resource Conservation*, 53 AUST. J. AGRICULTURAL AND RES. ECON. 1, 17, at 3 (2008) (hereinafter "Brewer").

concerned about harming efficient resource-allocation decision-making, and about becoming involved in resource-allocation decisions that should be made by more representative branches of government than by judges, as appropriate in a democracy.[228]

As a legal principle, the public trust doctrine had historically, and narrowly, been applied to the rights of the public to access navigable waterways without being impeded by private riparian owners. This doctrine was also extended in the nineteenth century to public ownership of certain tidelands and subsurface lake beds, and in the late twentieth century to non-navigable waters, wildlife and other natural resources held in trust by the state.[229] For example, in two cases dealing with wildlife, *Arnold v. Mundy*[230] and *Martin v. Waddell*,[231] the right to harvest oysters as a right to property was prohibited from being alienated, and the prohibition applied not merely to the submerged land from which the oysters were harvested. Justice Kirkpatrick said in *Arnold* that "the air, the running water, the sea, the fish, and the wild beasts"[232] are all common property. In *Martin*, "The people of New Jersey," said Chief Justice Taney, "have exercised and enjoyed the rights of fishery for shellfish and floating fish, as a common and undoubted right, without opposition or remonstrance from the proprietors."[233]

This doctrine and the idea of a public trust closely resemble what led to the regime established by UNCLOS, which regulates and manages the seabed resources via an intergovernmental body designed to act as a trustee for administering the common good for the benefits and interests of all states and/or humankind. Similar interpretations of "*the province of all mankind*" notion can be adopted in the case of space. However, though this doctrine has been argued in the U.S. to have a constitutional basis and roots in the police powers of the state,[234] it provides a judicially mandated reallocation and has also been criticized as the most costly and contentious method; it increases the costs of resolving debates over resource use and allocation, compared to other alternatives for reallocation and management of natural resources, such as market exchange where property rights are recognized.[235] Thus, it should not be trusted as an efficient solution for resource management in the case of space.

228. Araiza, *supra* note 226, at 388.
229. Brewer, *supra* note 227, at 2.
230. *Arnold v. Mundy*, 6 N.J.L. 1 (N.J. 1821) (hereinafter "Arnold").
231. *Martin v. Waddell*, 41 U.S. 367 (1842) (hereinafter "Martin").
232. Arnold, *supra* note 230, at 49.
233. Martin, *supra* note 231, at 417.
234. James L. Huffman, *Speaking of Inconvenient Truths—A History of the Public Trust Doctrine*, 18 Duke Envtl. L. Policy J. 1, 5-6 (2008); *see also* Araiza, *supra* note 226, at 450-51; Sax, *supra* note 227, at 185.
235. Brewer, *supra* note 227, at 3-4; *see also* Libecap, *The Tragedy of the Commons*, *supra* note 192, at 140-41.

F. MEASURES FOR DIVERTING RESOURCE SHARES FROM SPACE UNDER THE MOST EFFICIENT RESOURCE REGULATORY REGIME, SUCH AS PROPERTY RIGHTS

Alongside the most efficient resource management and ownership regime—yet to be decided among the options described above, even if by the creation of a hybrid type of ownership—a new tax base will be generated and will need to be allocated. Hence, an applicable tax method should be analyzed. Essentially, the chosen management regime will directly affect the economic value of space resources which the private sector aims to harvest and will impact the decisions made regarding investments for doing so. As such, it is essential that with the formation of the resource management regime, concurrent and accompanying tax measures and the tax system, as a whole, be designed for commercial space activities so that they may support an attractive and stable investment environment.

Indeed, there are few alternatives for diverting shares of resource rents to the public, including nontax measures for splitting up the new resources in space, such as when a share of equity in the firm is allotted or when public ownership is created. This alternative is analogous to imposing a cash flow tax, since both have a similar impact, by making the public sector a partner in the ownership of the firm and profiting from it; however, with cash flow taxation, the public resembles a silent partner, who does not have a say in the firm, as is more typical in public ownership.[236] However, the alternative to giving an equity share to the international community and making it an active partner in mining operations is facing challenges in its implementation and could discourage private investment in these emerging industries.

Therefore, another way to divert a share of resource rent to the public must be found. This could be done by requiring that firms place bids to gain the rights that would allow them to exploit resources and purchase leases from the public sector for exploration (as is typical in the oil and gas industries, where a bonus bid is sometimes offered in addition to any royalties paid on oil or gas produced from the lease, as a one-time payment in exchange for exclusive access to explore a parcel and the grant of an exclusive lease for a set period of time) or for the exploitation of a particular resource (as is typical in the fishery industry).[237] Usually, competitive bidding is the preferred method, since an open auction insures that the rights are first obtained by the most productive user, as each bidder would offer up to the value of the mining rights package.[238]

From the perspective of economic efficiency, a competitive bidding system is more efficient than a system that embraces the rule of "first possession."[239] Competing

236. Robin Boadway et al., *The Taxation of Natural Resources: Principles and Policy Issues by Robin Policy Research Department* World Bank, at 5 (1993) (hereinafter "Boadway").
237. *Id.*, at 2, 4 and 50. For "bonus bid," *see* in general U.S. Department of the Interior, *They Said It Couldn't Be Done: Trump Admin Dominates with Billion-Dollar Oil and Gas Sale* (Sep. 6, 2018); *see also* Nicole Gentile, *Federal Oil and Gas Royalty and Revenue Reform, Center for American Progress* (Jun. 19, 2015).
238. Ross, *Exploitation of Deep Ocean Minerals*, *supra* note 145, at 152.
239. Dean Lueck, *supra* note 105, at 414-16.

bidders drive the price to the present discounted value of the expected surplus, eliminating any private incentive to invest prematurely in exploitation.[240] However, in the case of space, a bidding system might be inefficient, not merely because under this bidding mechanism net rents must be paid entirely up front, unlike rent taxes (or royalties) which are spread out into the future,[241] but also because, under this bidding system, nations, including developing nations, will bid to gain rights over space resources before they have even attained the economic wherewithal to exploit such resources. Moreover, it is uncertain that the engagement in premature exploitation should be hindered, since space development has other noneconomic spillover benefits for society beyond generating profits.[242] For examples of this, *see* the discussion above in section 2.B.2.

Furthermore, in order for a bidding system to work, it must be associated with obtaining perpetual property rights, so that the value of the bid would equal expected future net rents (the net of future expected taxes) as indexed by risk factors. For example, an indefinite duration of a lease would be equivalent to full private ownership rights. Otherwise, the operator would be incentivized to extract the resource inefficiently and not at an optimal level. Therefore, the bidding system as a preassigning method (which ignores the real economic value to be generated from space and relies only on the anticipated one) might be politically unacceptable and less appropriate in the case of space mining.[243]

Nevertheless, it is not a simple task to offer rights-based solutions to open access. How property rights are designed, formed, allocated and enforced is a complex and costly process, and the results vary according to the empirical setting at hand and based on the political, social, environmental/ecological and economic conditions involved, as discussed above in section 2.E.3. It is crucial that research is done so that there is clarity on when, how and for whom these rights should be defined, and by so doing, determine when these are appropriate choices for addressing open access.[244]

In the case of space, property rights that accompany user rights may be too incomplete for efficient markets to exist. The basic features of a property rights system contain four components, which, when unmet, deem the whole system inefficient. These features include:[245] (1) an unambiguous description of the resource—or in the case of land, well-defined procedures for delimiting and delineating boundaries—since the higher the ambiguity in the definition of resource or in rights, the higher the costs of negotiation or litigation; the costs of exchange or the restriction on it also rise (it should be highlighted that for as much as the transaction costs associated with rights are positive, as explained below, the assigned property rights are not complete); (2) exclusivity in capturing the benefits and the full value derived from the use of the resource, since without exclusivity the rewards from investment decrease and the

240. Haddock, *supra* note 106, at 786.
241. Boadway, *supra* note 236, at 3-5 and 45.
242. Merges, *supra* note 153, at 123.
243. Boadway, *supra* note 236, at 40-41 and 45.
244. Libecap, *The Tragedy of the Commons*, *supra* note 192, at 136.
245. Clas G., *Outer Space Resources*, *supra* note 40. *See also* Ross, *Exploitation of Deep Ocean Minerals*, *supra* note 145, at 152.

enforcement costs of preventing trespass increase (the right to exclude others is an important feature of property rights, since it encourages everyone to invest time, labor and capital into the development of resources; this exclusive control enables owners to identify other owners, and, thus, allows to facilitate exchanges of the fruits of their labors until the resources arrive in the hands of the most productive users—those who value them the most—and, thus, to reach to the most efficient production level and, ultimately, to foster the well-being of the community);[246] (3) enforcement at a low cost against unauthorized use, such as trespass, since high enforcement costs reduce rewards from investment; and (4) procedures for recording and registering claims (a tract index, for example, in the case of land) for facilitating transfers among economic agents. Any restraints or legal procedures that increase the costs of exchange diminish incentives for allocating rights to more productive users. The higher the costs of exchange, the more important it becomes to define and assign rights optimally at the start, and, vice versa, low-exchange costs do not justify property rights assignments, but an allocation of rights through the market might instead be sufficient and more efficient.

When dealing with space resources, it is uncertain whether the policing and enforcement costs of property rights will exceed the market allocation values of these, creating a situation where these rights become prohibitively costly, while remaining poorly delineated. There are multiple lines of reasoning which support this perspective, including: (1) the distance from Earth for enforcing and policing the allocation of property rights making this more complex and costly; (2) the lack of complete information by either the current or the prospective owners concerning the real attributes of the assets, or their future activities and functions, resulting in the absence of full knowledge of the parties of what the value of space resources will be[247] (this situation imposes difficulties in giving exclusivity over the benefits, and raises the exchange, transfer and enforcement costs, since it is difficult to specify the precise content of property rights before the economic activity they will cover has matured);[248] and (3) the highly ambiguous outcomes embedded in working with nature, particularly when the definition and the limits of space resources as "common" property increases both the potential for complexity and the adverse repercussions which space resource allocations might pose globally, increasing the exchange costs. Additionally, when transaction costs (charges associated with transferring, capturing and protecting rights) soar, the full protection and the full transfer of rights may become prohibitively expensive. Consequently, property rights may never be fully completed as long as "owners" never find it worthwhile to gain the entire potential value of "their" assets. In order for the rights to an asset to be complete or fully defined, its owner and those others who are potentially keen on acquiring the asset must hold full information on

246. Carol Rose, *supra* note 26, at 711-12.
247. An example to potential evaluation difficulties of resources in space can be found in the potential prospects for usage of CO_2 in space, for which NASA has initiated a competition aiming to find ways to convert carbon dioxide into useful compound, such as glucose. *See* NASA, *New NASA Competition Aims to Convert Carbon Dioxide into Exploration Sweet Success* (Aug. 30, 2018).
248. Merges, *supra* note 153, at 114; *see also* Barzel, Economic Analysis, *supra* note 108.

the value of the asset and its attributes. Otherwise, the asset would be misallocated before it could be transferred into the hands of those who value it most highly, thereby increasing the transaction costs even more. When rights are fully defined and formed, obtaining product information must be free of charge, and, hence, the costs of transactions, or the cost of producing the transaction, need to be zero.[249]

In the case of space, it is uncertain whether the costs of assigning and enforcing property rights will exceed the value of space resources when allocated via the market, or if the benefits from creating a property right system would outweigh its costs. In the first situation, when assignment and enforcements of rights are cost-prohibitive, property rights may merely increase the price of space resources, especially at the beginning, before space mining activities mature. However, as the access to space becomes cheaper and more prevalent, so does the knowledge that could be obtained on the valued attributes of space resources, and as space opens up for more countries to exploit, the transaction costs can be expected to be reduced and the need for coordination among the private players in space is expected to increase. Therefore, the design of a coordinated property rights system with greater specification of rights is not excluded, as this also grows to become more feasible and efficient. Furthermore, "[w]hen property rights are protected and maintained in any context, transaction costs exist," a coordinated framework with regard to space resources for establishing any type of property rights may ultimately lead to a more efficient management regime.[250]

In case a system of private ownership is not workable, it is expected that the negative consequences and externalities associated mostly with environmental implications (e.g., the costs of space debris removal) will not be internalized by commercial space users themselves or impact their decisions, but will become a burden on the community at large.[251] This conclusion can also be supported by the *Coase Theorem*,[252] which is the basis for a theory of externality and the evolution of property rights.[253] According to the Theorem, as rights are defined, resources will be used where they are most valued. Thus, the income is maximized regardless of who owns these rights.[254]

When trying to decide on the most efficient ownership pattern, the Coase Theorem becomes relevant to discuss. Consistent with this Theorem, when property rights are clearly delineated and there are zero transactions costs, resource allocations are efficient and optimally exploited, independent of the pattern of ownership.

---

249. Barzel, Economic Analysis, *supra* note 108, at 4. *See also* Lee Anne Fennell, *The Problem of Resource Access*, 126 Harvard L. Rev. 1471, 1477, 1481-82, 1484, 1487 and 1515 (2013); and Robert C. Ellickson, *The Case for Coase and Against "Coaseanism,"* 99 Yale L.J. 611, 612-15 (1989).
250. Merges, *supra* note 153, at 115-6. *See also* Douglas W. Allen, *Transaction Costs*, in 1 Encyclopedia of Law and Economics 893, 898-99 (Boudewijn Bouckaert & Gerrit De Geest eds. 2000).
251. *Id.*
252. Ronald Coase argued that private bargaining among parties can achieve a socially effective outcome and ensure that the market equilibrium is efficient even if there are externalities when the following two conditions are met: first, the property rights are clearly defined; second, the transaction costs are low. *See* Ronald H. Coase, *The Problem of Social Cost*, 3 J.L. Econs. 1-44 (1960).
253. Robert Cooter, *The Cost of Coase*, 11 J. Legal Stud. 1 (1982), at 14.
254. Barzel, Economic Analysis, *supra* note 108, at 8-9 and 77.

However, since costless transactions are a sufficient condition for clearly defining property rights, the requirement of well-defined rights might seem redundant.[255]

The same rationale behind the Coase Theorem indicates that where property rights are vague and the costs of transactions are high, the property ownership system is unworkable. For example, several questions remain unclear. Who owns the rights to space free from debris? Who owns the rights to the commercial use of space, and what do these rights include? Does space law authorize commercial benefits for the whole of humankind, including the profits from space resources? Is it sufficient to globally share technology and the possibilities this encompasses, such as better communication and weather predictions, as external or secondary benefits? The answers to these sorts of questions can contribute to potential ambiguities associated with property rights and directly impact transaction costs, such as the transfer, capture, and protection of rights, including, in the case of space, the cost of exchange and the cost of time and effort to reach an agreement at the international level. After all, in many cases, since transactions are costly, the Coase Theorem cannot be invoked.

Thus, a new pattern of ownership for securing rights over space resources should be found, and this pattern should most effectively optimize the resource allocation system in space and maximize the net value of the space resources. In addition, since the value of exchanging an asset is a result of the gross income it can create, along with the charges of measuring and protecting its exchange, and when the highest income the asset can generate is achieved by an exchange, the net income an asset can produce depends on the delineation of rights.[256] When the value of rights over exchanged assets increases, as can be expected in the case of space, disputes between parties may erupt. These disputes can be resolved by delineation of the contested rights.[257]

Moreover, where the market cannot efficiently resolve the problem of externalities, an alternative solution for imposing a share of the negative externalities and the environmental costs from the commercial space sector—which derives most, if not all, of the economic benefits from space—must be found. If the international community can reduce transaction costs by gaining even a bit of command and control, as needed for defining certain aspects of property rights, this solution might be achieved. The adoption of an international royalty regime by the international community could be an efficient method for gaining this control and maximizing political support for delineating rights. At the same time, it would provide a method for compensating the international community for the harm imposed on its commons, the externalities.

Furthermore, this international royalty regime can serve as a tool for achieving and ensuring peaceful space development and the growth of a sustainable industry. A tool for maintaining "intergenerational equity," which might also help pave the way for establishing a space property rights system in the future.[258] These royalties, once they

---

255. *Id.*
256. *Id.*, at 8-10.
257. *Id.*, at 104.
258. Merges, *supra* note 153, at 123-24. In this article, the idea of setting aside preserved areas for the developing countries as keeping for them the "opportunity to exploit near-Earth resources well after the initial development period by advanced 'nations has passed" has been offered as a solution for the problems associated with the allocation of property rights in space.

gain international consent, will help divide the pie without shrinking it too much, by reducing transaction and exchange costs.

In addition to the general income tax as applicable to all companies, a royalty regime could involve two more levies: a royalty to secure a minimum payment and a progressive royalty, also known as resource rent tax, which is an additional or progressive profit tax designed to capture more of the economic rent and a larger share of the profits as the project becomes more profitable (i.e., this tax can be contingent on the volume or value of production, or even on some profit ratio).[259] The less elastic the demand for trade in space resources, as will likely be expected when these resources are used in space, the less chance that its taxes will deter many trades, and the smaller the lost gains. Furthermore, the lost tax revenue that would have been made from trades is lost (the deadweight loss is smaller, and so are the secondary losses for others, such as employees). Additionally, the trades that do occur will maximize tax revenues.

It should be noted that one of the solutions to the problem of pooling the "commons," that is, the common-pool problem, which has also been adopted for mineral rights on the continental shelf of the U.S., is for the sovereign nations to usurp titles, and then auction or barter them, or barter them as these assets become economically viable. In the case of space, when the sovereign's wealth increases, more national sovereigns compete to be the one to usurp this title. Therefore, this competition will increase the dissipation of wealth on an international basis.[260]

On the other hand, when there is an international royalty system that provides the benefit of simplicity and ease of administration, more countries will adhere to space law and consent to the registration and liability obligations as applied to objects in space. Yet this system would also include sufficient coordination among countries to make property transactions feasible and mitigate the distribution of global wealth. Indeed, in the case of the oceans, the "*common heritage*" of mankind is often linked to tax revenues to be derived from marine exploitation. Similarly, in the case of space, it may very well be that revenue-sharing is a desirable way of making the concept of "*the province of all mankind*" operational. However, it would only be by chance that the taxation and regulations designed to ensure efficiency will generate an exactly "fair" amount of revenue for sharing. It would be an error to tie revenue-sharing too closely to taxation for regulation, for this would cause needless trade-offs between efficiency and revenue-sharing.[261] In the case of space, tailoring a property rights regime alongside a congruent royalty regime can help set the right balance for these trade-offs, as will be further discussed in this book.

---

259. Emil Sunley et al., *Revenue from the Oil and Gas Sector: Issues and Country Experience*, in FISCAL POLICY FORMULATION AND IMPLEMENTATION IN OIL-PRODUCING COUNTRIES 153-83 (J.M. Davis et al. eds., International Monetary Fund 2003); *see also* Steve Rozner, *Taxing Oil: Issues and Trends, In Best Practices in Fiscal Reform and Economic Governance* (2009).
260. Haddock, *supra* note 106, at 786.
261. Sweeney, *supra* note 33, at 179-80.

G. CONCLUSION

The similarities between the space and the ocean in many ways provide a justification to adopt a resource management regime in space that is similar to the regime of the oceans. The physical nature of each area as being outside of any jurisdictions, the nature of the resources available to be exploited by mankind as their commons, the technological and economic feasibility of future explorations, and the environmental concerns surrounding mineral resource development (whether stemming from over-exploitation, generated debris or pollution) all support the need for finding an international agreement regarding the regulatory and resource ownership framework for the space mining industry, the same as has happened in the case of the seas. In both realms, there is no overriding sovereign authority, and neither regulation nor property rights may be feasible without collective international action. Whereas the research on resource management dilemma demonstrates a world of possibility rather than of necessity, the optimal resource management regime needs to be subject to international obligations and principles, such as the notions regarding the "common heritage," and the common-pool problems. In order to foster the space mining industry and create an attractive business environment for private space entrepreneurs, this management regime should be accompanied by an efficient and fair tax regime. Both the tax and the resource allocation regimes should be consistent with one other, and accordingly support the maintenance and stability of both. An international royalty regime, as will be analyzed later in this book, can serve as a tool for achieving these goals while ensuring peaceful space development and the growth of a sustainable industry. This royalty regime can be adjusted to and support any type of ownership regime that has yet to be developed and evolved in space. With this sort of future contingency in mind, as with respect to the development of the most efficient resource management regime in space, the royalty regime would enable the formation of an attractive investment climate for the space industry supported by a stable international tax system that will settle global expectations.

However, due to the uniqueness of certain space features—such as the nonstationary positioning of space (space has no proximity to any jurisdiction on the planet) and the liability owed by the launching states for potential hazards created by space objects—and the potential uses of resources being different (e.g., space resources are not meant to only be used on Earth, but also in space itself), differences in the tax field should also be explored.

Chapter 3

Policy and Key Objective Considerations for Designing a Competitive Space Mining Tax Regime

A. INTRODUCTION

In the context of the oceans and DSM—the *"common heritage"* of mankind—there exists an acknowledgment among participating states within and beyond their Extended Continental Shelf (ECS), beyond 200 nm from shore, for the need to shape a comprehensive fiscal policy to encompass the application of taxes; income and withholding taxes; royalties; import/export duties; and fees, such as license fees, rental fees, entry fees, levies and other monetary burdens that delineate how gross income is divided between the government and investors, including any other material benefits to government. This policy would also need to decide how to manage the host state's share of money raised from DSM. The policy, which each state can decide for itself, needs to ensure maximum benefits from this new industry to the host state, which should be financially compensated for the loss of its finite resources (at least when dealing with the states' ECS areas which are subject to their quasi-territorial jurisdiction as set by UNCLOS, as will be further discussed in detail). At the same time, this policy must reach in to protect the attractiveness of new investment opportunities in the view of developers assessing both risks and returns, mainly their after-tax returns (both are, to date, unproven). Otherwise, these developers could funnel their mining capital to other competitive jurisdictions.[262]

262. Tearinaki Tanielu, *Establishment of a National Regulatory Framework for the Exploration and Exploitation of Deep Sea Minerals: A Case Study for Kiribati*, U.N. Nippon Found. of Japan Fellowship Programme at 47-48 (2013) (hereinafter "Tanielu, *Establishment of a National Regulatory Framework*"); *see also* Secretariat of the Pacific Community, *Pacific-ACP States Regional Legislative and Regulatory Framework for Deep Sea Minerals Exploration and Exploitation* at 15 (2012) (hereinafter "Secretariat of the Pacific Community").

As with any economic activity, an important feature of any risk assessment associated with investments is the sustainability and stability of the existing tax regime. Before companies invest high upfront capital in new mining operations, they want to be assured that once their capital investments have been made (and which therefore have become immobile), there will be no possible changes in the tax burden, similar to securing their ownership allocation (as discussed in Chapter 2).[263] As a result, it can be concluded that in the case of "global commons," including space, the particular nature of these resources is expected to be entangled with and impact the attractiveness and stability of the chosen tax policy/regime, at both domestic and international levels.

B. SHOULD THE TAX PRINCIPLE IN SPACE MINING BE BASED ON THE CONCEPT OF THE "COMMON HERITAGE OF MANKIND"?

In the case of the oceans, UNCLOS has created the concept of the "common heritage of mankind" to govern the exploitation of minerals on the deep seabed.[264] According to the UNCLOS preamble, "the area of the seabed and ocean floor and the subsoil thereof, beyond the limits of national jurisdiction (the Area), as well as its resources, are the common heritage of mankind, the exploration and exploitation of which shall be carried out for the benefit of mankind as a whole, irrespective of the geographical location of States."[265]

Like UNCLOS, but with respect to Space Law, the world's nations have signed the Agreement Governing the Activities of States on the Moon and Other Celestial Bodies (Moon Treaty[266]) to control the exploitation of lunar and other space minerals by adopting the "common heritage" concept. This treaty declares that the mineral resources found on the moon are the "common heritage of mankind."[267] Although the "common heritage" concepts in both treaties (UNCLOS and the Moon Treaty) were not intended to have the same meaning and content, because both terms were negotiated under those treaties during approximately the same period of time, their interpretation for the seas as well as for outer space can shed light on the meaning and intention behind the concept.[268]

263. Fehr Ernst et al., *Fairness and the Optimal Allocation of Ownership Rights*, 118.531 The Econ. J. 1262-84 (2008); *see also* Otto J. et al., *Mining Royalties: A Global Study of Their Impact on Investors, Government, and Civil Society*, World Bank, Washington, D.C. (2006) 1-296, at 12 (hereinafter "Otto, *Mining Royalties*").
264. UNCLOS, *supra* note 5, under Part XI, Arts. 136 and 137 of the Convention; *see also* UNCLOS, *supra* note 5; Wikipedia, *List of the parties to the United Nations Convention on the Law of the Sea* (hereinafter "List of the parties to the United Nations Convention on the Law of the Sea"), https://en.wikipedia.org/wiki/List_of_parties_to_the_United_Nations_Convention_on_the_Law_of_ the_Sea.
265. UNCLOS, *supra* note 5, under its Preamble.
266. Moon Treaty, *supra* note 47. As of November 2016, it had been ratified by seventeen states. Four more states had signed (and not yet ratified) the Treaty—France, Guatemala, India and Romania. *See* Wikipedia, *Moon Treaty*, https://en.wikipedia.org/wiki/Moon_Treaty#cite_note-untdb-1.
267. Moon Treaty, *supra* note 47, at Art. 11(1).
268. Roberts B. Owen, legal advisor to the Department of State, in his statements before the Senate Subcommittee, while discussing the Moon Treaty (which was opened for signature by the

However, different from the high seas realm,[269] the Moon Treaty was ratified by a group of seven U.N. Member States; none of the space powers engage in self-launched manned space exploration nor have plans to do so (e.g., the U.S., Russia, People's Republic of China, Japan).[270] This simple fact can, essentially, also impact the practical interpretation of the legal concept of the "*common heritage*" when dealing with space resources.

Admittedly, some commentators trace the genesis of the term "Common Heritage of the Mankind" to the language of the Outer Space Treaty, which states that "[t]he exploration and use of outer space ... shall be the province of all mankind,"[271] by claiming that the "[p]resumably common heritage is an extension of province [of all mankind]."[272] Other commentators claim that the idea of the "common heritage" means the following: (1) no state shall claim or exercise sovereignty or sovereign rights over any part of the area or its resources; (2) all rights in the resources of the area are vested in mankind as a whole;[273] and (3) this idea is generally construed to require the equitable sharing of that resource. Nevertheless, the phrase "province of all mankind" may allow for some dispute regarding this point. The poor ratification of the Moon Treaty is another reflection of the existence of such a dispute.[274]

Regardless of the debate over significant differences in the formulation, and the way the marine law and the space law regimes have been labeled, most scholars agree that the "province" term stems from the Roman property notion of *res communis*,

Secretary-General of the U.N. on Dec. 18, 1979) and its effect on future use of space, commentated that the "negotiating history of the [Moon] Treaty demonstrates that the negotiators did not intend that the Common Heritage concept had to have the same meaning and content in both treaties [the UNCLOS and Moon Treaties]." *See* Agreement Governing the Activities of States on the Moon and Other Celestial Bodies: Hearings Before the Subcomm. on Science, Technology, and Space of the Senate Comm. on Commerce, Science, and Transportation, 96th Cong., 2d Sess. at 5 (1980). Moreover, it is being articulated in the Moon Treaty that the meaning of the "common heritage" term lies within the treaty itself. *See* Moon Treaty, *supra* note 47, at Art. 1; Staff of Senate Comm. on Commerce, Science, and Transportation, 96th Cong., 2nd Sess., Report on Agreement Governing the Activities of States on the Moon and Other Celestial Bodies 281 (Comm. Print 1980), at 5 (hereinafter "Comm. Print"); Brian M. Hoffstadt, *Moving the Heavens: Lunar Mining and the "Common Heritage of Mankind" in the Moon Treaty*, 42 UCLA L. Rev. 575, 593-94 (1994), (hereinafter "Hoffstadt").

269. Note that the UNCLOS has been ratified by 168 parties, which includes 164 United Nations Member States plus the U.N. Observer state Palestine, as well as the Cook Islands and Niue, and the European Union. An additional fourteen U.N. Member States have signed, but not ratified the Convention. *See* List of the parties to the United Nations Convention on the Law of the Sea, *supra* note 264.
270. Hoffstadt, *supra* note 268, at 580-81.
271. Outer Space Treaty, *supra* note 17, at Art. I.
272. Hoffstadt, *supra* note 268, at 587; *see also* Comm. Print, *supra* note 268, at 58.
273. Part XI, Art. 137 of the UNCLOS, *supra* note 5. *See also* Marjorie Ann Browne Foreign Affairs, Cong, Research Serv., IB95010, CRS, Defense, and Trade Division, The Law of the Sea Convention and U.S. Policy (2006) at CRS-6 (hereinafter "Marjorie").
274. Anupam Chander, *The New, New Property*, 81 Tex. L. Rev. 753 (2003) (hereinafter "Chander"); *see also* David Tan, *Toward a New Regime for the Protection of Outer Space as the "Province of All Mankind,"* 25 Yale J. Int'l L. 145, 162-79 (2000) (asserting that the concept of the "province of all mankind" should not be equated with the concept of a "common heritage of mankind" and discussing the possible meaning of the former in international law).

literally "thing of the community," hence, giving everyone the right to access and use common resources without ownership rights.[275]

Under the *res communis* rule, upon which maritime law and the "freedom of the high seas" principle[276] are based, no member has exclusive ownership rights to the property, but all members have the right to access and use the property, even without the approval of the community. This rule contrasts with the *res nullius* rule, where the resource lies unclaimed for the taking, which allows a person to claim sovereignty and ownership over property, as on land. The claimant does not have to share his bounty with the community. This is what took place in the California Gold Rush of 1849, when gold diggers claimed sovereignty over land they had staked out.[277] However, different from the case of the high seas, with the evolution of colonies in space, it is uncertain whether the *res communis* rule will not be replaced, as occurred during the California Gold Rush.

To conclude, it can be assumed that critical questions and concerns about which rules should govern the exploitation of resources in outer space will resemble the questions and concerns currently being debated in the context of the high seas and the utilization of seabed resources. Where the leading spacefaring nations are not bound by the Moon Treaty, unilateral attempts (other than unilateral domination[278]) have been taken to provide a legal framework for private enterprises to harvest the ocean and the heavens, as reflected in the Deep Seabed Hard Mineral Resources Act of 1980[279] (DSHMRA) and the Space Act of 2015 in the U.S. (Space Act).[280] However, the instability and uncertainty that characterizes this area of international law needs to be settled by the international community. The need to resolve this instability and uncertainty might only be exacerbated in space, as compared to the oceans, where jurisdictional limits are less certain and the connection to Earth is weaker. Without first resolving these concerns, no significant investments can be expected to be made to support the development of emerging mining industries.

275. Hoffstadt, *supra* note 268, at 587.
276. Note that until the mid-twentieth century the international doctrine known as the "freedom of the seas," which was a pure model of *res communis*, governed the ocean floor. This was a principle put forth in the seventeenth century essentially limiting national rights and jurisdiction over the oceans to a narrow belt of sea surrounding a nation's coastline, and by that practically leaving the remainder of the seas to be free to all and belonging to none. *See* the United Nations Convention on the Law of the Sea (A historical perspective), Div. for Ocean Affairs and the Law of the Sea, Office of Legal Affairs (2012); *see also* Hoffstadt, *supra* note 268, at 592.
277. Hoffstadt, *supra* note 268, at 587 under footnote 59.
278. Note that the outer space and any celestial bodies are "*not subject to national appropriation by claim of sovereignty, by means of use or occupation, or by any other means*" as per Art. II of the Outer Space Treaty.
279. Deep Seabed Hard Mineral Resources Act of 1980 (DSHMRA), H.R. 2759, 116th Cong. (2000) (hereinafter "DSHMRA").
280. On Nov. 25, 2015, President Barack Obama signed the bill under its full name, Spurring Private Aerospace Competitiveness and Entrepreneurship Act of 2015, a bill which gives a U.S. citizen engaged in commercial space resources the right to possess, own, transport, use, and sell the asteroid resource or space resources. The bill is intended to spur private space exploration by limiting governmental regulations until Oct. 1, 2023. *See* U.S. Commercial Space Launch Competitiveness Act, H.R.2262, 114th Congress (2015) (hereinafter referred to as "Space Act of 2015").

Although the rule of *res communis* has been developed as a general international legal principle, it has remained controversial as an overreaching principle of international law. More specifically, this debate hinges on the question whether the *res communis* rule applies to all areas outside of national jurisdiction, and if it is a part of customary international law with regard to how areas are used beyond national jurisdiction.[281] If it does not apply, it is due to a lack of consensus required for general applicability.[282] Thus, it is uncertain whether the *res communis* rule could be integrated into the space law regime, and, if it does, how it should be so.

One area of certainty is that, while the rule is clearly articulated in the law of the high seas, in the space realm, it is being left to the whims of certain members of the international community,[283] most notably to the developing countries. Naturally, developing countries tend to be concerned that richer countries will harvest the resources of the ocean beds, outer space and Antarctica as "first comers." The technological and economic advantages of the developed states allow them to exploit and loot the far reaches of Earth and space far faster and at the expense of the developing countries. By the time the latter acquire the resources to reach those frontiers, unless the rule of *res communis* provides the developing countries their rights as "second comers," or unless there exist appropriate protections to assure them at least a fair, if not equitable, share from those extracted riches, there will be nothing left. After all, this resource management regime should ultimately seek a balance between the need to make exploitation worthwhile for the developed countries, who risk their capital, and the desire to share benefits of exploitation as the "*province of all mankind*" without harming the efficient use of resources (since over-benefiting the "second comers" would impede the willingness of "first comers" to proceed). While this balance seems to be similar to socialism, in that it operationally defies the spirit of capitalism with regard to stateless and common property, the international regime tends to defy the first possession regime that gives the first claimant (usually the best positioned to win the race) the property regardless of its value.[284] As will be further explained, not only is the first possession rule in effect a civilized form of mightiest possession, but it could also be flawed even as a normative (efficiency) construct whenever first possession yields economic rents, as expected in the case of space mining.[285]

---

281. Rüdiger Wolfrum, *Common Heritage of Mankind*, IN MAX PLANCK ENCYCLOPEDIA OF PUB. INT'L L. 692, 694 (Rudolf Bernhardt ed. 1992). *See also* John E. Noyes, *The Common Heritage of Mankind: Past, Present, and Future*, 40 DENV J. INT'L L. & POL'Y 447 (2012); Chander, *supra* note 274, at 750-51; Aust, *supra* note 6, at 40.
282. JONATHAN I. CHARNEY, THE ANTARCTIC SYSTEM AND CUSTOMARY INTERNATIONAL LAW (1987); FRANCESCO FRANCIONI AND TULLIO SCOVAZZI EDS, INTERNATIONAL LAW FOR ANTARCTICA, 51, 75 (2d ed. 1996).
283. FRANCIONI & SCOVAZZI, *supra* note 282, at 76.
284. Chander, *supra* note 274, at 718, 733, 736, 740 and 752-53; *see also* Dean Lueck, *supra* note 105.
285. Haddock, *supra* note 106, at 775-76. Moreover, it can be noted that an allegedly socialist approach to the mining industry, which might seem to create tension between developing and developed countries, is not a new or unusual concept; the idea of a universal cash-transfer program has been adopted even in developed countries. For example, in 1976, Alaska amended its constitution to dedicate a part of its yearly oil revenues to a state investment fund, called the Alaska Permanent Fund (APF). The goal of the fund was to ensure that every Alaskan would

Nevertheless, the U.S. refrained from ratifying the Moon Treaty, as it also refrained from ratifying UNCLOS. Moreover, in the context of the oceans from 1982 to 1990 (before the 1994 Agreement on Implementation of Part XI of UNCLOS was adopted as a binding international convention), the U.S. agreed to accept all UNCLOS provisions, except Part XI, as a customary international law.[286] Despite the fact that the American position, supported by U.S. administrations from President Reagan onwards, has always been that a major part of the 1982 Law of the Sea Convention was for fulfilling U.S. interests in having "a comprehensive legal framework relating to competing uses of the world's oceans," it has continued to avoid ratifying UNCLOS.[287] During the Final session of the UNCLOS, on July 9, 1982, President Reagan made the decision that the U.S. would not sign on the Convention. He identified the following problems with the DSM regime: provisions that would actually deter future development of deep seabed mineral resources, when such development should serve the interest of all countries; a decision-making process that would not give the U.S. or others a role that fairly reflects and protects their interests; provisions that would allow amendments to enter into force for the U.S. without its approval; stipulations relating to mandatory transfer of private technology and the possibility of national liberation movements sharing in benefits; and the absence of assured access for future qualified deep seabed miners to promote the development of these resources.[288] However, on July 28, 1994, the U.S. reached a resolution by supporting a new agreement that amends the deep seabed regime (Part XI) of the 1982 UNCLOS.[289]

Part XI of UNCLOS establishes an ISA to authorize seabed exploration and mining and collect and distribute the seabed mining royalties to developing and landlocked countries. One of the reasons the U.S. objected to this regime, with regard to seabed minerals outside any state's territorial waters, was its concern that such a regime would harm American economic and security interests.[290]

---

benefit from the state's decision to exploit its oil resources, and that they could continue to benefit even after oil production ended. *See* Alaska Constitution, under Art. IX §.15, it is stated that "[a]ll income from the permanent fund shall be deposited in the general fund unless otherwise provided by law." *See* also Karl Widerquist, *About the Alaska Dividend*, Alaska Dividend Blog. Note that in 1982 the state's legislature passed a plan that paid each Alaska resident regardless of age an equal amount out of the appropriable earnings of the Permanent Fund.

286. Note that the "Agreement relating to the implementation of Part XI of the United Nations Convention on the Law of the Sea" was signed in 1994, amending the original Convention. The agreement has been ratified by 150 parties (all of which are parties to the Convention), which includes 146 United Nations Member States plus the U.N. Observer state Palestine, as well as the Cook Islands and Niue, and the European Union. An additional three U.N. Member States have signed, but not ratified the agreement. *See* List of the parties to the United Nations Convention on the Law of the Sea, *supra* note 264.

287. Roncevert Ganan Almond, *U.S. Ratification of the Law of the Sea Convention*, THE DIPLOMAT (May 24, 2017); *see also* Marjorie, *supra* note 273.

288. Statement by the President, 18 Weekly Comp. Press. Doc. 887 (Jul. 9, 1982); *see* Jonathan I. Charney, *The United States and the Revision of the 1982 Convention on the Law of the Sea*, 23 OCEAN DEV. & INT'L L. 279, at 285-86 (1992).

289. Jonathan I. Charney, *The Marine Environment and the 1982 United Nations Conventions on the Law of the Sea*, 28 INT'L L. 879, 880-81 (1994).

290. *See* List of the parties to the United Nations Convention on the Law of the Sea, *supra* note 264; *see also* Edward Guntrip, *The Common Heritage of Mankind: An Adequate Regime for*

In order to confront challenges with the seabed mining provisions contained in Part XI of UNCLOS, which were mostly addressed by major industrialized countries including the U.S., the U.N. Secretary-General initiated a series of informal consultations in July 1990, which ended on July 28, 1994 with the adoption of the Agreement on Implementation of Part XI of the UNCLOS of December 10, 1982 (IA). This agreement entered into enforcement on July 28, 1996.[291]

The IA modified the provisions of UNCLOS that the industrialized states had objected to. These objections included the mandatory transfer of technology, training of personnel and the decision-making process of the ISA. (The ISA is composed of a Secretariat and a Council of thirty-six countries, where all members, including the U.S., if it accedes to the Convention and takes its guaranteed seat on the council, have an effective power to veto all substantive decisions of the ISA, including those relating to budgetary or financial matters, such as how seabed mining fees paid to ISA will be spent under a distribution formula.) Additionally, the ISA contains an assembly of all parties in UNCLOS, numbering 168 members, which include the European Union, as of March 2020. This is the "supreme organ" of the Authority.[292]

Further modifications of importance were also included. The IA provides that a review of UNCLOS may occur at any time, and not only by a review conference. Additionally, modifications have occurred to remove production limitations, establish an economic assistance fund for land-based producers, and alter the financial terms of contracts. The IA finalized the operations of the Finance Committee and clarified aspects of the Pioneer Investor Scheme, which was established for those states that had invested in deep seabed technology. Any investment in DSM already made by states was factored into the regime governing the exploitation of DSM resources. Moreover, the IA includes precautions that make sure that market-oriented approaches are used for managing the resources of the deep seabeds, replacing Part XI's interventionist and centralized economic planning approach, and provide that the U.S. can bar funding for any liberation movements, as distribution of revenues derived from royalties may only occur after a consensus decision is reached in the Council.[293]

Although the IA does not alter the meaning within the "*common heritage of mankind*" principle, due to conflicting opinions, the substantive elements of the concept still remain vague. The IA merely reworks the provisions preventing universal

---

Managing the Deep Seabed?, 4.2 MELBOURNE J. INT'L L. 376 (2003) (hereinafter "Edward, *The Common Heritage of Mankind*").

291. Oceans and Law of the Sea, United States, Agreement relating to the implementation of Part XI of the United Nations Convention on the Law of the Sea of 10 December 1982 Overview, Division For Ocean Affairs and the Law of the Sea, Office of Legal Affairs, United Nations, last updated Sept. 2, 2016.
292. The Law of the Sea Convention Treaty Doc. No. 103-39, (1982) (hereinafter "The Law of the Sea Convention Hearing"); *see also* International Seabed Authority, *Structure and Mandate of the Council*, ISA (2017); International Seabed Authority, *Organs of the Authority*, ISA (2017).
293. The United States of America and the United Nations Convention on the Law of the Sea, the Convention on the Law of the Sea Oceans Conference, Monterey, California, June 1998, Archive Site for State Department information prior to January 20, 2001.

participation and acceptance by adapting them to the political and economic climate of a market-oriented economy.[294]

So far, 168 members have signed and ratified the treaty, which became effective in 1994. Developed states were induced to enter into the IA and consequently into UNCLOS. Despite support from the majority of states, and even though Canada has signed both UNCLOS and the IA but has ratified neither, the U.S. has neither signed nor ratified UNCLOS and has signed but not ratified the IA.[295]

Nevertheless, with the U.S.' signing of the IA to the Law of the Sea Convention, it can be argued that the alignment in interest in the exploitation of the deep seabeds between the U.S. government and private enterprise has been called into doubt.[296] Although the State Department position was that "the Agreement [IA], by restructuring the seabed mining regime along free market lines, endorses the consistent view of the United States that the common heritage principle fully comports with private economic activity in accordance with market principles," and whereas the supporters of UNCLOS might argue that the of the common heritage of mankind found within the Convention is not *jus cogens*,[297] the opponents to UNCLOS might still argue that mining under the common heritage concept is impossible.[298] Therefore, it might even be argued that, in contrast to the state of affairs with regard to ocean riches, U.S. interests in the commercialization of outer space resources by the private sector have been more firmly maintained (as reflected by the avoidance of even signing the Moon Treaty), and these commercial interests have already started to emerge and gain a legal foothold under the Space Act by the U.S. (which resembles, from some perspectives, the U.S. domestic law in the context of ocean mining, the Deep Seabed Hard Mineral Resources Act of 1980, as further discussed below), as well as under the domestic law of other countries, such as Luxembourg.[299] Furthermore, whereas under the Space Act, the U.S. took a more restrictive position by requiring that the majority of a company's stakeholders must be in the U.S., under the Luxembourg law, no restriction on stakeholder location is imposed. This lenient approach can merely indicate that global plans to reap the space riches, even by small countries such as Luxembourg, should not be ignored.

---

294. Edward, *The Common Heritage of Mankind*, *supra* note 290, at 385-86; *see also* Agreement relating to the implementation of Part XI of the United Nations Convention on the Law of the Sea, on its Forty-Eighth Session, U.N. Doc. A/RES/48/263 17 (1994) (hereinafter "United Nations, IA").
295. Edward, The Common Heritage of Mankind, *supra* note 290, at 386.
296. Hoffstadt, *supra* note 268, at 581 under footnote 31.
297. Note by the Secretariat, Extract from the Official Records of the Third United Nations Conference on the Law of the Sea, Volume XVII (Plenary Meetings, Summary Records and Verbatim Records, as well as Documents of the Conference, Resumed Eleventh Session and Final Part Eleventh Session and Conclusion), Third United Nations Conference on the Law of the Sea (1973-1982), Concluded at Montego Bay, Jamaica on Dec. 10, 1982 Doc. A/CONF.62/WS/37 and Add.1-2 (Mar. 8, 1983), at 243 (hereinafter "Note by the Secretariat").
298. Marjorie, *supra* note 273, at CRS-12.
299. The Government of the Grand Duchy of Luxembourg, Luxembourg is the First European Nation to Offer a Legal Framework for Space Resources Utilization, SPACERESOURCE.LU (Jul. 13, 2017); *see* The Government of the Grand Duchy of Luxembourg, Draft Law on the Exploration and Use of Space Resources, SPACERESOURCE.LU (Jul. 13, 2017).

While it can be argued that the Deep Seabed Hard Mineral Resources Act of 1980 protects the commercial interests of the U.S.' DSM sector, as the Space Act protects space mining's private players, the former act, unlike the latter, seems to have been enacted primarily as an interim law until the time when an international convention regarding the high seas will be signed,[300] as will be discussed in the next section 3.C.

Nevertheless, both space and ocean regimes seem to encourage and advocate commercial uses for the wider benefit of humanity, with a share of profits between all nations. Under UNCLOS, it has been clearly articulated: that the Area[301] and its resources are the common heritage of mankind,[302] and that the activities in the Area, that is, all activities in exploration for, and exploitation of, the Area's resources,[303] and the development of the common heritage will be for the benefit of humankind as a whole.[304]

According to UNCLOS, a share of profits derived from those activities will go to developing countries.[305] In a similar manner, Article 11(1) of the Moon Treaty[306] states that:

> "[t]he moon and its natural resources are the common heritage of mankind, which finds its expression in the provisions of this Agreement [i.e. treaty] and in particular in paragraph 5 of this article", according to which "States Parties to this Agreement hereby undertake to establish an international regime, including appropriate procedures, to govern the exploitation of the natural resources of the moon as such exploitation is about to become feasible. ..."

The Moon Treaty also adds under Article 11(7) that:

> [t]he main purposes of the international regime to be established shall include: ... (d) An equitable sharing by all States Parties in the benefits derived from those resources, whereby the interests and needs of the developing countries, as well as the efforts of those countries which have contributed either directly or indirectly to the exploration of the moon, shall be given special consideration.

However, due to the poor ratification of the Moon Treaty, as discussed above, it remains to be decided in the space context how Article I of the Outer Space Treaty, which declares that states are to continue exploring and using outer space "for the benefit and in the interests of all countries" as space is "the province of all mankind," would be interpreted with regard to profit-sharing from the space mining industry. The operational translation of the "common heritage" concept in shaping the tax regime for the space industry has yet to be determined, and it does not necessarily ensure an equal, but rather a just, amount of revenue-sharing among all countries, especially

300. Doug Bandow, *Developing the Mineral Resources of the Seabed*, 2 CATO J. 793-824, 815-16 (hereinafter "Bandow, *Developing the Mineral Resources of the Seabed*"); *see also* The Law of the Sea Convention Hearing, *supra* note 292, at 197 and 308.
301. UNCLOS, *supra* note 5, Art. 1(1).
302. *Id.*, Art. 136.
303. *Id.*, Art. 1(3).
304. *Id.*, Art. 150(i).
305. *Id.*, Art. 82.
306. Moon Treaty, *supra* note 47.

when it comes to the efficiency of the tax system as applied to new income from space mining.

In light of the similar notions and concepts embedded in both the ocean and space regimes, it is important that in the process of shaping space's new international framework, including its tax regime, further endeavors to correlate space mining regime to the high seas will be investigated as well. Similar interpretations of principles and concepts can be found in both arenas, which stretch far beyond any state's jurisdiction, and can certainly help formulate a firm and stable tax regime to be imposed on privately owned players in stateless realms.

Moreover, additional considerations and concepts should be taken into account in designing this tax regime, in light of the particular features of each stateless realm. From a futuristic perspective, whereas the high seas economy will always maintain its obvious terrestrial connection with Earth, when the space economy evolves, with its space settlements, this connection to Earth will necessarily diminish. This fragile Earth-based economic link, in addition to the special nature of space resources as "global commons," can and will impact the tailored tax regime and measures when determining the source for economic activities in space and providing a justification for imposing taxes on outer space activities.

C. THE NEED FOR ENSURING AN INTERNATIONAL LEGAL FRAMEWORK AS PART OF THE RISK-TAX REVENUE TRADE-OFF BETWEEN THE EMERGING MINING INDUSTRIES AND GOVERNMENTS

Since investors are largely influenced by expected returns after taxes, and by risks, the stability of the existing tax regime is an important component of any risk assessment. This stability is also important from the perspective of governments and can only be enhanced when dealing with international arenas and "global commons," such as on the high seas and in space, particularly when these regimes are subject to international conventions. These realms also greatly depend on political stability, which, in the case of the oceans, UNCLOS aims to provide. Given the role that the risk-return trade-off plays for incentivizing investors, the greater the perception of stability, the lower the expected return investors require, and, consequently, the greater the share of mining wealth that governments can collect in the form of taxes or other benefits, including non-fiscal related benefits, such as improvements in national infrastructure, business, employment or technology.[307]

Considering the claims and counterclaims regarding the option of joining UNCLOS, and the stable legal framework provided by the Convention, it is not surprising that the proponents of the Sea Treaty conclude that, overall, the Sea Treaty operates in the U.S.' national security, commercial, economic and environmental interests. The payments are minimal and reasonable in view of "the enormous economic value that

307. Otto, *Mining Royalties*, *supra* note 263, at 12; *see also* Tanielu, *Establishment of a National Regulatory Framework*, *supra* note 262, at 49.

would be received [and also remain within the U.S.' exclusive sovereign jurisdiction], and [this includes] the jobs that would be created, by the United States if its industry were to engage in oil, gas, and mineral development on the U.S. Extended Continental Shelf [ECS] in the Arctic."[308]

It has long been argued that the U.S. should accede to UNCLOS, in order to achieve the greater tax certainty and foreseeability which capital-intensive commercial enterprises require for managing financial risks in their investments, and to obtain the legal certainty necessary for major U.S. and foreign oil companies to secure government leases for the development of the ECS within the U.S. Due to the risks of legal challenges associated with mining activities, particularly when dealing with international arenas, not guaranteeing these legal assurances to U.S. companies would make them unwilling to invest the billions of dollars needed to develop in the Arctic or the deep seabeds. In order to develop this industry, U.S. corporations first need to obtain secured rights to DSM sites and indisputable title to minerals recovered in order to ultimately secure their mining business plans, which will only be possible if the U.S. accedes to UNCLOS.[309]

It should be noted that, consistent with any decision to invest, the "supply price of investment" is an important factor to be considered. This term, simply put, refers to the minimum expected rate of return (the minimum weighted average of possible outcomes, with weightings reflecting the probability of each outcome's occurrence) and is a function of normal, competitive returns to investment, according to the degree of monopoly in the industry, and the degree of economic and political risk associated with a project, and investors' attitudes on risk. In general, if there is a risk of substantial failure in a mining operation, a firm will not invest under *ex-ante* arrangements that would leave expected profits equal to the supply price of riskless investment. In addition, a firm will not invest under *ex-ante* arrangements that leave a substantial possibility for profits to be well below the supply price of riskless investment, even if the expected profits are significantly above this price. Some large investors while taking risk into account require the investment to yield a certain rate of return on "safe" *ex-ante* estimates of production costs and product prices, and where there is a high degree of political risk, some firms even demand shortening of the "pay back" period, which is the number of years whose income and expenditure streams are taken into consideration when calculating profitability. This has the effect of raising the supply price of investment in a way that highly depends on the timing of profits and taxation. However, usually there is also some trade-off between increased risk of failure of the operation, and the prospect of very high returns. On top of this, any taxation, even if confined to high profits and rents, also has an adverse impact when dealing with investments that are, *ex-ante*, not intra-marginal. However, as will be further explained

308. The Law of the Sea Convention Hearing, *supra* note 292, Statement of John B. Bellinger, Associate White House Counsel (Jun. 14, 2012), at 187. John Bellinger served from 2001 to 2005 in the White House as the associate counsel to President George W. Bush, and then as the Legal Adviser to the National Security Council. From 2005 to 2009, he was the Legal Adviser to the State Department.

309. *See* The Law of the Sea Convention Hearing, *supra* note 292, Statement of Hillary Rodham Clinton, U.S. Secretary of State, at 15.

below, this deterrence affect can be mitigated through taxation that focuses only on high yield returns expected in later years.[310] Since investors tend to assess political risks and the stability of an *ex-ante* negotiated taxation system, these mitigating tax measures should be included in the trade-off between the emerging miners and the government, and in any negotiated international resolution.

As a result, the U.S. private sector, including manufacturers and investors, all support the ratification of UNCLOS, while asserting that "[w]ith greater certainty and the predictability provided by the Law of the Sea Convention, industry will have greater incentive to fully take advantage of the significant advances in technology that allow us to extend operations into areas once considered out of reach or uneconomical,"[311] such as the oceans and outer space. This certainty would also allow American companies to remain competitive in the global market.[312] At a time when countries vie to expand their offshore jurisdictional claims, and as advances in technology push nations farther from their shores and into areas of harsher political and economic climates, the potential for conflicts with other nations' territorial claims, including tax jurisdictions, increases, as does the need for a stable and clear legal framework, and no ad-hoc arrangements can last as a substitute for this need.[313]

Today, as seabed mining becomes more economically viable, thanks to new technology and favorable market prices for deep seabed minerals, the emerging DSM industry, similar to the ESEs, seems to be accepting of a reliable legal framework that ensures them a license to engage in this start-up industry and enables them to calculate the cost of investments against the expected return on capital. This industry so far consists of engineering companies, consulting firms, exploration companies, exploration and mining equipment manufacturers, and mineral processing companies. It holds huge potential to boost the economic growth of the U.S. through the opening of new markets, an increase in jobs, and high profit revenues. This expected growth will be followed by increases in collected taxes and in market consumption, due to the lower prices for minerals and byproduct commodities, which are also taxed.[314] However, without obtaining clear legal title to specific claims in international waters, this industry will not invest the billions of dollars needed to engage in DSM. According to

310. Garnaut, *supra* note 67, at 272-75.
311. *See* The Law of the Sea Convention Hearing, *supra* note 292, Statement of Jack N. Gerard, President and CEO, American Petroleum Institute, at 273. *See also id.*, Statement of Jay Timmons, President and Chief Executive Officer, National Association of Manufacturers, at 275-76.
312. The Law of the Sea Convention Hearing, Statement of Jack N. Gerard, President and CEO, American Petroleum Institute, at 273, and to Timmons, President and Chief Executive Officer, National Association of Manufacturers, at 275-76.
313. The Law of the Sea Convention Hearing, *supra* note 292, Prepared Statement of Jack N. Gerard (President and CEO, American Petroleum Institute, Washington, D.C.), at 273.
314. For example, the oil or gas mining company would be taxed for its profits from selling the minerals to the electric company, which also be taxed on its profits from selling electricity to consumers.

the proponents of UNCLOS, this certainty can be achieved only through assent to UNCLOS.[315]

However, it should be noted that the U.S.' legal position regarding its right to engage in DSM was made clear in March 1983, during the final days of the Third U.N. Conference on the Law of the Sea, and has remained steadfast.[316] This position was created in response to statements from other U.N. Member States that UNCLOS nonparties would not have the right to engage in DSM.[317] At that time, along with the U.S. declaration of its continuous efforts to develop with other countries "a regime [outside the UNCLOS], free of unnecessary political and economic restraints, for mining deep seabed minerals beyond national jurisdictions,"[318] the U.S. also stated that:

> Article 137 of the Convention [forbidding claims of sovereignty over the deep seabed or its resources] may not as a matter of law prohibit sea-bed mining activities by nonparties to the Convention; nor may it relieve a party from the duty to respect the exercise of high seas freedoms, including the exploration for and exploitation of deep sea-bed minerals, by nonparties. Mining of the sea-bed is a lawful use of the high seas open to all States ... The practice of the United States and the other States principally interested in sea-bed mining makes it clear that sea-bed mining continues to be a lawful use of the high seas within the traditional meaning of the freedom of the high seas.[319]

This assertion was a restatement of the idea that "like the fish of the high seas the minerals of the deep sea-bed are open to anyone to take."[320]

Indeed, based on the position above, the U.S. unilaterally enacted the Deep Seabed Hard Mineral Resources Act of 1980[321] (which might resemble to some extent the 2015 Space Act, noting that neither really settles the legitimacy of ownership rights over minerals) to provide a legal framework for U.S. corporations to conduct, explore and exploit DSM. Thus, no nation is subject to any legal barrier that could ban U.S. companies from accessing, exploring, or exploiting the resources of the deep seabed. In fact, under customary international law, the DSM is a "high seas freedom" intrinsic right to all sovereign nations, regardless of their membership in UNCLOS or any other

315. *See* The Law of the Sea Convention Hearing, *supra* note 292, Additional Material Submitted for the Record (Responses of Thomas J. Donohue to Questions Submitted by Senator James E. Risch), at 307-08.
316. *See*, United States Ocean Policy (Statement of President Ronald Reagan), 19 Weekly Comp. Pres. Doc. 383 (Mar. 10, 1983); *see also* United States Oceans Policy, *Law of the Sea and Exclusive Economic Zone*, National Security Decision, Directive Number 82 (Mar. 10, 1983); Groves Steven, *The U.S. Can Mine the Deep Seabed Without Joining the U.N. Convention on the Law of the Sea*, Heritage Foundation: Washington, D.C. 1-18 (Dec. 04, 2012) (hereinafter "Groves, *The U.S. Can Mine the Deep Seabed Without Joining the U.N. Convention on the Law of the Sea*").
317. The Law of the Sea Convention Hearing, *supra* note 292, Statement of Steven Groves, Former Bernard and Barbara Lomas Senior Research Fellow at the Heritage Foundation, at 196-97.
318. United States Oceans Policy (Statement by the President, Administration of Ronald Reagan) at 384 (Mar. 10, 1983).
319. Note by the Secretariat, *supra* note 297, at 243.
320. The Law of the Sea Convention Hearing, *supra* note 292, Statement of Steven Groves, Former Bernard and Barbara Lomas Senior Research Fellow at the Heritage Foundation, at 196-97.
321. DSHMRA, *supra* note 279.

treaty.[322] Under DSHMRA, the U.S. position on the legality of DSM is stated as follows: "[I]t is the legal opinion of the United States that exploration for and commercial recovery of hard mineral resources of the deep seabed are freedoms of the high seas subject to a duty of reasonable regard to the interests of other states in their exercise of those and other freedoms recognized by general principles of international law."[323]

A conservative spokesman opposed to UNCLOS has even claimed that it is the Convention that "attempts to restrict access to the deep-seabed and infringe on the intrinsic rights of the U.S. and other nations that have chosen to remain non-parties."[324] This contention can simply imply on the strong motive why not to accede the "common heritage" concept when dealing with the emerging industries in both the oceans and space.

Nevertheless, the proponents of UNCLOS assert that DSHMRA, which was enacted not to serve as a unilateral substitute for an international legal authority, but merely as an interim program to regulate DSM until an acceptable convention is ratified, does not provide the clear international legal title that U.S. companies—especially public companies that owe special obligations to public investors—require before investing billions of dollars in exploration and resource extraction. These concerns for the need to form a secure investment climate had already been expressed in the U.S., even before a regulatory framework was adopted under DSHMRA or UNCLOS. For example, in 1973, Leigh S. Ratiner, a member of the Inter-Agency Task Force on the Law of the Sea stated, "*[T]he freedom of the seas would permit American companies to mine [nodules] today, although there could be no legal assurance that other countries would respect all the rights and other elements necessary for a secure investment climate.*"[325] Another example of the call and the rationale for regulation in the case of ocean mining was stated in 1972 by a representative of the American Mining Congress, C. H. Burgess of Kennecott Copper Corporation, who said that:

> [a]lthough the exploration and development phases cost many millions of dollars, the critical financial problem is the $150 to $300 million required for a commercial plant. Financing of this magnitude will require that the legal status of the operation be reasonably clear and that the operation be under some kind of national or international government sponsorship. This proper financial climate must be created in advance of committing such funds; if it is not, private industry cannot make these large investments, and potential operators must withdraw ... If some sort of interim arrangement [before a firm treaty is negotiated] is not achieved with satisfactory protection, these deposits and the technological lead may be lost from

322. Groves, *The U.S. Can Mine the Deep Seabed Without Joining the U.N. Convention on the Law of the Sea, supra* note 316.
323. DSHMRA, *supra* note 279, at s. 2(a)(12).
324. Groves, *The U.S. Can Mine the Deep Seabed Without Joining the U.N. Convention on the Law of the Sea, supra* note 316.
325. *See* Statement of Leigh S. Ratiner, U.S. Dep't of the Int., an appendix to a report from the State Dep't to Senator Henry M. Jackson, Mar. 1, 1973, in Mineral Resources of the Deep Seabed, Hearings on s. 1134 Before the Subcomm. on Minerals, Materials and Fuels of the Senate Comm. on Interior and Insular Affairs, 93d Cong., 1st Sess. 29 (1973), at 35.

the United States to others who may be less reticent about protecting their own interests. Prompt action is required.[326]

Similar apprehensions and legal uncertainties and concerns continue and are being expressed today, and likely to arose in the case of space as well. Furthermore, in an unprecedented move under President Trump's administration, the U.S. has aligned itself on the side of the international law as reflected under UNCLOS when it stood with the international community in defense of freedom of the seas and respect for sovereignty in the South China Sea. The U.S. took the position that China has no lawful territorial or maritime claim neither to Mischief Reef and Second Thomas Shoal, which fall under the territorial jurisdiction of the Philippines, nor to James Shoal, which is located 50 nm from Malaysia and some 1,000 nm from China's coast. The question of how this approach will be further followed by the current or any future U.S. administrations is still pending and unclear. These types of moves surrounded by unclarified policies while not being abided under international treaty—all can eventually hinder the economic development of the global commons in both the oceans and space. For example, Lockheed Martin, after applying under DSHMRA to the National Oceanic and Atmospheric Administration (NOAA) for an extension of its licenses to engage in deep seabed exploration, announced that it would engage in preparatory activities on land but would not make the "substantial investment in at-sea exploration" until it has the "adequate assurance of security of tenure at the international level" that would be provided by a U.S. ratification of UNCLOS.[327] These sorts of concerns arising in the private sector can pose obstacles to the development of a U.S.-owned DSM industry, and, unless resolved, might end the opportunities and potentials for thousands of new jobs.

As long as the U.S. is not a party to the Convention or any other acceptable convention—while the international community moves forward to define the legal landscape affecting over 70% of the world's surface, and other parties to the Convention apply for licenses and approval of contractors to engage in seabed exploitation (e.g., applications by the Republic of Korea, France, the United Kingdom (U.K.), Kiribati and Belgium)—U.S. companies' interests are not represented in the race to mine the ocean. Such a state of affairs could likely result in major revenue losses.[328]

These private sector concerns do not appear capable of being resolved through domestic law and bilateral agreements. Today, states are no longer the only producers

326. *See Development of Hard Mineral Resources of the Deep Seabed,* Hearing on s. 2801 Before the Subcomm. on Minerals, Materials & Fuels, 1972 92d Cong. 2d Sess. (statements of T.S. Ary, Union Carbide Exploration Corp. et al.) at 35-36.

327. Michael R. Pompeo, Secretary of State, U.S. Position on Maritime Claims in the South China Sea, U.S. Department of State (Jul. 13, 2020). *See also* Edward Wong and Michael Crowley, *U.S. Says Most of China's Claims in South China Sea Are Illegal,* The N.Y. Times (Jul. 13, 2020); Bill Hayton, *Pompeo Draws a Line Against Beijing in the South China Sea,* FP (Jul. 15, 2020). The Law of the Sea Convention Hearing, *supra* note 292, Responses of Thomas J. Donohue to Questions Submitted by Senator James E. Risch, at 308; *see also* Fed. Reg. 77(40), 12246 (Feb. 29, 2012); *see also* The Daily Journal of the United States Government, *Deep Seabed Mining: Request for Extension of Exploration Licenses,* Fed. Reg. 2012-4613 (Feb. 29, 2012).

328. The Law of the Sea Convention Hearing, *supra* note 292, Responses of Thomas J. Donohue to Questions Submitted by Senator James E. Risch, at 308-09.

of laws, and the internationalization of different customary laws, for example, contract law, business law, torts and tax, has to be observed. International organizations such as the World Trade Organization (WTO) or the EU create binding rules for both public and private actors in their Member States. Furthermore, with the growth in international trade and multinational corporations, international private law has gained stature. At a time when the nation state can no longer guarantee complete legal certainty and is reluctant to participate in an international resolution that attracts other countries, the private sectors may try to create their own legal certainty by shopping for business-friendly laws and competitive environments with a stable legal framework,[329] as can be observed in the "treaty shopping" phenomenon in the tax field.

However, it should be noted that under UNCLOS, companies from nonparty nations, such as the U.S., may not be sponsored for licenses to engage in DSM by countries that are members of the Convention. Article 4(3) of Annex III to UNCLOS provides that "[e]ach applicant [for a license] shall be sponsored by the State Party of which it is a national unless the applicant has more than one nationality, as in the case of a partnership or consortium of entities from several States, in which event all States Parties involved shall sponsor the application ... ." Therefore, for applications by a joint venture, partnership or consortium, each company must be sponsored by the country of its nationality.

Nevertheless, a U.S. company could avoid this obstacle by establishing a foreign subsidiary that might be sponsored by another country for a license, for the sole purpose of engaging in seabed mining. (For example, U.K. Seabed Resources is a subsidiary of the British arm of Lockheed Martin, the American defense giant.)[330] This action would also ensure U.S. companies that their commercial interests are being represented in ISA by the same sponsoring foreign country member, whereas the U.S. government as a nonparty to the convention cannot properly speak for them.

In spite of this, such a course of action might also have numerous commercial and economic disadvantages for the company involved, since this company would lack U.S. domestic legal framework and support. This would, most certainly, also lead to numerous commercial and economic disadvantages for the U.S., including losing license and tax revenues (excepting the potential imposition of new taxes described below, e.g., the Base Erosion and Anti-Abuse Tax, that would probably be required to be withheld from interest or royalty payments by U.S. parent companies of any foreign DSM subsidiaries, and excepting the global intangible low-taxed income tax, as discussed below), and benefits from the expected growth in jobs[331] and other monetary and non-monetary benefits.

329. Anne Hartl, *Online Dispute Resolution—A Promising Alternative for Resolving Disputes in the Future?, The Law of the Future: Maastricht Students' Perspectives on the role of the law in a globalization world*, 2 HILL INNOVATIVE JUSTICE, 27, 9-13; *see also* the U.S. Chamber of Commerce, *Statement of the U.S. Chamber of Commerce-Hearing on the United Nations Law of the Sea Convention* (Testimony of Thomas J. Donohue President and Chief Executive Officer U.S. Chamber of Commerce), 1-8, 4 (Jun. 28, 2012).

330. David Shukman, *UK Seabed Resources Joins Deep-Ocean Mineral-Mining Rush, Science & Environment*, BBC NEWS (Mar. 14, 2013).

331. An example for the expected revenue from opening the high seas to commercial use can be demonstrated from the decision made by President Trump Administration on Jan. 4, 2018, to

Moreover, there is the imposition of the Base Erosion and Anti-Abuse Tax[332] (BEAT) and global intangible low-taxed income tax[333] (GILTI) (assuming the sponsoring country's corporate tax rate is not higher than 13.125%, so that GILTI can be applied), which was enacted on December 22, 2017, under H.R. 1, informally known as the Tax Cuts and Jobs Act[334] (TCJA) and is effective for taxable years beginning after

---

open more than a billion acres in the Arctic offshore and along the Eastern Seaboard to drilling. *See* Lisa Friedman, *Trump Moves to Open Nearly All Offshore Waters to Drilling*, THE N.Y. TIMES (Jan. 4, 2018).

332. §59A of the Tax Cuts and Jobs Act (hereinafter "TCJA"). According to this section, a tax will be imposed on deductible amounts (including most royalties, rents, service fees, interest and payments made under a cost sharing agreement, and excluding cost of goods sold, certain amounts paid with respect to services, and certain qualified derivative payments unless payments made to a surrogate foreign corporation that first became a surrogate foreign corporation after Nov. 9, 2017) paid to foreign-related entities by large U.S. companies or foreign corporations with U.S. branches that: (1) has average annual gross receipts over a three-year look-back period of at least USD 500 million (which should include only effectively connected income to a U.S. trade or business if paid by non-U.S. corporations); and (2) has a "base erosion percentage" of 3% (2% for banks and certain security dealers) or higher. For purposes of these rules, foreign-related parties include any 25% owner of the taxpayer (by vote or value) and any person who is related to the taxpayer under the s. 482 transfer pricing rules. The BEAT has a potential for double taxation, unless the amount to the related foreign entity is either exempt or eligible for an indirect credit, and as such, it is equivalent to raising the U.S. effective corporate tax rate and, thus, can function as an alternative minimum tax in some cases. Broadly and conceptually, the BEAT can be considered as a thin capitalization rule that is intended to protect the U.S. corporate tax base. *See* McDermott Will & Emery, *US Tax Reform Measures Affecting Foreign Multinationals,* NAT. L. REV., (Jan. 12, 2018); *see also* Reuven S. Avi-Yonah, *BEAT It: Tax Reform and Tax Treaties, Public Law and Legal Theory Research Paper Series*, Paper No. 587, LAW & ECONOMICS RESEARCH PAPER SERIES, PAPER NO. 18-003 (2018); Davis Polk, *GOP Tax Cuts and Jobs Act: Preview of the New Tax Regime* (Dec. 20, 2017 client memorandum) (hereinafter "Davis Polk").

333. §951A of the TCJA. Under this new section, a 10% U.S. shareholder of a controlled foreign corporation (hereinafter "CFC," *see also* footnote 73) must include in income for a taxable year its share of its CFCs' GILTI, which is the deemed company's intangible income calculated as the aggregate return of CFCs in excess of 10% of the value of its "qualified business asset investment" ("QBAI"), meaning 10% of the CFCs' aggregate basis in associated tangible depreciable business property minus certain interest expenses allocable to the aggregate net income of the CFCs. GILTI can only be applied to CFC, but not to foreign branches or U.S. resident companies, although the latter, i.e., U.S. resident companies, are subject to, beginning after December 201,7 under s. 250(a) of the TCJA to foreign-derived intangible income tax (hereinafter "FDII"), which can be referred to as a "patent box" and is intended to capture income over a base return on tangible assets, earned from property sold or services provided in foreign markets. FDII tax is applied to the income return of the U.S. resident company in excess of 10% of its QBAI and practically taxed at a reduced tax rate of 13.125% by applying 37.5% deduction, thus leaving 62.5% of the FDII to be taxed at 21%. Note that FDII is allegedly providing U.S. companies an export subsidy, thus it can be challenged by the WTO. While a GILTI inclusion by a U.S. shareholder is taxable at the regular 21% corporate rate, s. 250(a)(1)(B) of the TCJA provides 10% U.S. shareholders of CFCs that are corporations special tax deductions reducing the amount of the GILTI inclusion to 50% (and beginning after 2026 to 37.5%), thus resulting in an effective rate of 10.5% (and 13.125% after 2026). *See* Davis Polk, *supra* note 332.

334. The Act is Public Law No. 115-97. The unwieldy name of the Act is "To provide for reconciliation pursuant to titles II and V of the concurrent resolution on the budget for fiscal year 2018." Note that shortly before the Act has been finally approved by Congress, the Senate parliamentarian ruled that the previously attached short title, the "Tax Cuts and Jobs Act" (TCJA), as appeared under s. 11000(b) of the Conference Report (Dec. 15, 2017), violated procedural rules governing the Senate's consideration of the legislation. Therefore, the Act

December 31, 2017. In addition to the corporate income tax imposed by the sponsoring state (assuming the sponsoring corporate tax rate is lower than 13.125%),[335] the competitiveness of these U.S.-owned subsidiaries and controlled foreign corporations[336] (CFC) (which are left with no other practical alternative for participating in DSM) might even be significantly harmed. Ultimately, avoidance in regulating the exploitation of American ECS under multilateral tools and international conventions could lead to serious consequences from profit losses, as a result of mining operations being shifted overseas.[337]

Clearly, just as there are benefits and revenue losses for not entering into DSM agreements, there is also a potential for similar losses for failing to agree on space mining. Both emerging industries hold similar expectations regarding significant economic growth through increasing jobs and tax revenues. In order to foster the development of both industries, high taxpayer-funded public budgets must be designated for the exploration of both realms, which entitle the supporting nations to tax returns once these industries begin to bloom. By comparing ocean and space exploration funding, it has been found that NASA's space exploration budget dominates NOAA's ocean exploration budget by a large margin,[338] even though "[t]he high seas are the biggest reserve of biodiversity on the planet," as stated by Peter Thomson, the ambassador of Fiji and former president of the U.N. General Assembly, who was appointed in September 2017 as the Secretary-General's Special Envoy for the Ocean.[339]

Economic activities in the ocean and in space are both vulnerable as a result of their statelessness, and with projected long-term periods of production after high initial costs, these types of investments are particularly vulnerable to policy instabilities and

bears no short title, although the short title—the TCJA—has continued to be used when referring to the actual Act. *See* Watkins Eli, *Senate Rules Force Republicans to Go with Lengthy Name for Tax Plan*, CNN (retrieved Dec. 20, 2017).

335. §960(d) under the TCJA provides U.S. shareholders of CFCs that are corporations a deemed foreign tax credit equal to 80% of the foreign taxes imposed on the CFC income included as GILTI of the CFC. The practical result of this latter section is that any foreign corporate tax rate imposed on a CFC which equals or exceeds 13.125% will not trigger any GILTI inclusion. No carryover is allowed for excess credits.

336. A CFC as defined under I.R.C. §957(a) is a foreign corporation over 50% of the stock of which, by vote or by value, is owned by U.S. shareholders, which is defined as any U.S. person that owns at least 10% of a foreign corporation's stock by vote or by value. Under the TCJA new attribution of ownership rules (so-called downward attribution) have been included for calculating the holding percentage of U.S. shareholders, intended to expand the treatment of foreign corporations as having CFC status. For example, under the new attribution of ownership rules foreign-parented group owns a U.S. subsidiary will become now CFC. *See* ss 14213 and 14214 of TCJA.

337. The Law of the Sea Convention Hearing, *supra* note 292, Additional Material Submitted for the Record (Responses of Thomas J. Donohue to Questions Submitted by Senator James E. Risch), at 308-09; *id.*, Responses of Lowell C. Mcadam to Questions Submitted by Senator Jim Demint, at 309.

338. Michael Conathan, *Rockets Top Submarines: Space Exploration Dollars Dwarf Ocean Spending, Energy and Environment*, Ctr. for Amer. Progress (Jun. 18, 2013).

339. Sengupta, *Nations Will Start Talks to Protect Fish of the High Seas*, *supra* note 13; Peter Thomson comments in an interview after negotiations aiming to create coordination to protect and conserve the biodiversity of the high seas have been started.

ill-defined legal boundaries. As a result, it becomes necessary to create agreements shaped by supporters among the international community to ensure an ultimately sustainable regime.

In the case of space, the U.S. has the opportunity to further its leadership in the international community on international zone issues, including the global free trade of space resources. Ultimately, debates around the stateless areas of the oceans and space and their resolutions are (and should be) performed at the level of the international community. The results would also likely impact the way in which the tax regimes for the ocean and space mining industries are shaped. These regimes need to be tailored to guarantee that the participating nations, either actively or passively, have access to the wealth below and above them through a stable tax-revenue flow.

In addition, pan-regional cooperation and integration with regard to DSM and space mining tax regimes is recommended when dealing with income sourced in international areas, outside any jurisdiction. Cooperation and integration of the tax structures for these emerging industries would facilitate international negotiations particularly if issues arise when deposits cross boundaries, or when the DSM's and space mining operation's rather mobile natures—where a mining vessel and equipment may need to pass between jurisdictions. In the latter situation, mining operators might try to claim tax benefits in different jurisdictions, thereby creating different non-double taxation scenarios, for example, by writing-down depreciations in one jurisdiction and then passing into another jurisdiction, where a second tax break may be sought on the same equipment by writing up the value of the same asset again. The tax regime of international mining areas should consider the existence of activity funded by overseas companies and investors, without hindering foreign investments. Therefore, cross-border cooperation and information-sharing would also be crucial when addressing these potentials for tax avoidance and for maximizing the benefits that DSM and space mining may bring to states, or even in order to avoid a "race to the bottom" scenario. In such situations, imposing a reasonable tax on expatriate assets and equipment might even be considered.[340]

The acknowledgment of the importance of the need for international cooperation in regulating international areas is demonstrated by the fact that in late July 2017, after two years of talks, U.N. diplomats recommended that treaty negotiations begin in order to establish marine protected regions in waters outside of national jurisdictions.[341]

It is expected that intergovernmental negotiations on a new high seas treaty, which started in 2018 and continues at the General Assembly of the U.N.,[342] and which involves 193 countries, will ultimately decide which are the protected areas in waters

340. Secretariat of the Pacific Community, *supra* note 262, at 17, 18 and 46. *See also* Tanielu, *Establishment of a National Regulatory Framework*, *supra* note 262, at 51.
341. Sengupta, *Nations Will Start Talks to Protect Fish of the High Seas*, *supra* note 13; *see PNG Deep Sea Mining*, BBC News (Dec. 18, 2017).
342. The General Assembly of the United Nations is a unique forum and organ at the United Nations, where all Member States have equal representation: one nation, one vote. In this forum member countries discuss and work together on a wide array of international issues covered by the U.N. Charter, such as development, peace and security, international law, and so on.

beyond national jurisdictions that will support biodiversity and marine life.[343] This decision is expected to settle diplomatic bargaining involving powerful commercial interests, and to replace existing regional organizations and rules. While Russian and Norwegian vessels fish the high seas for krill, Japanese and Chinese vessels go there for tuna, and India and China continue their explorations for minerals in seabeds in international waters.[344]

Furthermore, similar endeavors to mitigate concerns regarding future tax jurisdiction conflicts and tax avoidance, including non-double taxation attempts by emerging mining industries, should be investigated at the international level to ensure that these industries' investments are being lured and benefit both sectors, the private and the public, which should gain a fair share out of the generated profits.

While the commercial exploitation of seafloor materials has yet to begin and, in fact, may still be years off[345] (though some report this may be in the next couple of years), DSM is now viewed as being in a crucial transitional period regarding exploitation. It is expected that the race to explore both the deep seas and space will accelerate,[346] and will likely be followed by a parallel race to tax the new tax base generated by this new emerging industry, between the states who are competing as hubs for this industry.

Since more than half of the world's oceans belong to all people and countries, meaning they belong to no single entity, it has been argued that the lack of a new international system to regulate human activity on the high seas would deem international waters a "pirate zone," where the riches of the high seas lay ripe for plunder.[347] Similar assertions and concerns should be raised in the context of the commercial uses of space. The way these concerns are dealt with and resolved in the oceans could provide guidance and inspiration for similar dilemmas in space mining. This would play a significant role in deciding the extent of a fair profit share between the space

343. For News—Meetings Coverage and Press Releases by U.N.—regarding Intergovernmental Conference on Marine Biodiversity of Areas Beyond National Jurisdiction, *see* https://www.un.org/press/en/highlights/BBNJ.

344. Sengupta, *Nations Will Start Talks to Protect Fish of the High Seas*, *supra* note 13.

345. Some say that DSM will start in the next couple of years. Plans for the world's first deep sea mine are already taking shape in the waters off Papua New Guinea. *See* PNG Deep Sea Mining, *supra* note 341; Randy Showstack, *Deep-Seabed Mining May Come Soon, Says Head of Governing Group,* DEEPSEA CONSERVATION COAL. (Nov. 22, 2017) (hereinafter "Showstack, *Deep-Seabed Mining*").

346. On Nov. 14, 2017, at the 88th Meeting of the Ocean Studies Board (Joint Session with the Board on Earth Sciences and Resources) of the National Academies of Science in Washington, D.C., Michael Lodge, Secretary-General of the International Seabed Authority (ISA), stated that the world is "on the threshold of a new industry," while describing the environmental and other challenges that the deep-sea mining industry faces and while maintaining that a new workable regulatory system, that incentivizes contractors to commit significant investment and resources to develop exploitation project, could allow the seabed operations to proceed in a systematic manner. Mr. Lodge also added that "All the indications are that we are at a decisive point in the long history of attempts to mine the deep seabed"; *see* 88th Meeting of the Ocean Studies Board, Remarks by Michael W. Lodge, Secretary-General of the International Seabed Authority (Nov. 14, 2017); *see also* Showstack, *Deep-Seabed Mining, supra* note 345.

347. Sengupta, *Nations Will Start Talks to Protect Fish of the High Seas*, *supra* note 13.

mining industry and "all mankind"—the countries that support this and have either allowed or would allow it to evolve.

D. THE PARTICULARITY OF TAX CONSIDERATIONS CONCERNING TURNING THE "GLOBAL COMMONS" INTO A FUTURE HUB FOR MULTINATIONALS

As history has shown, technological developments oftentimes have unexpected consequences; and these developments may lead to huge and unexpected boons. Bill Gates, who co-founded Microsoft, described once his own inability to foresee the internet's rather remarkable development and its astounding reshaping of our lives and culture.[348] Furthermore, for many years, the internet—specifically, the ability to order digital products and services—has created distinctive issues for tax authorities.[349] These tax challenges, posed at the state, national, and international levels, arise from the challenges and confusions which technology created for authorities seeking to locate a source-state (the state where the income is derived, which is the main state able to collect tax internationally).[350] This twenty-first-century economic platform is still evolving around the world and expanding. Furthermore, given human ingenuity, it might never cease to do so. The same symptom (the tax authorities' confusion) may very well reappear as we struggle with the rapid economic expansions expected from a very different ecosystem outside the reach of any state: the expanse of outer space.

348. In Spring 1998, Bill Gates and Warren Buffett came to the campus of the University of Washington in Seattle for a conversation with students from the business school. During the meeting, Bill Gates conveyed how he was taken by surprise by the rapid development of the Internet as a deep phenomenon, which was not even prioritized by his strategy. *See* Video: Buffet and Gates on Success (May 10, 2013). *See also* Savir, *Tax Infinity & Beyond*, *supra* note 10, at 6.

349. *See, e.g.*, Reuven S. Avi-Yonah, *International Taxation of Electronic Commerce*, 52 Tax L. Rev. 507 (1997); Doernerg et al., *Electronic Commerce and International Taxation*, 24 Suffolk Transnat'l L. Rev. 233 (2000-2001) (discussing the notion of the Internet becoming a tax-free zone); Peter A. Glicklich, *United States: Internet Sales Pose International Tax Challenges*, Mondaq (Dec. 14, 200) ("The threshold issue arising under a typical bilateral treaty of the U.S. is whether the server used by the seller constitutes a "permanent establishment" of the seller in the host country.").

350. Organization for Economic Cooperation and Development, *Addressing the Tax Challenges of the Digital Economy*, OECD/G20 Base Erosion and Profit Shifting Project 123-39 (2014). "(T)he main policy challenges raised by the digital economy fall into three broad categories: • Nexus: The continual increase in the potential of digital technologies and the reduced need in many cases for extensive physical presence in order to carry on business ... can raise questions as to whether the current rules to determine nexus with a jurisdiction for tax purposes are appropriate. • Data: The growth in sophistication of information technologies ... raises the issues of how to attribute value created from the generation of data through digital products and services, and of how to characterise for tax purposes a person or entity's supply of data in a transaction ...• Characterisation: ... the proper characterisation of payments made in the context of new business models. These challenges raise questions as to whether the current international tax framework continues to be appropriate to deal with the changes brought about ... and also relate to the allocation of taxing rights between source and residence jurisdictions. These challenges also raise questions regarding the paradigm used to determine where economic activities are carried out and value is created for tax purposes, which is based on an analysis of the functions performed, assets used and risks assumed." *Id.* at 125-26.

The tax challenges which outer space presents are analogous to the international tax issues derived from e-commerce. But these challenges may be even more daunting, given the certainty that taxable assets might be outside any jurisdiction.

As blurred as the tax boundaries concerning revenues stemming from digital businesses are here on Earth, the boundaries concerning the billions of dollars stemming from future commercial space mining industries will likely be far less distinct. In digital companies, the need to overcome the difficulties involved in determining to whom tax liabilities should be allocated (whether the country of residence or a source marketplace where a significant digital presence exists) has been addressed as a major global concern under the OECD's Base Erosion and Profit Shifting Project (BEPS Project)[351] and has caused the "physical presence" notion to become outdated for tax purposes.[352] In the case of space, where tax boundaries of billions of dollars are expected to be generated by future commercial space industries, while exploiting and exhausting space resources in a place thought of as the "global commons," the nexus of business models operating from space with another ecosystem jurisdiction on Earth would further complicate and challenge tax systems worldwide that look to take a bite of Earth's biggest apple.

In addition to the tax challenges stemming from the inherent nature of space as stateless income, that is, outside of any tax jurisdiction—which in some sense could resemble the problems imposed by digital commerce—there are further tax challenges which the commercialization of space poses at both the domestic and international levels. The equal and analogous tax treatment with respect to the three stateless realms (i.e., the oceans, space and Antarctica) can be justified when comparing the domestic legal framework that governs the oceans (i.e., Deep Seabed Hard Mineral Resources Act of 1980)[353] and space (i.e., the Space Act of 2015). Additionally, the international legal framework (Law of the Sea Convention in the case of the former, and the Outer Space Treaty in the case of the latter), can help when analyzing how these regimes could impact the taxation methodology of both realms (excluding Antarctica, where the sovereignties of any individual state remains controversial).

As commercial space activities evolve in the hands of the private sector that is pledged to the expansion of the space economy, different scenarios, including the ability to incorporate in space, might create opportunities for space companies to erode every country's tax base by shifting their profits to space. As soon as space becomes a hub for companies to incorporate, it will likely become an expanding tax shelter for multinational enterprises. This latter scenario would likely eliminate the attractiveness of any residence-based tax system, as is currently being imposed by the U.S. with respect to space activities under section 863 of the Internal Revenue Code (hereinafter "Code"). This code section was enacted in 1986, and it includes a source rule based on citizenship and residency (Source Rule) for taxing other stateless areas, such as the

351. OECD, *Action Plan on Base Erosion and Profit Shifting*, 14-15 (OECD Publishing 2013) (hereinafter "OECD, Action Plan on Base Erosion").
352. *South Dakota v. Wayfair*, 138 S. Ct. 2080, 2099 (2018). *See also* Savir, *Tax Infinity & Beyond*, *supra* note 10, at 7 and 78.
353. DSHMRA, *supra* note 279.

oceans and Antarctica, in order to ensure that income derived outside any source jurisdiction (i.e., any jurisdiction as recognized by the U.S.) is not nontaxable.[354]

The U.S. space source rule gained a broad scope when considered within the definition of "Space" under the regulations, which were enacted only 20 years after section 863(d) had been added to the Code[355] (hereinafter "Regs"), probably due to the rapid and dramatic technological advances in the satellite and communications industries. Under these Regs, "Space" is defined as *"any area not within the jurisdiction (as recognized by the United States) of a foreign country, possession of the United States, or the United States, and not in international water(s)."*[356] This definition ignores the exact extent to which national air space extends above the Earth's surface.[357] However, even at this early stage, a U.N. Working Group on the Definition and Delimitation of Outer Space from COPUOS addresses the need to demarcate the boundary between air space and outer space in light of the pace of technological and scientific developments in the space and aviation industries and their commercialization. Various nations claim that, in light of such developments, the absence of such a delineation produces legal uncertainties that might lead to conflicts among countries. Similar arguments, along with the constant evolution of space technology and activities, lead the U.N. COPUOS to recognize the importance of a final decision on the definition and delimitation of outer space, which is not merely a legal but also a political need that should be resolved under an international framework and "taken on a basis that would suit the interests of all States and [the decision] would not necessarily be similar to the current positions taken by States."[358] It can be assumed that, as the space industry continues to evolve, similar disputes will arise in the international tax field. In light of this, the current U.S. Code might be perceived as anachronistic. At the very least, ESEs will need to be assured that, from a legal standpoint, they need not worry about double taxation, for

354. Staff of the Joint Committee on Taxation, General Explanation of the Tax Reform Act of 1986, H.R. 3838, 1st Sess., 99th Congress (1987). *See also* Savir, *Tax Infinity & Beyond*, *supra* note 10, at 28-29.
355. Regulations §1.863-8 (hereinafter referred to as the "Regs"). *See also* Regs. *§1.863-9.* The first time that the Regs under *§ 863(d)* have been proposed was in Jan. 17, 2001 under Prop. Regs. *§ 1.863-8*, 66 Fed. Reg. 3903, 3910 (2001) and Prop. Regs. *§1.863-9*, 66 Fed. Reg. 3903, 3914 (2001) (they contain numerous examples in Prop. Regs. *§1.863-8(f)*). The 2001 Prop. Regs. on space, ocean and communications activities were withdrawn and reproposed in September 2005. After revising, the reproposed regs were adopted as final regs on Dec. 27, 2006. *See* TC 9305, adopting Regs. §§ 1.863-8 and 1.863-9 (generally effective for 2007, and without major change). For comments on the proposed regs, *see* Kennedy & Fox, *Careful Planning May Avail Foreign-Source Income Under Section 863(b) Prop. Regs.*, 84 J. TAX'N 232 (1996); Nadel & Gate, *863(b) Prop. Regs. May Increase Some Taxpayers' Foreign-Source Income*, 7 J. INT'L TAX'N 265 (1996); *see also* Michael S. Lebowitz and Stacy Paz, *IRS Reproposes Regulations for Taxing the "Final Frontier,"* 84 TAXES 21-28, 22 (Jan 2006).
356. Regs. §1.863-8(d).
357. Gbenga Oduntan, *The Never Ending Dispute*, *supra* note 10.
358. Delimitation of Outer Space, *supra* note 64. *See also* Comm. on the Peaceful Uses of Outer Space, *Historical Summary on the Consideration of the Question on the Definition and Delimitation of Outer Space*, U.N. Secretary-General, U.N. Doc. A/AC.105/769/Add.1, at 7-8, 1-14 (2020); U.N. Secretary-General, *Report of the Committee on the Peaceful Uses of Outer Space*, U.N. Doc. A/58/20, at 29-30, 1-57 (2003).

example, being bound by the territorial air space rules of one nation, while at the same time owing taxes based on their corporation's country of residence in another.[359]

Complex dilemmas might arise in the international tax field by either simply adopting different concepts about where outer space actually begins above the Earth's surface (including the high seas), or, in more far-fetched scenarios, even overhauling the very definition of "outer space." Certain nations might try to nationalize—read: claim—whole segments of outer space in an attempt to apply and broaden their own tax jurisdictions. Such concepts would be expected to evolve as even more game-changing technologies are developed (if not during today's Space Age, then during the next one, when colonies on Mars, for example, become independent[360]). Under such circumstances, the current legal perceptions that regard outer space, the oceans, and Antarctica as analogous, would likely become outdated.

In fact, when considering this analogous treatment under the tax code, it should be mentioned that, in 1992, in *Smith v. United States*, Antarctica was deemed a foreign country for the purposes of the Federal Tort Claims Act (FTCA).[361] The court's reasoning might also render space a "foreign country" under FTCA, as well as in other judicial contexts, including those for tax purposes. Since the court stated that the commonsense definition of "country" is not particularly limited to a "sovereign state" but simply to a "region or tract of land,"[362] there might even be a basis for claiming that space is a "foreign source" governed by any jurisdiction recognizable by the U.S., as found in international space law. Although the court's decision to date seems to stand as settled law,[363] applying such an analysis to the other two sovereign-less zones (space and the oceans) can emphasize the legal discord captured within the basic definition of outer space under today's tax Regs, and points to the conflict within the general rule under section 863(d) describing how to tax space activities derived by a U.S. person as a U.S. source income.[364]

With this American move to a territorial tax system, another important (and current) question is whether the Source Rule will continue to be relevant and viable with respect to space activities, or if it would essentially disincentivize the development of US commercial space activities by deeming this development to be 100% U.S. income, and thus subject to a 21% tax, even when its services and goods are sold to a non-U.S. person in space. The answer to this question is crucial in light of the adoption of a new provision under the TCJA, which allows for a reduced tax rate (13.125% until

359. Bin Cheng, Commercial Development of Space, *supra* note 65. *See also* Savir, *Tax Infinity & Beyond*, *supra* note 10, at 47.
360. Konstantin Tsiolkovsky (1895): "The Earth is the cradle of mankind, but one cannot stay in the cradle forever."
361. *Smith v. United States*, 507 U.S. 197 (1993).
362. *Id.*, at 201-02.
363. *Id.*, at 205-06. It should be noted the Justice Steven in his dissenting expressed his concern that "[t]he negligence that is alleged in this case will surely have its parallels in outer space as our astronauts continue their exploration of ungoverned regions far beyond the jurisdictional boundaries that were familiar to the Congress that enacted the Federal Tort Claims Act ('FTCA') in 1946."
364. William Lee Andrews, The Taxation of Space Commerce 59-60 (2001). *See also* Savir, *Tax Infinity & Beyond*, *supra* note 10, at 48.

2025) on income earned directly by corporate U.S. taxpayers from selling property or providing services outside of the U.S. This provision, aimed at taxing foreign-derived intangible income (FDII),[365] essentially provides an export subsidy for U.S. corporations. If all sales and services income in space by U.S. ESEs were to be treated as income from the exploitation of domestically-held intangible assets in the U.S., they might thus be subject to the regular corporate rate (i.e., 21%), and the space industry might be deemed to suffer a discriminatory tax treatment (even if unintentional) and be harmed as a whole.

Nevertheless, under the Source Rule, three activities are excluded: transportation income (as defined in section 863(c)); international communications income;[366] and "any activity with respect to mines, oil and gas wells, or other natural deposits, to the extent [the mines, wells or natural deposits are located] within the United States or any foreign country or possession of the United States (as defined in section 638)."[367] According to the third exception, and in light of the new rule under the TCJA, which determines the source of income from sales of manufactured inventory solely on the basis of production,[368] space mining activities are likely to be treated as pure space activities, thus generating 100% U.S. income when conducted by U.S. ESEs, except "to the extent the income, based on all the facts and circumstances, is attributable to functions performed, resources employed, and risks assumed in a foreign country or countries,"[369] as provided under the Regs. These tax rules are about to raise numerous legal challenges on both domestic and international fronts.

365. Section 250(a) of the TCJA, under which U.S. resident companies are subject, beginning after December 2017, to FDII, which can be referred to as a "patent box" and is intended to capture income over a base return on tangible assets, earned from property sold or services provided in foreign markets. FDII tax is applied to the income return of the U.S. resident company in excess of 10% of its QBAI and practically taxed at a reduced tax rate of 13.125% by applying 37.5% deduction, thus leaving 62.5% of the FDII to be taxed at 21%. For taxable years after 2025, the deduction is reduced to 21.875% of FDII. Assuming a 21% corporate tax rate, this will result in an effective tax rate of 16.406% on FDII. Note that FDII is allegedly providing U.S. companies an export subsidy, thus it can be challenged by the WTO. *See generally* Davis Polk, *supra* note 332.
366. I.R.C. §863(e) covers communication between U.S. and non-U.S. end point. According to I.R.C. §863(e) international communications income earned by a U.S. person shall be considered to be 50% U.S. source income and 50% foreign source income; and international communications income earned by a non-U.S. person shall be considered to be entirely foreign source income except to the extent such income is attributable to an office or fixed place of business in the U.S. However, income from transmitting communication between two points in space or international waters (space/ocean communications income) is sourced under the space and ocean rules of I.R.C. § 863(d) and the Regs. §§1.863-9 (effective Dec. 27, 2006, and without major change). In addition, income which is not derived from the "transmission of communications" but rather from the rental of the property utilized in providing transmission of communications, such as leasing of a satellite or cable, does not appear to be International Communication Income.
367. I.R.C. §863(d)(2)(B)(iii).
368. Note that under pre-TCJA under the Code s. 863(b), sales of inventory property produced in one jurisdiction and sold in another were sourced by allocating 50% of the sales income to one jurisdiction and 50% to the other. §14303 of the TCJA changed this sourcing rule so that the entire amount is sourced to the jurisdiction of production.
369. Reg. §1.863-8(b)(1), (b)(2)(ii).

As we are about to enter this new age in space, an age where fortunes can be made from our solar system for the benefit of the people of Earth, space mining is likely to be a turning point for our civilization, reminiscent of the colonization period, when an abundance of new (albeit occupied) land became accessible to trailblazers and pioneers. This turning point may even lead us to a debate regarding tax emancipation, for instance, on Mars ("no taxation without representation"). Needless to say, it is quite clear that there are many legal considerations for the tax field that must soon be resolved.

As space activities increase and commercial enterprises develop in space, governments will need to examine these tax challenges. The more ESEs seeking the right set of regulatory regimes for supporting the development of commercial space activities, the stronger the probability that conflicts will develop among nations vying to become the hub for these ESEs, and, thereby, benefit their own tax base. To achieve this goal of becoming an attractive hub for future space commerce, nations might start competing by making revisions and adjustments to their current tax regimes, both at the international and domestic levels. When adapting these regimes, we should remember that tax regulations for space activities need to be carefully crafted. These should attract (not repel) the ESEs into developing an idyllic future in outer space for all mankind. However, these regulations should also be designed to mitigate the repercussions of emerging space business models in order to prevent the participants in space commercialization (the ESEs) from extracting profits from new enterprises that are outside of any source-based jurisdiction, or even beyond this, any tax jurisdiction (e.g., by relinquishing Earth residency and/or incorporating in space).

Generally, space-oriented policies seem to be trying to enable the Emerging Space Industry to flourish by avoiding over-regulations. However, tax-oriented policies should also be advised to target the preservation of tax-bases of the states which supported the development and growth of the ESEs initially. An appropriate tax regime would likely enable new ESEs to recoup the economic benefits from the "global commons," thereby luring the development of the commercial space economy, while ensuring that a just tax base is allocated to the applicable tax jurisdiction, and that a just compensation is given to the international community for the exhaustion of its shared resources. This regime should also be tailored in a way that would support an investment climate that leaves no room for vagueness regarding any legal rights and entitlements.

E. ADDITIONAL TAX POLICY CONSIDERATIONS

Ultimately, the international best practices and best competitive fiscal regimes in related areas, such as the most prominent ones in terrestrial mining, will most likely be adapted and modified by the states' ocean (the DSM) and space mining fiscal regimes, and impact the structure of their tax regimes in order to maintain international competitiveness and horizontal equity objectives.[370] Therefore, the new fiscal framework for the emerging industries requires a rethinking of an appropriate tax regime.

Since taxation of mining activities, specifically in international areas, is an important public policy issue that raises questions of fairness regarding the exploitation of nations' natural capitals, the tax regime of these upcoming mining industries will be evaluated through the following key questions:[371]

- Are payments to society for exploiting its nonrenewable resources adequate?
- Are investors receiving a fair return?
- Is the system competitive with those of other states or provinces?

For example, similarly to the case of terrestrial mining where the division of wealth between companies and the host state is important, in the case of mining in international areas (outside of any state's jurisdiction) the division of wealth between companies and all states and, in fact, all of humankind, will probably become at least as important as the division found in terrestrial mining. How these divisions are decided will likely be subject to international community pressures, and special-case lobbying by the industry, which is aware of and responsible for the high risk nature of capital investments. Ultimately, both sorts of pressures could lead to distortions in economic efficiency, which might even be exacerbated, due to government incentives and special tax stability agreements provided for these emerging mining industries.[372]

Providing incentives for the development of those mining industries and ensuring stable tax-rate structures during the period of an agreement or of a mining project might appear desirable, particularly at a time when Earth's resources are being exhausted, especially as the cyclic and volatile mining business model might require flexibility. (Cyclic phases of the mining industry are discussed further below.) However, the imminent risk of economic deficiencies resulting from increasing pressures accompanied with the provision of such incentives or other tax agreements might be best resolved through global uniform tax regimes applied to those industries.[373]

A uniform tax regime with standards and rules largely set by legislative bodies, and which disallows special tax agreements, would help in reducing the complexity of the tax codes, thus making them easier to administer and enforce. Such a regime would mitigate concerns regarding discriminatory treatment, and thus, might alleviate different pressures. However, as tax systems increasingly converge, the question of how mining tax revenues are being distributed and utilized might become even more

370. Tanielu, *Establishment of a National Regulatory Framework*, *supra* note 262, at 48.
371. P. Mitchell, *Taxation and Investment Issues in Mining*, in ADVANCING THE EITI IN THE MINING SECTOR: A CONSULTATION WITH STAKEHOLDERS, EXTRACTIVE INDUSTRIES TRANSPARENCY INITIATIVE 27-31, 29 (Christopher Eads et al. eds. 2009) (hereinafter "Mitchell, *Taxation and Investment Issues in Mining*").
372. *Id.*, at 29 and 31; *see also* Otto, *Mining Royalties*, *supra* note 263, at 140.
373. Mitchell, *Taxation and Investment Issues in Mining*, *supra* note 371, at 28-29; *see also* Otto, *Mining Royalties*, *supra* note 263, at 12 and 15.

important with regard to the fruits of extraterritorial resources, such as of the province of all mankind.[374]

Before the DSM and space mining industries evolve, it is important for governments to understand the effects of their general tax system on investments and respond accordingly, excluding, of course, the incorporation of mining-specific features (as will be discussed below, regarding mining royalties). There is a ready measure which can be used, as recommended by the Extractive Industries Transparency Initiative[375] (EITI) and based on relative exploration expenditures:

> all things being equal (including tax), a country should attract exploration investment proportional to its international geological attractiveness rating. If investment is less, it implies other faults in the investment climate, such as excessive tax. However, if investment is greater than geological [oceanography/space research] potential, investment conditions may be overly generous.[376]

This same measure may also facilitate the search for an optimal level of taxation, since if taxation is too high or excessive, investors will eventually shift their focus to other alternatives. If taxation is too low or generous, the country will lose revenue useful in serving the public welfare. In addition, the timing of tax charges should be considered, as it influences both investment patterns and the government tax revenue. Although raising tax rates will increase government receipts in the short term, if the increase is excessive, it will discourage exploration and development, and, in marginal cases, it will even keep some mines from operating. Therefore, over the long term, it will reduce tax revenues generated by the sector.[377]

Consequently, the investment climate and investors' perceptions are important in deciding the tax structure and rates, aside from taking into account the fiscal interest of countries.[378] These might be even more important when nations compete for minerals and resources that lay in open common areas, and in areas previously considered inaccessible, since in this case the high risks and costs associated with investments can merely increase the volatility of investors to any changes in the tax

---

374. Mitchell, *Taxation and Investment Issues in Mining*, *supra* note 371, at 28-29 and 31; *see also* Otto, *Mining Royalties*, *supra* note 263, at 14; Secretariat of the Pacific Community, *supra* note 262, at 22; International Seabed Authority (ISA), *Making the Most of Deep Seabed Mineral Resources*, Developing Financial Terms for Deep Sea Mining Exploitation, ISA (2014), at 51 and 59 (hereinafter "ISA, *Making the Most of Deep Seabed Mineral Resources*").
375. PwC, *Tax Transparency and Country by Country Reporting BEPS and Beyond*, at 24 (2016); *see also* EITI.ORG at https://eiti.org; and ISA, *Making the Most of Deep Seabed Mineral Resources*, *supra* note 374 at 2, 18-19. Note that the EITI is a standard that promotes revenue transparency and accountability in the extractive sector by requiring companies in the extractive industries to report what they pay to governments and equally for governments to make public the payments they receive. Whereas the decision by a country to implement the EITI is a voluntary one, the EITI aims to strengthen governance in resource-rich countries by improving transparency and accountability as to how natural resource wealth is generated and used.
376. Mitchell, *Taxation and Investment Issues in Mining*, *supra* note 371, at 29.
377. *Id.*, at 27.
378. Controller General Indian Bureau of Mines Nagpur, *Mineral Royalties*, GOV. OF INDIA, MINISTRY OF MINES 19 (2011) (hereinafter "Controller General Indian Bureau of Mines Nagpur, Mineral Royalties").

rates or structure as, in general, it can be expected from firms to respond to tax risks by choosing safer projects and, thereby, reducing the risks they take.[379] An efficient tax structure can help sustain a stable investment climate either by mitigating investors' risks, which can adversely affect innovation and economic growth, or by leaving the incentives to invest unaffected while increasing tax certainty.[380]

When designing a tax system for those new start-up mining industries, policy-makers should be aware of the cumulative and ripple effects which taxes (including any required upfront fees and/or financial bonds) have on the economics of mining and potential levels of future investments. This insight must acknowledge how each tax type helps achieve specific objectives, including the implications of the combined effects of all taxes.[381] To demonstrate the significance of each type of tax on investment decisions, the case of mining royalties should further be discussed and considered. For example, unit-based royalties, which are in rem taxes (as will be further discussed in Chapter IV), generally seem to have a more distortional impact on production decision-making pertaining to cut-off ore grades (i.e., the break-even grade when costs associated with mining and mineral processing are equal to revenues, but at a level below this, it is no longer economically viable to mine the ore), mine life, and mineral reserves compared to the impact profit-based royalties have, which are in personam taxes.[382] As a result, nations dependent on mineral exports, who are more vulnerable to mineral commodity prices, would allot a higher importance to in rem taxes than to in personam, particularly since the first are imposed irrespective of the net revenue and profitability of the mining sector.[383]

However, mineral sector investors will become anxious about how the "bottom-line" appears on their balance sheet and their overall tax share, that is, the effective tax rate (as is further discussed below in this section), and the extent of the total tax burden, particularly the imposed in rem taxes, which are not based on profitability, and which hold a larger significance when losses occur even under poor operating conditions. Note that it has become a practice across the globe to lower the applicability

379. Alexander Ljungqvist, Liandong Zhang, and Luo Zuo, *Sharing Risk with the Government: How Taxes Affect Corporate Risk Taking*, 55.3 J. Accounting Research 669-707 (2017). An argument can be made that although the expectation that firms will try to take safer projects in the case of tax increase, this prediction can be modified if there are loss-offsets rules in place. However, since in many cases there are limitations on the latter loss-offset rules and only partial deduction is allowed, the downside associated with a risky project is higher than its upside where losses cannot be completely written off against past or future profits. *See also* Buchholz Wolfgang and Kai A. Konrad, *Taxes on Risky Returns—An Update*, Working Paper 2014-10, MPI for Tax Law and Public Finance, Max Planck Society (2014).

380. Michael P. Devereux, *Taxing Risky Investment*, Working Papers 0919, Oxford University Centre for Business Taxation (2009).

381. Tanielu, *Establishment of a National Regulatory Framework*, *supra* note 262, at 49; *see also* Secretariat of the Pacific Community, *supra* note 262, at 16.

382. Tanielu, *Establishment of a National Regulatory Framework*, *supra* note 262, at 49; *see also* Secretariat of the Pacific Community, *supra* note 262, at 16; Otto, *Mining Royalties*, *supra* note 263, at 31.

383. Laporte Bertrand and De Quartrebarbes Celine, *What Do We Know About Mineral Resource Rent Sharing in Africa?* (Aug. 1, 2015), at 9 (hereinafter "Laporte Bertrand, *What Do We Know About Mineral Resource Rent Sharing in Africa?*"); *see also* Otto, *Mining Royalties*, *supra* note 263, at 31.

and level of in rem taxes in the mining sector.[384] Yet, it is uncertain if this is the right approach when dealing with the emerging industry in space, which is based on developed knowledge and capabilities resulting from large government investments, and where high expectations for supernormal profits exist.

Ultimately, a competitive tax regime should maintain several important objectives:[385]

- Stability, predictability, and transparency of the tax system.
- Administrative efficiency, enforceability and simplicity of the tax system, especially where there may be a low administrative capacity to calculate, collect and audit the sums due. In general, greater complexity may be a genuine constraint in developing countries with limited administrative capacities. Moreover, complexity may create higher compliance costs and cause a greater potential for corruption and tax fraud, two key concerns in the EITI context.[386] Note that similar objectives have been implied under the IA, which states that "[t]he [payment] system should not be complicated and should not impose major administration costs."[387] Typically, the presence of fewer taxing instruments under a tax regime translates to greater simplicity.[388]
- Equitability (*see* further below in this section regarding equitable distribution of revenues and a fair revenue) and sustainability of the mining industry, by providing domestic and foreign investors sufficient returns in order to encourage industry development.
- Recognition of the non-monetary benefits and further value-adding generated by this industry, such as the increase in industry diversification; the development of downstream processing and other economic sectors; employment opportunities; development in domestic infrastructure; and technology.
- Acknowledgment of the unique profile of the emerging mining industry as a cyclical industry, where separate mines have differing capacities to pay taxes at various stages of development. To better understand the meaning of this objective, it should be noted that, even before the extraction/production stage (as is explained below in this section, regarding each mining phase), mining generally involves high capital investment, including upfront fees and financial bonds; high exploration risks; development of sophisticated technology; sensitive environmental impacts; stakeholder scrutiny; volatile marketplaces; and highly fluctuating commodity prices.

384. Laporte Bertrand, *What Do We Know About Mineral Resource Rent Sharing in Africa?, supra* note 383; *see also* Otto, *Mining Royalties, supra* note 263, at 31-35.
385. Mangondo Kismore, The Economics of Gold Mining Taxation, 29-38 (University of South Africa 2006); *see also* Tanielu, *Establishment of a National Regulatory Framework, supra* note 262, at 49; Secretariat of the Pacific Community, *supra* note 262, at 16-17; ISA, *Making the Most of Deep Seabed Mineral Resources, supra* note 374, at 32 and 41.
386. Mitchell, *Taxation and Investment Issues in Mining, supra* note 371, at 28.
387. Annex under United Nations, IA, *supra* note 294, at s. 8(1)I, 20.
388. ISA, *Making the Most of Deep Seabed Mineral Resources, supra* note 374, at 76.

All of these features have led to the need for a balanced trade-off between two more objectives, flexibility and certainty. Both objectives are required in order to create a stable tax regime, as the DSM and space industry evolve through the investment and learning processes.[389]

There are four main phases in mining, as follows:[390]

(1) *Exploration*: a high-cost and highly risky phase before income begins to be generated. Losses resulting from this stage are usually allowed to be carried forward and offset against profits from the production phase, in order to encourage mining beyond this initial phase;
(2) *Development*: a high-cost phase of investment, as it involves the purchase of substantial capital inputs, most of which involve imports. As a response, accelerated recovery (depreciation) of capital costs is usually allowed once production begins, and low import duties and value added taxes (VATs) are imposed;
(3) *Production*: the longest and most profitable phase, where income and profits are expected. During this phase, corporate income tax is usually imposed on net profits, and additional profit taxes, such as rent resource taxes may kick in to catch any "supernormal" profits/rents. In addition, due to fluctuations in mineral prices and a volatile and competitive marketplace, tax flexibility is usually implemented to allow relief from export duties and VATs, and even relief from other substantive taxes;[391]
(4) *Post-mining phase*: the last phase in the cycle, which involves rehabilitation costs when mining ceases as income.

In the emerging mining industry sectors, it should be decided which costs would be managed as capital assets and, thereby, depreciated or amortized for tax purposes over the economic life of a mine. Some regimes provide tax deductibility in order to encourage companies to set a progressive fund during the production stage, to cover post-mining costs. However, regimes opposed to this tax deductibility claim this phase is part of the miners' social responsibility.[392]

Similar to post-production costs (also referred to as the rehabilitation or closure phase), special rules should be enacted on the deduction of other feasibility costs, including pre-production exploration costs, development costs and assets, and production costs. Providing special depreciations and tax incentives for R&D activities, due to

389. Tanielu, *Establishment of a National Regulatory Framework*, *supra* note 262, at 49; *see also* ISA, *Making the Most of Deep Seabed Mineral Resources*, *supra* note 374, at 28.
390. Mitchell, *Taxation and Investment Issues in Mining*, *supra* note 371, at 28.
391. ISA, *Making the Most of Deep Seabed Mineral Resources*, *supra* note 374, at 56. *See also* United Nations Handbook on Selected Issues for Taxation of the Extractive Industries by Developing Countries, United Nations 1-477, at 441-45 (2017).
392. H. Choudhury, O. Fjellsa, C. Sanger and Dr. B.G. Twomey, *Extractives Industries Taxation: CRP.3-Attachment A*, United Nations Tax Committee's Subcommittee on Extractive Industries Taxation Issues for Developing Countries, 1-48, at 37-38 (2016) (hereinafter "Choudhury, *Extractive Industries Taxation*"). *See also* Mitchell, *Taxation and Investment Issues in Mining*, *supra* note 371, at 28.

the inherent risks embedded in the new mining industries, would encourage capital investments. However, it should be decided how those costs can be apportioned between different mining projects, such as exploration costs or when a plant or machinery is shared, or where there is a central administration. It also needs to be decided if the nature of each expense is of a capital or a revenue type (i.e., an operating expense). Whereas the former expense needs to be deducted over time, either depreciated or amortized, the latter expense can be fully deducted immediately.[393]

The TCJA demonstrates how changes in the rules governing allowable deductions, such as the depletion deduction, R&D and NOL, can impact the mining industry. After the repeal of the alternative minimum tax (AMT) under the TCJA, which allowed many sector companies to pay taxes at a 20% tax rate, the way and the extent to which these kinds of deductions are set will have a major impact on every domestic and multinational mining companies with operations within the U.S. Note that the single largest tax incentive targeted at the mining sector, percentage depletion, was not eliminated as part of the TCJA. Percentage depletion allows miners to claim depletion deductions equal to the lesser of 50% of net mining income or a fixed statutory percentage of gross income, at varying rates based on the type of mineral being mined. With the repeal of the corporate AMT, percentage depletion is expected to be more important than ever for this sector, and so is the utilization of the R&D credit. Note that in the pre-TCJA period, the research credit was not often used by the mining industry since it was not allowed to offset companies' AMT liabilities, except for eligible small businesses.[394] Whereas many companies chose not to fully explore all opportunities to claim the full amount of percentage depletion to which they were entitled because of AMT consequences, after the TCJA, these companies will probably want to immediately explore all opportunities to claim the full amount of allowable percentage depletion deductions. Under the TCJA, 50% of the net mining income limit, as percentage depletion, is also burdened by depreciation expenses, as well as bonus depreciation. This bonus depreciation increased under the TCJA, from 50% to 100% for "qualified property" placed in service after September 27, 2017, and before 2023, and will start to phase down in 2023 by 20% for each of the following five years, and reach 0% by the beginning of 2027. In addition, under the TCJA, the NOL deduction has been limited to 80% of taxable income.[395] While NOLs incurred in tax years beginning after 2017 will have an unlimited carryforward, no carryback is allowed.[396] It should be noted that the ability to carryback NOLs provided a helpful benefit for most sector companies, specifically in times of market downturns, and especially for sectors

393. ISA, *Making the Most of Deep Seabed Mineral Resources, supra* note 374, at 46-48.

394. *See* §613. *See also* §174 of TCJA dealing with Amortization of Research and Experimental Expenditures; Ernst&Young LLP, U.S. Tax Cuts and Jobs Act, *Effects of the Tax Cuts and Jobs Act and Its Impact on the Energy Sector*, Tax News Update, U.S. Edition (Jan. 5, 2018). *See also* Yair Holtzman and Sharlene Sylvia of Anchin, *INSIGHT: 2017 Tax Law Changes Increases Value of R&D Tax Credit*, Bloomberg Tax (Jan. 23, 2019). As explained in the latter "[s]tarting in 2016, the PATH Act of 2015 allowed eligible small businesses—privately held businesses with $50 million or less in average gross receipts for the three preceding tax years—to utilize the credit against their AMT."

395. I.R.C. §172(a).

396. I.R.C. §172(b)(1)(A).

in which rapid commodity pricing moves could disrupt the profitability and financial health of a company, as typically occurs in the mining industry. As commodity pricing decreased, and large losses were incurred, companies were able to carry these losses back to prior profitable periods.[397]

To conclude, all allowable deductions would adjust the mining companies' tax base. Therefore, there are a few options to which the tax base for space mining operating entities could be subject. The first is the regular corporate income tax rules as applied to any normal business sector. The second are specific (and beneficial) mining sector rules for adjusting the tax base, which would be enacted to foster the space mining industry, for example, by providing a bonus deduction in the first year and by repealing the 50% net mining income limit (as explained in the paragraph above). Alternatively, perhaps a ring-fencing could be applied to the emerging mining industry, which would allow for a loss carryback at the end of a mining operation's life, i.e., when the project reaches the closure of the mining phase, in order to allow mining operations a tax relief through deduction of the actual costs incurred.[398]

Additionally, while it is important to provide multinational mining companies with protections against double taxation, it is crucial that the tax base be adjusted in accordance with appropriate anti-avoidance rules, to avoid profit-shifting. These anti-avoidance rules should prevent mining multinationals from segregating profits from the economic activities that created it by using a group of affiliated/consolidated mining companies to maximize deductions (including interest deductions) for reducing sales revenues in a nation with higher tax, and later shifting their profits to a country with lower tax. In order to limit the problem of excessive interest deductions, Action 4 under the BEPS project has been developed to help host countries to ensure that a company's net interest expense deductions (i.e., interest expense that exceeds any interest income) are directly linked to the taxable income it generates from its economic activities. As part of the OECD recommendations under Action 4, the need for implementing a unique approach for the terrestrial mining sector has also been acknowledged and justified, despite the fact that "[t]ax policies implemented sector by sector are not usually encouraged, since treating sectors differently can drive resource allocation across the economy," by explaining that "where extractive industries are a significant portion of the economy (and by extension, potentially a significant part of the revenue base), this can justify special interest limitation rules for the sector. This would be especially the case if there is evidence of acute base erosion. And in any case, mining companies often face separate fiscal arrangements and ring-fencing, meaning the decision to apply sectoral rules has already been made."[399] Similarly, the BEAT enacted under TCJA can be seen as another example of an anti-avoidance measure

397. Ernst&Young LLP, *Effects of the Tax Cuts and Jobs Act on the Mining and Metals Industry*, TAX NEWS UPDATE, U.S. EDITION (Jan. 12, 2018).

398. ISA, *Making the Most of Deep Seabed Mineral Resources*, *supra* note 374, at 63 and 74. *See also* Choudhury, *Extractive Industries Taxation*, *supra* note 392, at 15.

399. ISA, *Making the Most of Deep Seabed Mineral Resources*, *supra* note 374, at 48. *See also* OECD, *Limiting the Impact of Excessive Interest Deductions on Mining Revenues, IGF-OECD Program to Address Beps in Mining*, at 23-26 (OECD Publishing 2018).

adopted unilaterally by a country, here the U.S., and as a type of thin capitalization rule.

However, whereas in DSM, land and ocean-based activities can easily be defined on Earth and can indicate trends in cross-border profit shifting, because economic activities evolve in space, this analysis will likely become obscured. For example, whether on Mars or in attempts to develop Asgardia (also known as the Space Kingdom of Asgardia),[400] space nations could be established and become hubs for the incorporation of space mining companies. Later, they might grow into hubs to send out mining expeditions, and for trading with mining resources and other by-products. At that point, all the industry's upstream and downstream will likely be conducted in space. Distinct from seabed minerals, which are meant to be used and sold on Earth, the consumption market for utilizing space resources is anticipated to be developed in space itself for the long-term and on a large-scale basis (at least in its first phase), since the utilization of space resources is likely to first become economically viable and commercially recoverable in space itself, unless Earth suffers from a threatening lack of accessible resources, and land-based resource prices inflate at extreme rates.

Ultimately, the goal is to make the space economy increasingly independent and based on self-production of its resources alone. Therefore, by using extracted space minerals in space, for example, by selling water from asteroids to refuel satellites or for watering space agriculture, or even for turning water into liquid oxygen in space, the above form of tax planning—that is, the incorporation in space for selling space resources and rendering services—is also where the potential for a total erosion of the tax base can occur or where the issue of transfer pricing might emerge. Whereas the economic feasibility and success of the DSM industry depends on potential profitable margins influenced by the price of similar terrestrial minerals,[401] the marginal profit of asteroid-derived minerals cannot be compared or tested under any other market conditions when consumed in space.

This could be a major area of concern, especially when dealing with a new industry based on economic assumptions, which also bears a potential for companies to be incorporated in international jurisdictions (as further explained below in this section). As a result, noncommercial, in effect, non-arm's length intercompany costs and prices for goods and services and excessive interest deductions for intercompany financing (i.e., "thin capitalization") would have to be assessed, since all these factors have not yet been proven in market conditions. In the context of terrestrial mining, the OECD Secretariat Proposal document released in October 2019 ("OECD Secretariat Proposal") declared that extractive industries and commodities should be considered beyond the scope of the new tax approach being proposed under Pillar One. This approach primarily aims at applying new nexus and profit allocation rules to solve tax challenges that were imposed by the digital commerce, by allowing a jurisdiction to tax

400. Asgardia, https://asgardia.space/en/; *see also* Andrea Lo, *Asgardia, The World's First "Space Nation," Takes Flight*, CNN STYLE (Nov. 15, 2017); Humaid Alshamsi et al., *Space Station Asgardia 2117: From Theoretical Science to a New Nation in Outer Space*, 16 SANTA CLARA J. INT'L L. 37 (2018).

401. Bandow, *Developing the Mineral Resources of the Seabed*, *supra* note 300, at 801-03.

e-commerce companies at the international level even if the latter has no physical presence within it. However, no similar relief has been guaranteed to the mining industry from new international tax rules enacted under Pillar Two. Under Pillar Two, mining companies may be subject to a minimum tax where little to no tax is paid in the mining jurisdiction in which such companies operate. James Ferguson, Global Mining & Metals Tax Leader, and Deloitte U.K. already stated that "[a]lthough the sector may be exempted from the proposed new nexus rules, the BEPS 2.0 deliberations have spurred tax authorities and nongovernmental organizations (NGOs) alike to revisit some of the tax rules that apply to resource companies," adding that "[a]s a result, mining companies may once again find themselves being challenged by the ever-evolving rulebook for tax in the host countries and the international chain back to their investors." Similar and new commercial complexities, for which the terrestrial mining industry's tax rules are overseen and reexamined, would have to be dealt with in the case of space mining and may cause the OECD and NGOs to keep an eye on new space commodities evaluation measures, transfer pricing and excessive interest deduction cases, including new thin capitalization rules and interest withholding taxes. All of this should be done in order to secure a fair share for the host jurisdiction to which the space mining operation continues to maintain a nexus and which helps, either directly or indirectly, enhance the value of the operator's asset.[402] It is uncertain whether the OECD guidelines for keeping arm's length standards and for ensuring non-double taxation and single taxation at the same time could be justified under the new conditions that can be expected in the case of the emerging space industry. Similarly, the question remains whether the OECD reasons to object to the adoption of a global formulary apportionment approach as an alternative to the arm's length principle, which are mainly concerning potential political and administrative complexities and high compliance costs, are justified as well.[403]

For example, one of the reasons for the OECD objection to applying a global formulary apportionment, instead of the arm's length standard, is that it would be time-consuming and extremely difficult to reach an agreement on the measurement of the global tax base and the factors used to apportion the tax base between different jurisdictions.[404] However, in opposition to this reasoning, it could be argued that this agreement is necessary given the international nature of the space mining areas and in light of other international obligations with regard to this arena. Furthermore, the endeavor to protect marine life globally and develop DSM demonstrate that this course can be successful, despite political disagreements and pressures, as well as similar difficulties.

402. ISA, *Making the Most of Deep Seabed Mineral Resources*, *supra* note 374, at 48. *See also* OECD, *Secretariat Proposal for a "Unified Approach" under Pillar One* (Oct. 9-Nov. 12, 2019); James Ferguson and Ben-Schoeman Geldenhuys, *Trend 10: Tax tribulations, Concerns over "Transfer Mispricing" Puts Miners in the Spotlight*, in TRACKING THE TRENDS 2020, Deloitte (February 2020); Aengus Barry and Mark Barker (Deloitte), *Transfer Pricing Disputes and Implications for Centralised Commodity Trading Hubs*, INT'L TAX REV. (Mar. 5, 2019).

403. OECD, *Transfer Pricing Guidelines for Multinational Enterprises and Tax Administrations* (2017), *see* Chapter I-C, *A Non-arm's-length Approach: Global Formulary Apportionment*, at 39-43.

404. *Id.* C.2.(1.22), at 40.

Additionally, it is also uncertain if the arm's length standard can provide emerging entrepreneurs in the space industry the certainty they need for sustainable development. This uncertainty might even be enhanced in light of the "province of all mankind" principle under the space regime, along with other international obligations that govern the space regime, such as the risk liability principle, all of which increase the need for international consensus and cooperation. Therefore, in opposition to the tax rules and cases on Earth, a universal formula might turn out to be a more workable, achievable, realistic and sustainable solution as a new tax framework for the space industry. This formula would have to adapt new factors beyond the traditional ones, such as payroll, property, and sales in order to secure the nexus to Earth when the space industry matures and develops into a stable ongoing operation phase where most of its services and products are being consumed in space. At this phase, the only link to Earth would be accounting for intangibles, in addition to any remaining liability risks carried by the launching states, as will be further discussed in this section.

A certain amount of guesswork would be at play in developing a tax regime for an industry that is still developing and whose viability is not yet established, particularly with regard to economics, and thus, should be carefully handled. Some of these include: predictions regarding investment levels and revenue flow that should be gathered; assumptions regarding prices, costs and production volumes and the fluctuation rates that should be made; considerations that need to be made regarding the allocation of risk (with input from industry); and the key objectives described above (e.g., tax policy criteria of equity, simplicity, efficiency, stability and sustainability) that need careful consideration.[405] As a result of existing difficulties in calculating optimal tax revenues when the tax system is based on economic theory, and when there are technical and terrain considerations—for example, oceanography, space research and other highly expensive and incomparable technological capabilities, and systems never yet experienced at terrestrial mining sites and that would need to be recovered[406]—simpler systems should be strongly recommended for efficient administration.[407]

Nevertheless, another important feature which the tax structure should adopt is progressivity, which ensures higher government revenue as the mining industry blooms, thus encouraging both investments and profitable, technologically advanced industries. This feature also benefits investors, particularly when dealing with marginal mines, where the costs of production tend to be high due to low grades of ore, and when mineral prices are low. In a progressive tax system, tax payments are correlated

405. Secretariat of the Pacific Community, *supra* note 262, at 15. *See also* Secretariat of the Pacific Community, *SPC—EU Deep Sea Minerals Project Response to the ISA Stakeholder Engagement Survey on Developing a Regulatory Framework for Mineral Exploitation in the Area*, at 3 (May 2014) (hereinafter "SPC, *SPC—EU Deep Sea Minerals Project*"); Tanielu, *Establishment of a National Regulatory Framework*, *supra* note 262, at 48.

406. Note that in order to get a seabed mine site into commercial operation an initial investment of approximately USD 1.5 billion is required. *See* Bandow, *Developing the Mineral Resources of the Seabed*, *supra* note 300, at 800-01.

407. Mitchell, *Taxation and Investment Issues in Mining*, *supra* note 371, at 29.

with profitability; therefore, a progressive tax system helps mines that are marginally economic and less profitable to be subject to a lower overall effective tax.[408]

Unlike regressive taxes, which discourage investment by taking increasing shares of profits, progressivity motivates corporate innovation and profit-seeking since the extent to which revenues increase depends on both the price of the commodities and the cost of production. This progressivity shapes the risk-sharing model between investors and governments in a way that requires investors to allocate gains out of the upside associated with their investments, and, at the same time, protects investors from some of the downsides.[409] However, this risk-sharing balance may need to be adjusted when dealing with the emergent space industry since efficiency policies indicate that risk should be borne by the party who is better capable of bearing it. In light of the unique risks associated with the space industry, such as the liability risk of the "launching states," the risk balance, even at the outset, may seem to be tilted against private investors. Since progressivity is considered to be more politically attractive for investors, if governments are interested in promoting this emerging industry for the benefit of all, more risk should be shifted away from the ESEs, particularly while the portfolio of their projects is still developing and cannot be satisfactorily diversified. Therefore, ways for shaping a limited progressive system that provides flexibility for the fiscal regime of the emerging industry and that can help this private industry to mature and evolve might better be sought. Nevertheless, this flexibility might also be formed by using different tax tools and incentives that could be provided for ring-fencing this industry, such as through the adoption of a royalty regime, a specific type of royalty, rates of royalty, and a deferral of royalty payments, as will be discussed further below.

In addition to progressive models of taxation that secure higher government revenues, as long as the operating margin on a mining project is higher, some regimes use profitability ratios (operating margins) as trigger points, above which profits are subject to taxation. Therefore, to create progressivity, more profit taxes can be introduced and imposed in the mining sector. There are various types of such profit taxes, including: "windfall taxes," which propose capturing windfall profits made during high commodity price cycles,[410] "resource rent" taxes, such as the formerly used Minerals Resource Rent Tax in Australia,[411] and "excess profit" taxes, which are

408. Tanielu, *Establishment of a National Regulatory Framework, supra* note 262, at 49; *see also* Secretariat of the Pacific Community, *supra* note 262, at 17; *see also* Durbandude, *Marginal Mines in a Bull Market*, GOLD-EAGLE (Jun. 5, 2002); James Otto, *Position of the Peruvian Taxation System as Compared to Mining Taxation Systems in Other Nations*, Ministry of Economy and Finance, at 23 (March 2002).

409. Mitchell, *Taxation and Investment Issues in Mining, supra* note 371, at 29. *See also* Carlo Cottarelli, *Fiscal Regimes for Extractive Industries: Design and Implementation*, IMF 1-80, 14-15 (Aug. 15, 2012) ("Cottarelli, *Fiscal Regimes*").

410. ISA, *Making the Most of Deep Seabed Mineral Resources, supra* note 374, at 49.

411. Minerals Resource Rent Tax, "*Economic Rent,*" Henrygeorgefoundation.org., HENRY GEORGE FOUNDATION. *See also* Peter Martin, *Henry Recommend Resource Rent Tax*, THE SYDNEY MORNING HERALD 22 (2010). The Minerals Resource Rent Tax (MRRT) was set as a tax on profits generated from the mining of nonrenewable resources in Australia and aimed to be levied at a rate of 30% on the "super profits" from the mining of iron ore and coal in Australia. Although, the nominal rate of the MRRT was 30%, the effective MRRT rate was 22.5% since the nominal

designed so that any super-profits for the DSM operator will trigger a higher tax to be taken by the state, and, at the same time, ensure that private investors are earning the required rates of return without such excessive taxes. Other variations on profit taxation are the so-called rate-of-return tax levied on rates of return in excess of a cut-off rate, and the so-called cash flow tax, which is levied on the real cash flow (as opposed to accrued) revenues of the firm, from the sale of output minus total cash outlays on both current and capital inputs as they occur.[412] All of these taxes, like royalties, are tax-deductible expenses under a corporate income tax. These taxes are perceived to be imposed on "economic rent," meaning the total revenue minus the total economic cost. Since the economic rent is the rent obtained after deducting capital and labor costs from the price of minerals sold, the tax is effectively levied on the revenues derived from the efforts of others, or from simple luck. This tax constitutes compensation to the landowner—here considered to be all mankind—for the use of its original and indestructible powers.[413] This tax is also responsive to changes in profits, particularly in the case of output-based royalties, by securing an increasing share of the community return from its resources over a period of increasing profitability in the resource sector. Those who support the imposition of tax on the "economic rent" also contend it is an efficient tax, because it does not distort behavior (as applied to investment and production decisions) in the same way a tax on income or capital distorts employment or investment decisions, and it neither reduces productivity nor raises the price of produced output.[414] However, mining companies in space and on the seabed are likely to advocate against these "windfall" or resource rent taxes, asserting their entitlement to any "super-profits" as a reward for assuming the "super-risk" of investing in pioneering industries, and be entitled to the merits of the "economic rent" resulting from economic growth driven mainly by their investments. Conversely, opponents might try to identify protective regulatory tools and leave room for profit taxation mechanisms within the fiscal regime, for any upsides.[415]

Admittedly, few, if any, governments are attempting to impose royalty systems that capture resource rents, since the assessment, compliance, and auditing challenges these pose have proven far too great. In the case of space, similar challenges can only be exacerbated since governments need to track and closely monitor the costs of the ESEs. Furthermore, the ESEs can try reducing profit-related taxes by increasing deductible costs, and all of these still need to be unraveled. Nevertheless, deference of

---

rate has been reduced by an extraction factor of 7.5%, which is a factor that recognizes the specialist skills required to extract the resource and get it to the valuation point. The MRRT was enacted as a replacement for the proposed Resource Super Profit Tax (RSPT) that was initially announced as part of the initial response to the Australia's Future Tax System review, which is also known as the Henry Tax Review (published in 2010). The tax was introduced on Jul. 1, 2012 and was subsequently repealed in September 2014.

412. Boadway, *supra* note 236, at 3 and 10.

413. David Ricardo, The Principles of Political Economy and Taxation 34 (1911); *see also* J. McLaren, *A Uniform Land Tax in Australia: What Is the Potential for This to Be a Reality Post the "Henry Tax Review"?*, 29.1 Australian Tax Forum: A Journal of Taxation Policy, Law and Reform 43-58, 49-51 (2014) (hereinafter: "McLaren, *A Uniform Land Tax in Australia*").

414. McLaren, *A Uniform Land Tax in Australia*, at 51.

415. Secretariat of the Pacific Community, *supra* note 263, at 17. *See also* Cottarelli, *Fiscal Regimes*, *supra* note 409, at 14.

royalty payments through the greater reliance on rent-based royalties would help reduce risks assumed by the ESEs, thereby reducing the expected returns that the emerging industry will require for exploring and developing their operations.[416] Although, in practice, a "resource rent" tax has not been adopted, it can be argued that:

> [a] rent-based tax would, over time, earn for the community a greater return from the use of its resources while still attracting private investment. Such a tax would also require the government to accept a greater share of the risks than it currently bears.[417]

This is particularly true:

> [f]or non-renewable resources that are expected to generate significant amounts of economic rent [since], a rent-based tax is the most suitable charging mechanism, as the potential economic efficiency and revenue gains are likely to outweigh the higher administration and compliance costs of this tax compared with output-based royalties and income-based taxes.[418]

In setting the public-private shares of mining revenues, tax systems play an important role, particularly for the government, in terms of influencing the relative attractiveness of a jurisdiction for investors and the development of a sustainable mining industry.[419]

The equitable distribution of revenues between the state and corporations in extractive ventures is at the heart of the problems in setting a fair and balanced tax regime. The balance in the tax regime depends on two concepts: the ability-to pay and the benefit received. Adam Smith put the equity principle in taxation as follows:

> The subjects of every state ought to contribute towards the support of the government, as nearly as possible, in proportion to their respective abilities; that is, in proportion to the revenue which they respectively enjoy under the protection of the state (Smith, *An Inquiry into the Nature and Causes of the Wealth of Nations*, 1776: 371).

Generally, this is the main policy objective for a resource owner, accompanied with an appropriate balance of risk-sharing between the resource owner—or, in the case of the emerging industries, all mankind in addition to the host country—and the miner. Ultimately, the regulatory and fiscal regime should have no distortionary impact on reasonable commercial rewards (e.g., "excessive" royalties) and require relatively simple administration for all parties.[420]

While governments can impose a broad-based variety of taxes on their resource industries, such as corporate and general sales taxes, all of which are levied on a residency basis—meaning on the tax base of taxpayers residents in the nation levying

416. Otto, *Mining Royalties*, *supra* note 263, at 53. *See also* Cottarelli, *Fiscal Regimes*, *supra* note 409, at 14 and 19.
417. Commonwealth of Australia, *Australia's Future Tax System, Report to the Treasurer 2010, Part Two Detailed Analysis* 217 (2009) (hereinafter "Commonwealth of Australia, *Australia's Future Tax System*").
418. *Id.*, at 225.
419. Mitchell, *Taxation and Investment Issues in Mining*, *supra* note 371, at 28.
420. ISA, *Making the Most of Deep Seabed Mineral Resources*, *supra* note 374, at 13.

the tax—other taxes specific to resource industries are most often applied on a source basis, meaning on the tax base in the country where the base is generated.[421] However, due to the extraterritorial nature of DSM and space mining, it can be argued that it is unclear to whom the resource ownership should be referred. Note that under IA, it is required that the payment system be "fair," but no definition of fairness is included.[422] Moreover, in the DSM regime, the fair and equitable share should be subject to both the principles of the common heritage of humankind and the sustainable development of this industry. Both the principles and their interpretation can also influence a fair share in the space mining sector. On one hand, a regime that is too lenient would undermine the principle of mankind's common heritage, and may damage the yield optimum revenue for the host countries (including the launching states in the case of space). On the other hand, a regime that is too draconian would only discourage investments.[423]

A tailored tax regime should also try to balance international competitiveness (in order to incentivize and protect foreign companies interested in the theoretical host state's share in the common resources) with benefits for the host country, while acknowledging the right of that state to be financially compensated for the exhaustion of its share in the finite resources. However, this is a difficult balance to strike in the case of resources that are out-of-reach from any jurisdiction.[424]

Note that minerals are generally considered finite resources and are subject to property rights laws—in most countries, minerals are owned by the state. Thus, the states, as the owners of the minerals, try to recoup the loss of property rights by imposing royalties and encouraging companies to invest in infrastructure and other public goods.[425] However, the case of minerals extracted from international/common areas might require that the loss be defined in other terms.

Although minerals in the ECS of a state might still be perceived as subject to its quasi-territorial jurisdiction (most probably when conducted under international agreements, such as UNCLOS), the jurisdictional basis of the minerals embedded in an area beyond the ECS is uncertain, unless based merely on personal jurisdiction. In other words, the nationality of natural persons or juridical entities undertaking certain activities in DSM give the states (which also support DSM operations by providing a legal framework, for example, by being an ISA state party) the unbridled right to extend their judicial power over the extracted minerals beyond their boundaries. Therefore, a state taxing authority per se seems to carry no risk with regard to deep seabed minerals, though this authority may secure incremental revenues from DSM simply by taxing an enterprise on its worldwide income. The only risk that can be allocated to a state is when a sponsoring state tries to foster engagement in DSM and bears the risks, due to its responsibility to ensure legal and fiscal obligations in providing a framework for such an industry.[426]

421. Boadway, *supra* note 236, at 3.
422. United Nations, IA, *supra* note 294, at s. 8(1)(a) under the Annex.
423. ISA, *Making the Most of Deep Seabed Mineral Resources*, *supra* note 374, at 13 and 33.
424. Secretariat of the Pacific Community, *supra* note 262, at 15.
425. Mitchell, *Taxation and Investment Issues in Mining*, *supra* note 371, at 28.
426. ISA, *Making the Most of Deep Seabed Mineral Resources*, *supra* note 374, at 61.

In the context of space, it can be claimed that a balance should be designed under the tax regime to compensate a state jurisdiction from which the launch for space mineral exploitation takes place due to the liability risk it bears. This liability risk is embedded in the Convention on International Liability for Damage Caused by Space Objects[427] (Liability Convention) as a principle without limit.[428] The international liability factor is imposed on a "launching state"[429] for certain specified damages caused by a space object (and if damage is actually caused by private activities), through the fundamental involvement of such states in the launch of the object causing the damage in question.[430] This risk liability is a basic principle in international space law,[431] which rules that states will assume financial liability for damages caused by their space equipment. Under the Liability Convention, the third-party liability risk is imposed on states that are involved in the launch or procurement of the launch of a space object, with key involvement of private operators, or whose territory or facilities are used for such a launch.[432]

Since the launch country's government bears some of the risk and cost of providing the benefits necessary for earning income, this state should be entitled to a fair share of the taxable base. It should be noted that in order for a launching state not to be caught between an international obligation to pay damages and the inability to recoup any part of such payments from a private operator (the latter being responsible for the collision at issue), it should arrange for a legal system of national derogation vis-à-vis such private operators.[433]

The choice regarding the level of mandatory reimbursement is a policy choice, where potential issues of "flags of convenience" and "license shopping" might arise as soon as the competitiveness among the international jurisdictions participating in the space race accelerates. The seriousness of "flag of convenience" and "license-shopping" situations could be determined in light of the extent of divergence that would actually arise between states potentially qualifying as "launching states" of space objects for international third-party liability purposes.[434]

---

427. Space Liability Convention, *supra* note 212.
428. *Id.*, Under Art. XII of the Space Liability Convention, "*[t]he compensation which the launching State shall be liable to pay for damage under this Convention shall be determined in accordance with international law and the principles of justice and equity, in order to provide such reparation in respect of the damage as will restore the person, natural or juridical, State or international organization on whose behalf the claim is presented to the condition which would have existed if the damage had not occurred.*"
429. Space Liability Convention, *supra* note 212, Art. II; Space Liability Convention, provides for a fourfold alternative definition of the launching state, as comprising "*(i) A State which launches or procures the launching of a space object; (ii) A State from whose territory or facility a space object is launched*"; *see* further Arts. II-V.
430. Frans G. von der Dunk, *Towards "Flags of Convenience" in Space?, Space, Cyber, and Telecommunications Law Program*, 76 Faculty Publications U. Neb. Lincoln at 5 (2012) (hereinafter Frans G. von der Dunk, *Towards "Flags of Convenience"*).
431. Outer Space Treaty, *supra* note 17, at Art. VII. Article VII to the Outer Space Treaty posits the general principle of liability.
432. Frans G. von der Dunk, *Towards "Flags of Convenience," supra* note 430; *see also* Art. II, Space Liability Convention.
433. *Id.*, at 6.
434. *Id.*

It is reasonable to assume that the seriousness of these "flag of convenience" and "license-shopping" scenarios would also be influenced by the extent of global divergence in tax systems, and the desire of states to grab a bigger bite of the tax base generated by the emerging industries, all of which would also be affected by policy choices regarding the level of the risk of liability to each state, as further explained in the section below.

There are various policy choices that "launching states" could opt for in setting mandatory reimbursement levels, options that could be required of private space operators, including unlimited liability, mirroring the unlimited liability imposed on the launching state(s) under the Liability Convention (a policy that would lead to private parties likely being disincentivized from space activities), or setting a cap on damage reimbursement above which it would be held internationally liable (a policy that would be of concern to the state as a de facto partial insurer).[435] For example, in the U.S., commercial space companies currently have immunity against losses incurred as a result of an accident, and are entitled to an indemnification period, which requires the federal government to cover any third-party damages from a commercial launch accident. Those damages occur above a "maximum probable loss"[436] (MPL) level which the company holding the launch license is responsible for, up to a level of approximately USD 3 billion.[437]

Considering the risk-sharing agreement between the launching state and the private sector with regard to potential third-party liability claims, a competitive space tax regime should establish a balance for the risk-return trade-off between governments of the "launching states" and the private emerging space actors. To keep the U.S. commercial space launch industry in a competitive environment, it can be argued that, as the government's policy choices regarding international liability risk become more constrained or less generous, for instance, by adopting a higher MPL, the potential cost to taxpayers incurred from third-party liabilities and damages is minimized. Hence, the tax revenue share or the tax base applied to the space industry should be smaller. The differences in policy choices between countries acceding to different levels of risk liability would most likely be reflected in the differences in the tax burden that countries can offer to the emerging space industry players. As mentioned above, this might lead to the "flag of convenience" and "forum-shopping" phenomena in the space mining industry. Note that the state's absolute liability risk principle generally contrasts with private liabilities when applied to the high seas regime, where shipowners do not pay for liability for damages caused by their ships, but only in exceptional

435. *Id.*

436. Commercial Space Launch Activities, 51 U.S. Code § 50914(a)—Liability insurance and financial responsibility requirements. The amount of insurance coverage that FAA can require is capped at a maximum of USD 500 million for damages to third parties and USD 100 million for damages to federal government property and personnel. *See also* Space Act of 2015, *supra* note 280. The Space Act of 2015 extends this indemnification period for commercial spaceflight operators until 2025. *See also* Foust Jeff, *Congress Launches Commercial Space Legislation*, THE SPACE REV. (May 26, 2015).

437. Commercial Space Launch Activities, 51 U.S.C. § 50915(a)(1); *see also* U.S. Gov't Accountability Off., GAO, 17-366, *Commercial Space Launch Insurance, Weakness in FAA's Insurance Calculation May Expose the Federal Government to Excess Risk* (2017).

circumstances, such as high-risk or ultra-hazardous incidents, where treaty laws have been developed to provide for second-tier liabilities.[438]

Another important factor in evaluating the tax system, after incorporating all applicable fees and taxes, is the effective tax rate (ETR), computed by the value of payments to the government. This typically consists of production-based royalties, corporate income taxes, and even additional profit taxes, all fundamentally based on accrual accounting concepts (in the DSM context, this might also include fees and royalty payments to the ISA), divided by gross value or pre-tax profits. It is interesting to note that most countries fall within a range of 40-55% ETR imposed on terrestrial mining, which results in an approximately equal share between corporate profits and revenues for taxes.[439] The 40-55% effective rate range commonly consists of royalties (3-6%), corporate income taxes (21-35%), and additional profit taxes (15-25%). While corporate income tax is charged from the first dollar on "normal profits," meaning that it is imposed on the minimum return on capital expected by investors, an additional profit tax is also applied to "normal profits." This regime may be even more progressive, with higher rates of tax applied at higher operating margins, or similar to a corporate income tax but at lower rates.[440]

Therefore, further consideration should be given to whether the division described above could be applied to the DSM and space industries, or, alternatively, a larger share could be allotted to DSM and space mining companies in order to foster the development of these industries. All the above considerations, including the ability to predetermine tax liability, and the level and method of taxation, will facilitate tailoring a sustainable tax regime.[441] Moreover, in both DSM and space mining industries, it

---

438. Frans G. von der Dunk, Handbook of Space Law, at 89 footnote 220. *See, e.g.*, the International Convention on Civil Liability for Oil Pollution Damage, Brussels, done Nov. 29, 1969, entered into force Jun. 19, 1975; 973 U.N.T.S. 3; UKTS 1975 No. 106; Cmnd. 4403; ATS 1984 No. 3; 9 ILM 45 (1970); 64 AJIL 481 (1970). Article III of the Convention places a strict liability for oil pollution damage resulting from maritime casualties involving oil-carrying ships on the owner of the ship from which the polluting oil escaped or was discharged subject to a number of specific exceptions. Among these exceptions are wars and other forms of hostilities, natural disasters of an exceptional nature, acts or omissions of third parties done with intent to cause damage, or other wrongful acts of governments or other authorities responsible for the maintenance of navigational aids. Under Art. V of the Convention, the liability of the shipowner is limited in respect of each incident. This limitation is based on the tonnage of the ship, but there is a cap of approximately USD 14 million, unless the incident was a result of the actual fault or privity of the shipowner. *See* Thomas A. Mensah, *International Environmental Law: International Conventions Concerning Oil Pollution at Sea*, 8 Case W. Res. J. Int'l L., 110 (1976), at 126-27; *see* International Maritime Organization, *International Convention on Civil Liability for Oil Pollution Damage (CLC)* (Nov. 29, 1969) (being replaced by 1992 Protocol: adopted on Nov. 27, 1992).
439. *See* Clark, A. S., Cook Clark, J. L. M. & Pintz, S. *Towards the Development of a Regulatory Framework for Polymetallic Nodule Exploitation in the Area*, 81, at 51-53 (International Seabed Authority, Kingston, Jamaica, 2013); Mitchell, *Taxation and Investment Issues in Mining*, *supra* note 371, at 29; Secretariat of the Pacific Community, *supra* note 262, at 15; Cottarelli, *Fiscal Regimes*, *supra* note 409, at 35.
440. Emil M. Sunley, Selcuk Caner, Richard Krever, and Oana Luca, *Philippines: Reform of the Fiscal Regimes for Mining and Petroleum*, IMF, Country Report No. 12/219, 1-55, 39-40 (2012); *see also* ISA, *Making the Most of Deep Seabed Mineral Resources*, *supra* note 374, at 79-80.
441. Secretariat of the Pacific Community, *supra* note 262, at 15; *see also* ISA, *Making the Most of Deep Seabed Mineral Resources*, *supra* note 374, at 75 and 80.

should also be recommended that special aspects, such as their common stateless nature, unique risks, and their value as a part of the world's wealth, will be taken into account when forming a stable tax regime. The international royalty tax regime based on the simplest type of royalties (i.e., value- or volume-based royalties), which is capped at a maximum percentage and imposed only after a given relief period of several years from the start of mining production, can align best with the above key objectives required for tailoring a sustainable tax regime. Eventually, this royalty mechanism would help secure and embrace the development of these emerging industries, the expansion of the space economy, and the world's economy.

F. CONCLUSION

In both the space and oceans mining industries, a fair and equitable share of profits should be subject to both the principles of the common heritage of humankind and the sustainable development of this industry. Although there is a dispute regarding the practical interpretation of the "common heritage" notion articulated under the Outer Space and Moon treaties, the tax system to be applied to the space resources allocation regime will need to be tailored in a way that takes under consideration the particular characteristics and principles associated with space resources, such as stateless boundaries and the international obligations, among which are the liability risks of the launching states. The taken tax policy should aim to help mitigate concerns at both the international and domestic level in order to support a stable and attractive investment climate for the space industry.

The royalty regime can settle the conflicts between the collection of revenues by governments from the space mining industry while mitigating many risks on the one hand and preserving incentives to invest in this industry on the other. This regime, when imposed on gross basis, can aggregate tax revenues with very different risk characteristics, as applicable to space resources, in the most neural way without affecting the incentive compatibility conditions which are required to solve the control problem in the resource allocation management.

CHAPTER 4

The Role of a Space Resource Royalty Tax in Shaping an Overall Tax Regime

A. INTRODUCTION

Despite the U.S.' signature on the IA, concerns regarding the possibility to accede UNCLOS still persist. Some of these concerns stem from the usage of an "international royalty" system for splitting and sharing the proceeds derived from DSM. The same debate about a potential profit-sharing mechanism and its justification, and how to tailor such a system as part of the overall ocean tax regime, which can be applied and is relevant to the space mining industry, as will be further explained in this chapter.

B. PROS AND CONS FOR IMPOSING AN INTERNATIONAL SPACE MINING ROYALTY REGIME

In order to understand the pros and cons of these international royalties, it is necessary to delve into the ongoing arguments of the key stakeholders in this debate.

Despite the U.S.' signature on the IA, concerns regarding the possibility to accede UNCLOS are still expressed to this day. Some senators fear that the UNCLOS regime would yield U.S. sovereignty to international law, impose environmental pollution fees, and burden U.S. companies with royalties to the ISA (instead of to the U.S. Treasury for energy exploitation),[442] which are also considered as "international royalties" by ISA[443] or as a "U.N. tax" by American opponents of UNCLOS.[444] Several

442. Wong Kristina, *Rumsfeld still Opposes Law of Sea Treaty*, WASH. TIMES (Jun. 14, 2012) (hereinafter "Kristina, *Rumsfeld still Opposes Law of Sea Treaty*"); *see also* The Law of the Sea Convention Hearing, *supra* note 292, Statement of Hon. Donald Rumsfeld, U.S. Secretary of Defense, at 174.
443. The Law of the Sea Convention Hearing, *supra* note 292, Statement of Steven Groves, at 193.
444. *Id.* The Law of the Sea Convention Hearing, *supra* note 292, Statement of Hillary Rodham Clinton, at 11; *see also* Statement of John B. Bellinger, at 183.

American commentators and politicians opposed the ratification of UNCLOS, including former Secretary of Defense Donald Rumsfeld (under President George W. Bush), who warned that ratifying the Law of the Sea Treaty might create a precedent for the case of outer space resources.[445] This assertion may imply that the ratification of the Convention could establish a new premise for customary international law allowing international organizations to tax American citizens.

In 2012, during hearings at the U.S. senate in front of the Committee on Foreign Relations about the possibility that the U.S. would finally become party to and ratify UNCLOS, former Secretary of Defense Donald Rumsfeld commented that, under the treaty, industrialized countries pay royalties to less-developed nations for profits made while exploiting unclaimed energy resources.[446] In his statement Mr. Rumsfeld described the Law of the Sea Treaty as "a sweeping power grab that could prove to be the largest mechanism for the worldwide redistribution of wealth in human history."[447] According to him, this type of wealth redistribution is a "novel principle that has ... no clear limits" that "could become a precedent for the resources of outer space," adding that "[t]he treaty proposes to create a new global governance institution that would regulate American citizens and businesses, but which would not be accountable politically to the American people. Some of the Law of the Sea Treaty's proponents pay little attention to constitutional concerns about democratic legislative processes and principles of self-government, but I believe the American people take seriously threats to these foundations of our Nation."[448]

Other commentators opposing the U.S.' accession to UNCLOS claim that U.S. companies would be forced by this Convention to ultimately bear excessive costs and pay an undetermined percentage of royalties to developing countries. This radical accession to an international organization would impose an unprecedented bureaucratic and regulatory burden by an international authority on American companies.[449]

Consequently, even if the legal barriers (derived from international rules governing the nature of the space and ocean resources, as explained above) for mining in space and in DSM can be resolved by the adoption of international royalty mechanisms, which can accompany any international regulatory framework and be implemented under settled international or bilateral agreements, such as the Artemis Accords regime that NASA is currently aiming for, an economic barrier might still undermine the justification for such mechanisms, and therefore, this barrier needs to be addressed. This economic barrier was preliminarily pointed out in the context of the imposition of royalties on the DSM industry when the royalty regime was offered as a component of the regulatory legal regime of the DSM.[450] In the case of the ocean mining

445. *See supra* note 442.
446. Kristina, *Rumsfeld still Opposes Law of Sea Treaty*, *supra* note 442.
447. The Law of the Sea Convention Hearing, *supra* note 292, Statement of Hon. Donald Rumsfeld, at 175.
448. *Id.*, at 174 and 175-76.
449. Groves, *The U.S. Can Mine the Deep Seabed Without Joining the U.N. Convention on the Law of the Sea*, *supra* note 316.
450. Bandow, *Developing the Mineral Resources of the Seabed*, *supra* note 300, at 801-03. For the Artemis Accords Program, please *see* The White House, *Presidential Memorandum on Reinvigorating America's Human Space Exploration Program*, Presidential Memoranda, Dec. 11,

industry, the economic viability of this industry is highly dependent on the prices of terrestrial minerals, such as copper and nickel, and on the after-tax profits that the emerging industry can gain. Thus, the imposition of additional royalty taxes was criticized as a system that can only adversely impact the profitability of this mining industry and might have a distortionary economic effect on the whole terrestrial mining industry. This royalty tax would lead to higher mineral prices (by increasing the cost of recovery)[451] and might even damage the horizontal equity between deep seabed miners and terrestrial miners by applying an unjustifiable burden on the former.

Indeed, the imposition of added costs in both emerging industries, such as in the case of royalties, can always impede the economic viability of the new industries by eventually increasing the cost to the end user, and, thus, can be criticized for adding more costs. However, from an efficiency perspective, especially if land-based natural deposits are all mined out, and the quality of the remaining ore is steadily falling, or when new landed deposits become deeper and more expensive to extract, it is better to bear reasonable additional costs for gaining access to stateless minerals, all for the sake of the expansion of space and ocean economies in a sustainable manner.

Moreover, in the case of space mining, the adverse economic effects and barrier arguments discussed above should not be viable. Unlike DSM's minerals, the space mining industry is mostly directed at using resources from space for use in space, neither to be brought back to Earth's economy nor to be taken from Earth for use in space, due to the high cost associated with launching and importing resources. For example, a 1 gallon bottle of water, which costs around USD 1 at a local shop in a developed country, can cost, on board the International Space Station (hereinafter "ISS"), approximately USD 10,000 due to the high costs associated with delivering it to the ISS from Earth.[452] However, by mining water from asteroids for use in space, the price of water, which has the potential to become one of the most valuable commodities/elements in the future space economy,[453] could be lowered. The utilization of space minerals is primarily, and to a large extent, aimed at the markets based in

---

2017; Jamie Carter, *Trump Wants To Mine The Moon. This Is How NASA Will Do That Using "Roomba"-Sized Rovers*, FORBES (Apr. 9, 2020); David P. Fidler, *The Artemis Accords and the Next Generation of Outer Space Governance*, Council on Foreign Relations, Jun. 2, 2020; Joey Roulette, *Trump Administration Drafting "Artemis Accords" Pact for Moon Mining—Sources*, REUTERS (May 5, 2020). In October 2020, seven countries signed on to NASA's new Artemis Accords: Australia, the United Kingdom, Canada, Japan, Italy, Luxembourg, and the United Arab Emirates. *See* Christian Davenport, *Seven Nations Join the U.S. in Signing the Artemis Accords, Creating a Legal Framework for Behavior in Space*, WASH. POST, (Oct. 13, 2020).

451. Bandow, *Developing the Mineral Resources of the Seabed*, *supra* note 300, at 804.

452. Peter Ray Allison, *How Much Does a Bottle of Water Cost on the International Space Station*, SPACE (May 18, 2016). Note that the ISS orbits 400 km above the Earth's surface, which is in Low Earth Orbit (LEO), thus, considered to be not that far. However, launching water into Geostationary Orbit (GEO) is much more expensive. *See* spacex.com (noting the Capabilities & Services the Falcon 9 v1.1 can send a mass to LEO of 22,800 kg. The cost per launch is 61.2 million. Then the cost for launching 1 kg (i.e., which equals to 1 liter of water) to LEO is USD 2,684. Since 1 gallon equals to 3.78541 kg, the launching cost of 1 gallon of water to LEO is USD 2,684*3.78541 = USD 10,160 USD).

453. NASA, *In-Line Water Filtration: Better Hygenie, Less Expense*, (Sept. 28, 2009); Daniel Oberhaus, *How to Start an Asteroid Mining Company Without a Mine*, MOTHERBOARD (Oct. 2, 2016).

space itself and not at being exported from space to Earth, so the economic potential of the space mining industry is not impacted by or impacts the terrestrial mining industry. Therefore, from an economic allocative efficiency perspective, the implementation of a royalty system, which is set to ensure a modest cash flow to the international community without over-benefiting the nonparticipants on account of investors in this industry, would help settle and resolve any legal and economic barriers for space mining, and would ultimately encourage the risky investments required for this industry without harming the efficient use of space resources. The fact that the consumption of space resources is primarily aimed to be conducted in space itself should encourage governments supporting the space industry, including launching states, to find a rule of share that will ensure a modest and stable collection of taxes as the industry evolves. The trade-off between the costs due to the collection of royalties and the benefits due to a decrease of the political and compliance costs, when adopting royalties as a unique measure for mitigating wealth distribution pressures, will justify the establishment of a royalty mechanism that can secure a stable fiscal regime for this emerging industry and, at the same time, ensure a solid ground for the formation of a sustainable and efficient resource management regime. Thus, it would essentially support the viability of this industry. Collecting royalties as a mechanism that ensures the legal framework for the utilization of minerals in space can be advantageous to this emerging industry and would eventually guarantee the most productive use of space resources at the lowest possible price, and, as such, it is an economically efficient methodology.

In contrast to the arguments raised by opponents to the ratification of UNCLOS, supporters of the Convention describe the choice of whether to ratify the Law of the Sea Treaty as one of whether:

> companies will either mine in the deep-seabed and in the Extended Continental Shelf and are willing to pay a small amount of royalties after 5 years [1% per year starting in year 6, up to a maximum of 7% in year 12] or allow the U.S. Government to do it, or they won't do it at all. So the choice is either lots of royalties for the Treasury and lots and lots of money for U.S. companies and some small amount that goes to the ISA, or nothing at all.[454]

However, as was discussed in section 3.C., there could be another option for DSM with U.S. firms establishing subsidiaries in other nations that are members of UNCLOS.[455] This latter option would also jeopardize the tax revenue generated by U.S. DSM companies, which could be funneled to the U.S. Treasury, although after the TCJA, a minimum tax share from any U.S. owned subsidiary and CFC would be paid to the

454. The Law of the Sea Convention Hearing, *supra* note 292, Statement of John B. Bellinger, at 220; *see also* Art. 82(2) of UNCLOS, *supra* note 5.

455. William H. Taft, *Accession to the 1982 Law of the Sea Convention and Ratification of the 1994 Agreement Amending Part XI of the Law of the Sea Convention* (Statement of William H. Taft IV) (Apr. 8, 2004); *see also* Moore, *infra* note 457, at 221. *See* Hearing before the U.S. Committee on Foreign Relations, 110th Congress, First Session, Senate Hearing 110-592 (September 27 and Oct. 4, 2007). Treaty Doc. 103-39: Hearing on U.N. Conv. on the Law of the Sea Before the U.S. Committee on Foreign Relations, 110th Congress, First Sess. 210 (2007).

Treasury as GILTI and BEAT taxes would probably be imposed (as explained in the sections above).

The Convention provides two additional areas of economic benefits in the ECS, beyond 200 nm from shore, if certain criteria are met, and in the deep seabed areas beyond any country's jurisdiction. In accordance with UNCLOS, as asserted by proponents of the Convention, such as former Secretary of State Hillary Clinton, a coastal State could exercise sovereign rights over its ECF, including exploration, exploitation, conservation, and management of non-living resources, such as oil, gas, and other energy and mineral resources, and of living, "sedentary" species, such as clams, crabs, and sponges. According to Secretary of State Clinton "[t]he size of the U.S. Continental Shelf—just the portion beyond 200 miles from shore—is probably more than one and one-half times the size of Texas, and could be considerably larger than that. For this reason, the U.S. oil and gas industry, including the American Petroleum Institute, are in favor of joining the Convention."[456] Since the U.S. continental shelf is one of the largest in the world, it has also been argued by Professor John Norton Moore of the University of Virginia School of Law (in contrast to the assertion that the treaty would limit U.S. sovereignty) that the ratification of UNCLOS would actually "massively increase [U.S.] sovereign jurisdiction" by more than the size of the Louisiana Purchase and Alaska combined and "protect an extension of United States sovereign rights ... in an area roughly equal to our continental land mass"; hence "this Convention would be on the honor roll in its dramatic recognition of an expansive area of sovereign rights over resources."[457] Enlargement of the Area means higher opportunities for higher revenues, resulting in higher tax revenues. Thus, it is not surprising that, according to the Secretary of State Clinton, "[m]ore than 40 countries have made submissions regarding their Continental Shelves beyond 200 nautical miles to the expert Commission. Sixteen States, including Russia, Brazil, Australia, France, Indonesia, and Mexico, have received recommendations from the Commission and are proceeding to establish the outer limits of their Continental Shelves," while in the meantime adding that, "[a]s a nonparty, the United States is sitting on the sidelines while this happens."[458]

Based on the argument above, if the U.S. decides to impose a royalty fee of 18% on the value of production from the ECS of the U.S., then this would be 18% more than the U.S. would gain if it stays outside of the Convention. Even if the convention payment is at its highest rate of 7%, the U.S. Treasury would still be 11% better off, with respect to each production site, than it would be if the U.S. does not join the Convention and, by so doing, risks the whole 18% royalty tax to be left offshore as a

456. The Law of the Sea Convention Hearing, *supra* note 292, Statement of Hillary Rodham Clinton, U.S. Secretary of State, at 15.
457. Ernest Z. Bower et al., *Advancing the National Interests of the United States: Ratification of the Law of the Sea*, CTR. FOR STRATEGIC INT'L STUDIES (May 25, 2012). *See also* Statement of John Norton Moore, Walter L. Brown Professor of Law, and Director, Center for Oceans Law and Policy, University of Virginia School of Law; Treaty Doc. No. 108-136, Hearing on U.N. Conv. on the Law of the Sea Before the U.S. Committee on International Relations, 108th Congress, Second Sess. 131 (2004).
458. The Law of the Sea Convention Hearing, *supra* note 292, Statement of Hillary Rodham Clinton, at 15.

"trapped income" (or perhaps an even lower percentage if GILTI is imposed). Therefore, the supporters of UNCLOS believe that ratifying the Convention will have "an enormous benefit—not a loss—to the U.S. budget."[459]

Although this approach of gaining something or nothing might sound appropriate, there is room to argue whether the potential for gaining an extra 11% could become real or not. Unlike terrestrial mining, which deals with natural resources embedded in specific state's jurisdictions, as the access to these mining resources (on the high seas or in space, assuming royalties would apply to both arenas) becomes feasible from anywhere on Earth, it becomes more likely that tax jurisdictions will converge their tax systems as they compete internationally to be more attractive to investors. Therefore, the remaining royalty fees for each nation might be minimized unless the relevant tax jurisdiction would be able to compensate private mining investors for higher royalty rates. The way for compensation could be by providing investors with an effectively lower total tax rate or higher rates of return on investments by accelerating depreciation deductions on mining capital equipment or by allowing larger deductions, etc. Interestingly, this has been the case in terrestrial mining sectors where countries who do not adopt a royalty tax system do not necessarily provide investors with a lower overall effective tax rate compared to countries which impose royalty taxes. For example, although Mexico and Greenland do not impose royalty taxes (but instead rely only on the general income tax), they nevertheless hold relatively high effective tax rates. Conversely, Western Australia imposes a royalty, but has a lower total effective tax rate than in Chile, which does not impose a royalty. However, largely due to the payments from royalties in the early years of the project, the investor's rate of return in Western Australia is lower than in Chile.[460]

Nevertheless, the opponents to the UNCLOS argue that, practically, the Convention is allowing an international body, the U.N., to possess tax authority over the Convention parties, and the U.S. should never, under any circumstances, cede its taxing authority and accede to this kind of notion whatsoever.[461]

However, the proponents of the Sea Treaty refute this claim asserting that it is not a real tax but only a royalty, "a scale of some amount that will go to the landlocked nations in compensation for the rights of other countries to exploit the seabed of the Earth," to which the U.S. companies interested in maritime mining accede to pay.[462] In the view of the proponents, the royalties paid for mining the deep-sea minerals are not a "tax," in the same sense as when the Interior Department charges royalties to American oil companies for development of the oil and gas from the U.S. continental shelf, it is not exercising a "taxing power," but rather selling—or, more accurately—leasing, access to an asset. Therefore, these are not a tax on the American

459. The Law of the Sea Convention Hearing, *supra* note 292, Statement of John B. Bellinger, at 187.
460. Otto, *Mining Royalties*, *supra* note 263, at 35 and 53.
461. The Law of the Sea Convention Hearing, *supra* note 292, Comments of Senator James Inhofe, Oklahoma, at 44 and 133; *see also* comments by Senator Jim DeMint, South Carolina at 51.
462. The Law of the Sea Convention Hearing, *supra* note 292, Comments of the Chairman, John F. Kerry, Massachusetts, to Senator James Inhofe at 137; *see also* Art. 82 of UNCLOS, *supra* note 5.

taxpayers any more than royalties paid by U.S. mining companies to Chile or Indonesia to mine resources there.[463]

Either way, it has been argued by the opponents to UNCLOS that those "international royalties," evaluated to be at least USD 70 billion dollars (since USD 1 trillion in revenue is expected to be derived from DSM in the ECS of the U.S.), would otherwise go to the U.S. Treasury, whereas by ratifying UNCLOS they would not.[464] Moreover, the funds could even be distributed to unwanted hands (as happened, for instance, with the U.N. oil-for-food Programme in Iraq), as a "courtesy of the American taxpayers." By acceding to the UNCLOS regime "[i]t would be as if fishermen who exerted themselves to catch fish on the high seas were required, on the principle that those fish belonged to all people everywhere, to give a share of their take to countries that had nothing to do with their costly, dangerous, and arduous efforts."[465]

Considering the claims and counterclaims above regarding joining UNCLOS and acceding to the imposition of "international royalty" as a profit-sharing mechanism for extraterritorial resources, it is recommended that, in the next "gold rush," when the exploration of both the deep seas and space accelerates, the common property/areas not be left to unsettled fiscal regimes, including, of course, in the field of taxation. There appear to be common challenges in designing a tax system for both emerging mining industries, both of which are not yet viable nor profitable.

The key to fostering the emerging space industry is in advancing multilateral cooperation and in coordinating work on regulatory regime and tax matters. This multilateral solution can resemble efforts invested in the BEPS Project, where it has already been argued by the BEPS action plan that "the global economy requires countries to collaborate on tax matters in order to be able to protect their tax sovereignty,"[466] whereas unilateral measures "could lead to global tax chaos."[467] In the case of space, a similar dilemma to the one that the U.S. adherence to the UNCLOS evoked needs to be resolved. If there is no legal barrier to mine space minerals, under the Space Act, and in the case of the ocean the U.S. also refrain from ratifying the UNCLOS, why should the U.S. adhere to the royalty regime in the case of space?

Essentially, three options lay before the U.S. First, to adhere to an international regime and pay a small amount of royalties. Second, to not oblige to such a regime, but rather to do space mining by itself, and by that aiming that the big money goes solely to the U.S. Treasury. Third, to not mine and participate in the space mining industry. I contend that the two last options are the least realistic.

---

463. *See also* John Norton Moore et al., *The Senate Should Give Immediate Advice and Consent to the Law of the Sea Convention: Why the Critics Are Wrong*; Treaty Doc. 103-39: Hearing on U.N. Conv. on the Law of the Sea Before the U.S. Committee on Foreign Relations, 110th Congress, First Sess. 210 (2007) (hereinafter "Moore").
464. The Law of the Sea Convention Hearing, *supra* note 292, Comments of Senator James Inhofe, at 44-45, 133. *Id.*, Statement of Hon. Donald Rumsfeld, U.S. Secretary of Defense, at 176; *id.*, Prepared Statement of Steven Groves, at 191-94.
465. The Law of the Sea Convention, *supra* note 286, Statement of Hon. Donald Rumsfeld, U.S. Secretary of Defense, at 176. *See also* Art. 82 of UNCLOS, *supra* note 5.
466. OECD, Action Plan on Base Erosion, *supra* note 351, at 9.
467. *Id.*, at 10.

The maxim "each man-in this case, each country-for itself" cannot withstand the test of time.[468] The international tax regime of the twenty-first century has proven to be developed and shaped, as it still does, in a congruent way, and it is better if it can be done through a multilateral dialect and constructive dialogue. Although it is well-known that the U.S. international tax law is globally conceived to be a developed and very influencing tax system for the development of other countries' tax systems worldwide, the last decade has proven that this direction of influence can also be reversed.[469] This counter-direction can be reflected from the changes in the U.S. tax law, which were not merely dependent on the U.S. policy, but also a result of the OECD's BEPS Project influence. Although the U.S. declined to fully participate in the coordinated BEPS efforts, Congress did not seem to ignore the BEPS Project when implementing changes to the U.S. tax system. The changes adopted under the 2016 U.S. Model Income Tax Treaty and the provisions under the TCJA, including the imposition of excise tax on base erosion and outbound payments, such as the BEAT and the GILTI, the adoption of a favorable inbound minimum tax by lowering the corporate tax rate to 21%, and the enactment of territorial system—all were clearly affected by the BEPS Project and intended to achieve parity between the U.S. and other countries' tax systems, while keeping on an attractive investment climate under the U.S. tax system. The continuing efforts of Europe under BEPS 2, including the attempts to deal with the digital economy and address the Digital Services Tax (DST), are likely to continue affecting the U.S. tax system and leading to additional changes to the TCJA.[470]

In light of the congruent way that the international tax system is eventually being shaped, the U.S. should not fear its tax writing prerogative by adhering to international obligations. For an advantageous long-term policy, the U.S., as a leading space power, should be encouraging the adoption of an international royalty regime, rather than describing it as a measure for a tax war or another round of tax competition. This royalty regime should be seen as a constructive and collaborative solution between the U.S. and the international community in order to avoid future pressures to respond by revising more tax rules.

Addressing a multilateral dialogue over the taxation of our common future is important for the development of the space industry and for the future of space colonization. The U.S. should take a leading role in this dialogue and encourage other countries to participate in it. To shape a stable and sustainable tax regime that can support the most efficient management regime, this role cannot be done in a way of destructive unilateralism, but rather of constructive multilateralism. This solution can align with the same reason that drove OECD members to couple efforts during the BEPS

468. Rocha, Sergio André and Allison Christians eds., Tax Sovereignty in the BEPS Era, 187 (Kluwer Law International BV 2016).

469. *See*, in general, Reuven S. Avi-Yonah, *Constructive Dialogue: BEPS and the TCJA*, U of Michigan Public Law Research Paper No. 665, U of Michigan Law & Econ Research Paper No. 20-004, available at SSRN: https://ssrn.com/abstract=3544065 or http://dx.doi.org/10.2139/ssrn.3544065 (Feb. 24, 2020).

470. *Id. See also* Mindy Herzfeld, *New Analysis: Competition or Coordination: Responses to the Tax Cut and Job Acts*, Taxnotes (Jan. 16, 2018) (hereinafter "Herzfeld, *New Analysis*").

Project, which has been expressed in the OECD Secretary-General Angel Gurría's statement:

> [b]ase erosion and profit shifting affects all countries, not only economically but also as a matter of trust. BEPS is depriving countries of precious resources to jump-start growth, tackle the effects of the global economic crisis and create more and better opportunities for all. But beyond this, BEPS has been also eroding the trust of citizens in the fairness of tax systems worldwide. The measures we are presenting today represent the most fundamental changes to international tax rules in almost a century: they will put an end to double non-taxation, facilitate a better alignment of taxation with economic activity and value creation and, when fully implemented, these measures will render BEPS-inspired tax planning structures ineffective.[471]

Indeed, there is also room for criticism and skepticism regarding the viability of an act of constructive multilateral dialogue, which can rely on similar criticism to the success of the BEPS efforts. The dubious success of this type of collaborative efforts can be based on the criticism that the participants in the BEPS Project themselves, while representing different countries with diverse and conflicting interest, found it challenging to agree on the content of the reform and, as a result, dominant OECD countries who participated in the BEPS Project went on to "jump the gun" and adopt unilateral measures for taxing the digital economy under different domestic versions of the DST.[472]

However, since the pressures regarding the taxation of the digital economy continue and a global solution is still being sought through the continuance of negotiations under BEPS 2, and if judging by the way the international tax systems evolve and converge, it is the U.S.' interest to play an influencing and cooperative role for the future of the emerging space industry. The creation of artificial PE in space and the potential loss of residence base taxation all lead to the need of cooperation. This can be achieved by paying only a small amount of royalties.

Furthermore, the royalty regime is designed to support the most efficient management regime and help keep the value of space resources. This regime is not purported to generate an exact or equal share amount of revenue for each country, as this will be conceived as a needless trade-off between efficiency and global revenue-sharing. This regime, rather, aims to mitigate any potential wealth distribution pressures, and, thus, neutral parameters, such as GDP, can serve as indicia for splitting and sharing revenues derived from the exploitation of the world's commons.

C. TYPES OF ROYALTIES

Royalty payments, like any type of tax, consist of rates and a base, both of which are determined for each type of royalty. These royalty types need to be assessed differently

471. OECD Press Release, BEPS 2015 Final Reports (Oct. 5, 2015).
472. Moreno, A.B. and Brauner Yariv, *Taxing the Digital Economy Post BEPS-Seriously*, COLUM. J. TRANSNAT'L L. 58-1, 121, at 126, 162-63 and 187 (2019) (hereinafter "Moreno, A.B. and Brauner Yariv, *Taxing the Digital Economy Post BEPS-Seriously*").

and ultimately affect both investors and governments differently, as is further discussed in the sections below.

C.1. Value- or Unit-Based Royalties

While the rates are clearly stated under Article 82 of UNCLOS, the base yet needs to be decided. Article 82 of UNCLOS provides that "[t]he payments and contributions shall be made annually with respect to all production at a site after the first five years of production at that site. For the sixth year, the rate of payment or contribution shall be 1 % of the value or volume of production at the site. The rate shall increase by 1% for each subsequent year until the twelfth year and shall remain at 7% thereafter."

In general, value-based royalty is calculated as the product of a percentage/royalty rate times the value of the mineral, sometimes referred to as *ad valorem* royalties (in Latin; meaning "based on value"). Value-based royalty is measured as a revenue received from a sale, depending on whether the gross value, invoice value, billed value or market value[473] is taken into account.[474] In the seabed mining industry, it is also uncertain if the value of the minerals will be assessed by comparing them to the value of the same terrestrial minerals, or adding another hypothetical market value, the same uncertainty could also be applied to space minerals. In addition, it is uncertain what the reference price system should be. For example, could the London Metals Exchange daily quotation be used as such? Note that price reference systems for some minerals might not be found and that, quite often, the referenced price sale is for a product, a higher grade product such as a concentrate, which is different from the extracted product being sold in its natural form and has yet to be processed and refined. Due to commodity prices, the value-based royalty is much more likely to fluctuate. Moreover, this royalty method is more exposed to "transfer pricing" questions and tax avoidance techniques, when the sale value is less than the real market value, and many situations might arise from this. For example, suspicions might be preceded by situations that include sales to affiliated parties at abnormally low prices, poor estimations regarding the value of futures contracts, long-term sales agreements where prices are disconnected to market realities, so on. The picture becomes even more complicated when the value needs to be adjusted by deducting specified costs. As stated under UNCLOS "[p]roduction does not include resources used in connection with exploitation."[475] Whereas these costs need to be defined, they are usually not directly related to mineral extraction or beneficiation, such as transportation, insurance, and handling costs that are incurred between the mine site and the point of sale. Additionally, although this cost-adjusted mechanism for some nonproduction-related costs holds a potential for providing relief to the DSM or the

473. Note that companies can argue that invoice value is different from market value since market value would take into account certain costs, such as transportation, insurance, and handling fees incurred from the mine site to the point of export/sale. *See* Otto, *Mining Royalties*, *supra* note 263, at 52.
474. James M. Otto, *The Taxation of Extractive Industries: Mining*, No. 2017/75, WIDER Working Paper, at 9 (2017) (hereinafter "Otto, *The Taxation of Extractive Industries*").
475. UNCLOS, *supra* note 5, under Art. 82.

space industry, it might, at the same time, increase the administrative costs associated with such relief compliance.[476]

Similar to value-based royalty, unit-based (also known as flat-rate) royalty[477] is another type of output-based royalty, also called a "severance tax," when dealing with extraction/severance of nonrenewable natural resources. However, the unit-based royalty is a more straightforward method of royalty assessment because it is based on a fee levied per unit of output, either volume or weight, instead of on parameters subject to dispute, such as price, value and costs.[478] Under this type of royalty, a fixed monetary rate is applied to a physical rather than a financial base, for example, dollars per ton or dollars per cubic meter. Progressive adjustments to the fixed royalty rate for inflation or for shifts in commodity pricing might also be implemented. This type of royalty is administratively efficient and relatively easy to be audit.[479]

Although both royalty methods are conceptually simple and assure continual revenues to be paid to governments (and to the ISA as regards seabed minerals) by maintaining royalty flow during all production years, these royalties could be highly economically inefficient and distortionary. In fact, these could be deemed payable, regardless of whether the mine profitable or is losing money, and regardless of the financial feasibility in each mining project. In other words, the relative profitability of an operation is not taken into account because there is only the perspective of quantity of mineral produced or some measure of the value of mineral produced or sold.[480] This could be the reason why, under UNCLOS, a form of a tax relief is included, and royalty payments are required to be made only after the sixth year of production. However, it is not clear whether the adoption of a royalty deferral of five years will be a sufficient period of time for the space industry to reach profitability, or if the world's population would become hostile with this emerging industry if they feel deceived and cheated out of entitlements from the enormous profits found within the fruits of the province of all mankind; thus, an option for extending or shortening such a period of time should also be considered. For example, if the time needed to yield a large return and profits from space turns out to be much faster than the full five years, and the expectations for

476. Otto, *Mining Royalties*, *supra* note 263, at 52-53.
477. Pietro Guj, *Mineral Royalties and Other Mining-Specific Taxes, International Mining for Development Centre*, Mining for Development: Guide to Australian Practice, Center for Exploration Targeting, The University of Western Australia, 1-16, 6 (2012) (hereinafter "Guj, *Mineral Royalties and Other Mining-Specific Taxes*").
478. Statement of Robin M. Nazzaro, Director Natural Resources and Environment, Hardrock Mining Information on Types of State Royalties, Number of Abandoned Mines, and Financial Assurances on BLM Land, Testimony Before the Subcommittee on Energy and Mineral Resources, Committee on Natural Resources, House of Representatives, GAO, United States Government Accountability Office, at 4 (Feb. 26, 2009); *see also* United Nations' Committee of Experts on International Cooperation in Tax Matters, *Proposed Guidance on Fiscal Take in the Extractives Industries*, Agenda item 3(b)(ii), Thirteenth Session, E/C.18/2016/CRP.21, at 21-22 (2016); Otto, *Mining Royalties*, *supra* note 263, at 50; Commonwealth of Australia, *Australia's Future Tax System*, *supra* note 417, at 221.
479. Guj, *Mineral Royalties and Other Mining-Specific Taxes*, *supra* note 477, at 4.
480. Baunsgaard Thomas. *A Primer on Mineral Taxation*, No. 1-139, Int'l Monetary Fund, 10 (2001); *see also* Otto, *Mining Royalties*, *supra* note 263, at 50-53 and 268-69.

immense value from minerals in space materializes earlier in the lifecycle of a mining project, the deferral of royalty payments should be, obviously, phased out.

In the latter situation, increasing pressures by activist groups might force a reconsideration in order to further address the issues of what is a "reasonable" type and rate for royalties, and the way that this might be divided worldwide. Therefore, much preplanning and forethought on these issues should be adopted in order to avoid prompting similar political pressures on the space industry, such as the ones that plagued the DSM.[481]

A pre-consented criterion for meeting a minimum level of profitability or return on investment rate commensurate with the risks taken by the ESEs can help decide whether the deferral time of royalty payment should be shortened or extended. However, adding an instrument based on profitability to the fiscal and tax regime might become cost-prohibitive rather than an efficient tool. In order not to make the tax regime unclear in its results, the international community would need to agree upon a comprehensive and clear set of rules and regulations for determining how revenues should be calculated and what costs could be deducted. Since these calculations are in large part based on assumptions when dealing with the emerging space industry, and would likely pose high political and enforcement costs, countries may want to refrain from adopting this type of rules.

Note that under the IA agreement, there are no recommendations for setting an initial date for payments in the financial management system. However, under section 8(1)(d) in the Annex of the IA,[482] it has been stated that the annual fee shall be payable from the commencement of commercial production (*see* above regarding the four phases/cycles in mining). Thus, any royalty obligation is also likely to commence from that date in accordance with general practice in order to incentivize this industry to begin in the first place and allow it to develop. Any profit-mechanism will be dependent on the timing of profits to ensure optimum revenues can be generated, without compromising investments in this industry, and safeguard the ability of this industry to mature.[483]

It is also uncertain how marginal and undeveloped operating mines would be affected after six plus years of production, since unit-based and *ad valorem* royalties are technically neutral regarding economic allocative efficiency objectives. Both methods neither reward, nor penalize, improved or degraded mining efficiencies. On the one hand, it can be claimed that the UNCLOS policy, in general, is inefficient with respect to both the DSM and space policy objectives and the development of these industries. On the other hand, it can be counterclaimed that a five-year relief period from any

481. Otto, *Mining Royalties*, *supra* note 263, at 64.

482. *See* s. 8 Financial Terms of Contracts under United Nations, IA, *supra* note 294 at 20. Note that under s. 8(1)(c) in the Annex of the IA it is stated that: "*Consideration should be given to the adoption of a royalty system or a combination of a royalty and profit-sharing system. If alternative systems are decided upon, the contractor has the right to choose the system applicable to its contract. Any subsequent change in choice between alternative systems, however, shall be made by agreement between the Authority and the contractor.*"

483. ISA, *Making the Most of Deep Seabed Mineral Resources*, *supra* note 374, at 2 and 18-19. *See also* Industry Position Paper, ISA Royalty Regime (March 2020), (hereinafter "Industry Position Paper, ISA Royalty Regime").

royalty tax and the imposition of a 7% maximum cap on a royalty tax should outweigh any claims with respect to either neutrality or economic allocative efficiency.[484] Indeed, it can be argued that unit or value-based methods are essentially a "tax" on production, as well as on economic rent, hence, leading to a regressive tax system. These royalties often have distorting effects on production costs leading to high-grading by raising the marginal cost of extraction. As a consequence, the amount of resource being extracted is not as high as it would have been without imposing this tax and, as a result, the amount of the suboptimal ore reserve increases.[485] Nevertheless, the five-year relief and the cap applied to royalty rates can help to alleviate such concerns. Setting a cap of a 7% tax rate not only has already achieved a solid consensus in the context of the DSM, but it has also become sufficiently low to be accepted globally, considering tax rates imposed on base-eroding payments (i.e., "payments that give rise to domestic deductions and thereby erode the domestic tax base"),[486] or on other profits being shifted through sophisticated transactions in intangibles by avoiding having physical presence in the taxing jurisdiction. For example, the Digital Services Tax (DST) is proposed to tax the digital services at 3%, the BEAT is imposed at 5-12.5%, while GILTI is set as an effective tax rate of 10.5%. Therefore, it seems practical that, as long as the royalty is in the range between 3%-10%, it can be widely accepted and neutral so that it is not extrapolated from the currently imposed net taxation rate.[487]

In the case of DSM, the rate of royalty tax has been settled under section 8(1)(b) in the Annex of the IA, which articulates that "the rates of payments under the system shall be within the range of those prevailing in respect of land-based mining of the same or similar minerals in order to avoid giving deep seabed miners an artificial competitive advantage or imposing on them a competitive disadvantage." However, the question of what minerals can be considered to be the "same or similar" to space resources, particularly if these are transacted and consumed in space, has yet to be discovered and identified, and, in fact, there could be numerous justifications as for why tax incentives providing a competitive advantage for the space mining industry relative to its land-based mining counterpart should be adopted. Importantly, in the case of space, by setting a cap on the royalty tax at a balanced rate, a modest stream of collected tax is guaranteed as a tool for ensuring "intergenerational equity" and future compensation for the global community, among which are the governments and the ancestors of the taxpayers, who supported the emerging space industry and allowed it to bloom by investing high capital in researches, infrastructures, IP, and technology. This balanced stream of tax collection should be kept—and might also be mitigated and reduced, if needed—even at the time this emerging industry evolves so that all its

484. F.T. Cawood, *The South African Mineral and Petroleum Resources Royalty Act—Background and Fundamental Principles*, 35.3 Resources Policy 199-209, 203 (2010) (hereinafter "Cawood, *The South African Mineral and Petroleum Resources Royalty Act*"); *see also* Otto, *Mining Royalties*, *supra* note 263, at 64.
485. ISA, *Making the Most of Deep Seabed Mineral Resources*, *supra* note 374, at 44; Guj, *Mineral Royalties and Other Mining-Specific Taxes*, *supra* note 477, at 6.
486. Moreno, A.B. and Brauner Yariv, *Taxing the Digital Economy Post BEPS-Seriously*, *supra* note 472, at 128-29.
487. *Id.*, at 128-29, 160 and 166 (2019).

outputs be consumed only in space itself, whereas the only nexus to Earth would be left to intangibles generating economic value-added.

As the space industry evolves, it might be worthwhile to keep an option open for adjusting the royalty rates according to the level of profits, or the cumulative annual production, or even the cumulative annual sales, even though the simplicity of a fixed-rate royalty lowers the administrative costs borne by the governments (e.g., the ISA or any intergovernmental federation that would be established for the space industry). Fixing a scale for royalty rates based on the suggested measures above tends to complicate the royalty method and, thus, increases compliance and administrative costs. However, having such an option might serve as an improved incentive tool for the growth of the space industry, especially as it could offer higher flexibility and better adjustments for changing economic climates by providing a progressive tax system. This flexibility would enable, over the long term, alignment with important macroeconomic governance objectives, since the optimization goal should be to maximize the net present value of the social benefits derived from the space mineral sector, including government tax receipts. To achieve this goal, the tax level should be adjusted to maintain a balance between the social benefits that governments gain and the private costs that companies are willing to bear, in order to not harm the industry and the public shares derived from it. This balance stems from the fact that a taxation rate that is too high would cause the investments and the tax base to decrease, as investors would prefer shifting investments to other alternatives, whereas a taxation rate that is too low would cause the state to lose benefits and would reduce revenue shares that benefit the common good and public welfare. The design of a "two-tier" tax rate will provide a fair royalty system and profit-sharing mechanism among the ESEs and the governments, especially because once the space industry evolves, there will be two groups of entrants, the pioneers and those who come later. Accordingly, the financial and technological risks assumed by later participants, the newcomers to this industry, would be reduced and become lower relative to the risks born by the space pioneers, as will the minimum rates of return on investments expected by these late comers. This "two-tier" tax rate, which is typical in a hybrid royalty type system, as explained below, would adjust and conform to the royalty system as a fair trade-off mechanism between the lower risks assumed by the ESEs and the higher royalty rates and returns requested by the governments. Apart from this two-tiered tax rate mechanism, an additional flexibility could be provided under this framework by securing an updated royalty regime. This regime should allow the transfer to a value-based royalty system from a unit-based one. Apart from the potential addition of profit-based mechanisms, an updated royalty regime could be adopted as soon as the space industry matures and benchmark market prices for space resources and comparable minerals become available and are easily discoverable. These can be achieved through the development of best practices and arm's length transactions in either space itself, or between the ESEs and on-Earth contractors, processing operators and manufacturers. Given this additional flexibility, the royalty system would be able to support the efficiency of the space industry through its evolution from its start-up phase to a more stable phase of operations. Having a "two-phase" royalty mechanism would secure a design that is the simplest and fairest royalty system.[488] Nevertheless, it could be anticipated that the debate over the adoption of either the "two-tier" or the "two-phase" mechanism may be suspended or waived globally on political grounds. The possibility and suspiciousness that any shift in the royalty mechanism could evoke fiscal and political repercussions, and thus, become cost-prohibitive to adopt, may deter the incorporation of any contingent flexibility into the royalty system, especially when the space industry in its nascent stage.

C.2. Profit- or Income-Based Royalties

It should be noted that unlike the value- or unit-based royalty approaches, there are a variety of methods which allow for taking into account, in the royalty calculations, a broader set of costs for deductions, such as production, capital, marketing and restoration costs. These methods aim to create a taxation system that is based on the concept of the ability-to-pay, which is favored by most investors, and that allow for early recovery of capital and responds to downturns in the market. Such kinds of royalty approaches can lower the overall risk borne by private sector investors, and, at the same time, provide high-level long-term tax revenue.[489] The ability-to-pay concept can be adopted through either profit-based royalty approaches or income-based royalty approaches. These royalties have greater economic allocative efficiency, by better aligning the private investments and output levels with social objectives, but may lead to adverse consequences, such as unstable government revenues, and subjecting both the industry and the government to high compliance costs.[490] Both types of royalties include, in their calculations, sales revenues minus allowable costs which are pertinent to mining (although both, in their simple forms, may neglect returns on capital).[491]

Under profit-based systems, the royalty base consists of sales revenues from a single mine after deducting allowed costs, which can vary, but may include costs of extraction, processing, transportation, capital, marketing, and insurance. However, under income-based systems, the base is not limited to sales revenues from products, but may be comprised of other sorts of revenues, such as property sales, and may permit the aggregation of revenues by the taxpayer for all the taxpayer's mines. Note that profit-based royalties can be referred to under many names, including net profit royalty, net interest royalty, net proceeds royalty and mining tax.[492]

488. Otto, *Mining Royalties*, *supra* note 263, at 5, 56 and 67. *See also* Industry Position Paper, ISA Royalty Regime, *supra* note 483, at 5, 11 and 12.
489. Controller General Indian Bureau of Mines Nagpur, Mineral Royalties, *supra* note 378, at 18 and 64.
490. Guj, *Mineral Royalties and Other Mining-Specific Taxes*, *supra* note 477, at 4.
491. Harries Karl, *Mining Royalties Between Private Parties*, Centre for Resource Studies, Vol. 30, Queens University, Kingston, Canada, 117-21 (1996); *see also* Otto, *The Taxation of Extractive Industries*, *supra* note 474, at 16-17; *see also* Otto, *Mining Royalties*, *supra* note 263, at 30 and 53.
492. Otto, *Mining Royalties*, *supra* note 263, at 54; *see also* Pietro Guj, *Mineral Royalty Administration: The Acid Test of Policy*; Eric Lilford & Guj P., *Different Types of Mineral Royalties*, in MINING TAXATION, MODERN APPROACHES IN SOLID EARTH SCIENCES, Vol. 18, at 43-69 (Springer Cham 2020).

C.3. Hybrid Approaches

Additionally, there are approaches, called hybrid approaches, that combine profitability with unit or value-based royalties, by calculating, for example, profits, and adjusting the *ad valorem* royalty rate to the ratio of the costs to sales revenue, or to the rates of return, or to the ratio of price per unit to the reference price. This approach allows progressive sliding scale of royalties to be used where the percentage of government take is based on an agreed measure of profitability of the mine, or in other cases, the *ad valorem* royalty acts as a minimum tax where both the *ad valorem* and profit-based royalties are compared and the higher tax liability should be paid. However, a sliding-scale royalty under a hybrid approach may encourage tax-planning strategies that avoid a higher royalty bracket, thereby undermining government revenue.[493]

D. COMPARING AND CRITIQUING OBJECTIVES OF ROYALTY TYPES

When comparing the different objectives of each method, it can be argued that unit- or value-based royalties not only assure modest and constant revenue flow to governments, which usually are more risk averse than private investors, even at the early stages of mining, irrespective of the project circumstances, but they are also more transparent and easier to administer than profit- or income-based royalty taxes.[494] The latter kind of royalties are much more open to abuse and even to tax avoidance, since the royalties will not start being paid until the mining yields a return, which usually takes time in the mining industry, and often depends on the gathering of much information and applying financial accounting measures, which can be manipulated.[495]

Despite having similar flaws, given a choice between unit-based or value-based royalty, most companies would prefer a value-based method because such a method is sensitive to price changes and can easily be adjusted to market conditions. Generally, unit-based royalties, since they are the most administratively efficient method, are more appropriately applied to low-value bulk commodities. Nevertheless, these types of royalties have also been determined to be the most distortive, in terms of rational economic decisions, particularly when dealing with projects with small profit margins, which require companies to pay the state even when the costs of extraction are greater

493. Pietro Guj et al., *How to Improve Mining Tax Administration and Collection Frameworks: A Sourcebook*, 1-153, at 17 (World Bank Group 2013) (hereinafter "Pietro Guj et al., *How to Improve Mining Tax Administration*"); *see also* Otto, *Mining Royalties*, *supra* note 263, at 55; Natural Resource Governance Institute, *Fiscal Regime Design: What Revenues the Government Will be Entitled to Collect*, NRGI READER (March 2015) (hereinafter "NRGI, *Fiscal Regime Design*"); Readhead A., *Tax Incentives in Mining: Minimising Risks to Revenue*, The International Institute for Sustainable Development and the Organisation for Economic Co-operation and Development, at 15 and 39 (2018) (hereinafter "Readhead, *Tax Incentives in Mining*").

494. Pietro Guj et al., *How to Improve Mining Tax Administration*, at 17. It is explained that "Unit-based (specific) royalties": "...generally easy to administer and impose the lowest administrative compliance cost for industry and government alike."

495. Otto, *Mining Royalties*, *supra* note 263, at 53-54 and 64-65.

than revenues (as is explained further below). Consequently, there is a strong rationale to move from unit-based to value-based royalties in the case of higher-value commodities or large-volume operations, as the latter are more efficient than fixed-rate royalties based on units of output, such as volume or weight.[496]

However, given the choice between broader royalty types, the profit-or income-based royalties satisfy most investors' royalty preferences since they shift most of the risks, e.g., market, competence, and operational, away from the developer to the governments. In addition, hybrid methods are developed in order to balance between the objectives of economic allocative efficiency and administrative efficiency, which is influenced by the government's goal of ensuring modest and stable government revenue flow.[497]

Whereas unit-based royalties, based on units of volume or weight, are considered as the most administratively efficient method, *ad valorem* royalties, based on the value of sales, are ranked as second, and the profit-based royalties are ranked as the least administratively efficient method.[498] Revenue stability decreases and transparency challenges increase, in the same ranking order, when comparisons are made between the methods.[499]

However, the ranking would be reversed, if judged in terms of economically allocative efficiency,[500] since taxes based on units of production, irrespective of profitability, may create economic inefficiencies and result in suboptimal exploitation of a mineral resource by discouraging the exploitation of lower grade ores, and shortening the life span of some mines, particularly marginal mines.[501] By contrast, taxes on corporate profits (and to a lesser degree, incomes) are more efficient, when taking into consideration the inherent risks in mining operations, such as the wide fluctuations in international mineral pricing, and the difficulties of anticipating all the geological/oceanographic/space researches, and the technical, financial and political factors over a mine's lifetime.[502]

The same reversed ranking order could also be applied if judging the systems in terms of the opportunity (optimal tax base) to share upside increases, and in terms of their complexity or ambiguity level, i.e., profit-based royalties are ranked as having the highest opportunity to share upside increases, and as the most complex and ambiguous method, while unit-based are the least, as is further explained below.[503]

When selecting a royalty system and regulating the mining regime, a compromise between the above objectives should be made. The choice of the appropriate balance

---

496. *Id.*, at 65. *See also* Pietro Guj et al., *How to Improve Mining Tax Administration, supra* note 493, at 6, 15 and 17; NRGI, *Fiscal Regime Design, supra* note 493.
497. Pietro Guj, *Mineral Royalties and Other Mining-Specific Taxes, supra* note 477, at 6-7; *see also* Otto, *Mining Royalties, supra* note 263, at 64-65.
498. Pietro Guj et al., *How to Improve Mining Tax Administration, supra* note 493, at 6 and 17; *see also* Otto, *Mining Royalties, supra* note 263, at 65.
499. ISA, *Making the Most of Deep Seabed Mineral Resources, supra* note 374, at 77.
500. Otto, *Mining Royalties, supra* note 263, at 65.
501. Pietro Guj et al., *How to Improve Mining Tax Administration, supra* note 493, at 6.
502. Mitchell, *Taxation and Investment Issues in Mining, supra* note 371, at 27.
503. Otto, *Mining Royalties, supra* note 263, at 66; *see also* ISA, *Making the Most of Deep Seabed Mineral Resources, supra* note 374, at 77.

between these objectives is also a function of the size and diversity of mining operations, which affects the spread of administrative costs, and the institutional strength for regulating the mining, since the latter has to handle the administrative complexity of the mining regime effectively and without excessive delays. There are two categories of administrative costs that should be accounted for: (1) the category of the firm's costs, which are not dependent on the royalty calculation method, the scale of mining operation, or on the nature and value of the commodity mined; (2) the category of variable costs, which are a function of the calculation method and its administrative complexity, including potential disputes and efforts of compliance and verification by the companies and the governments.[504]

More considerations need to be recognized when balancing the different government objectives (i.e., the economic allocative and administrative efficiency), including the unit price of the commodity mined and its volatility, which affects the costs of errors in calculating royalties and the stability of the revenue flow. Another consideration to take into account is the size of the operation, which, if large, lowers the administrative cost per unit.[505]

Thus, it is not surprising that, given the projections of the high volume of highly valued minerals, or even of low-value bulk-mined commodities, the choice between value- or volume-based royalty methods has been adopted with regard to the DSM industry by UNCLOS. The same rationale works equally well with respect to the emerging space mining industry. Setting these royalty methods also as part of the tax regime in the emerging space industry is a way to ensure continual government revenue flow (though possibly through an international authority), even if, under less economically disruptive regimes, such as of the income- or profit-based royalty approach, larger mining producers and employers could be established. These larger operations might not outweigh the importance of guaranteeing a modest and continued government revenue flow generated from the exploitation of the world's shared wealth, especially where there are huge expectations for extremely high profits, as is likely to occur in the space mining industry. These high expectations for supernormal profits have existed for a long time. In fact, in 1852, a rare asteroid the size of Massachusetts (140 miles in diameter), known as 16 Psyche, was discovered. However, the significance of mining such a rare asteroid only started to gain attention worldwide at the beginning of the second millennium. This attention has gradually amplified over time and will only continue upon the revelations of new scientific proof for the astronomical value of resources embedded in asteroids, such as the one discovered in October 2020, when NASA's Hubble Telescope caught a closer look at 16 Psyche. This discovery provided further reasoning for future plans to launch a spacecraft to study it more closely in 2022. On the one hand, 16 Psyche is made of metal and offers a unique window into the violent history of collisions and accretion that created terrestrial planets. On the other hand, 16 Psyche could be worth USD 142

504. JAMES A. MIRRLEES AND STUART ADAM, DIMENSIONS OF TAX DESIGN: THE MIRRLEES REVIEW, 1-1346, at 1120-27 (Oxford University Press 2010); *see also* Otto, *Mining Royalties*, *supra* note 263, at 66.
505. Otto, *Mining Royalties*, *supra* note 263, at 66.

trillion, meaning 70,000 times more than the global economy. Given the very promising assumptions regarding the value and existence of this new source of wealth, the simplest and most just system to exploit and tax this source should be presettled.[506]

However, it seems that a basic assumption for adopting an output-based royalty regime is that all operations must be equal in their capacity to pay royalties, an approach which ultimately discriminates against less-profitable and marginal mining operations. The concerns about forming such an allegedly discriminating regime might be mitigated by setting provisions for royalty relief, similar to the one found in the first five-year period of production in DSM, which has been set to offer an incentive for the development of this industry through a royalty deferral. The significance of such an incentive has already been proven in the context of terrestrial mining. In this instance, the effect of this kind of royalty deferral has been realized to be more significant than that of an income tax holiday, given the potentially regressive nature of such a royalty.[507]

As a result of the objectives above, both profit- and income-based royalties, even though they are generally considered to be less economically disruptive, are usually less prevalent among most fiscal regimes of the mining industry. Typically, these royalty types expose governments to higher risks, which are shifted to them by mining developers, and, due to potential fluctuations in profits and income, if the latter can be established at all, are inherent in each mining project (when dealing with profit-based royalties) or in all projects together (when dealing with income-based royalties).[508]

Moreover, in contrast to income-based royalties, profit-based royalties should also be determined by which corporate items of expenditures can be allocated and deducted at the mining project level, and not at the corporate level. This challenge in itself makes the system even more complex. This complexity is further aggravated when adding the deductibility of many indirect items and noncash items on an accrual accounting basis, especially if accelerated depreciation deductions need to be applied.[509]

Additionally, the complexity of both of those royalty types results in higher additional administrative, compliance and auditing costs. All the latter costs can only increase where the financial accounting measure applied for calculating profits for royalty purposes is different from the traditional accounting measure of profit used for levying corporate income taxes.[510]

Moreover, the financial accounting measure might be open to manipulations and could subject taxpayers to keep a separate set of accounts. Nevertheless, in order to

506. Rachel Cormack, *NASA's Hubble Telescope Captures a Rare Metal Asteroid Worth 70,000 Times the Global Economy*, APPLE.NEWS (Oct. 28, 2020). *See also* NASA, 16 Psyche, NASA Science, Solar System Exploration (updated Jan. 11, 2021); Jamie Carter, *NASA Teases "Psyche," A Robot to Explore an Asteroid Worth More Than Our Global Economy*, FORBES (Jul. 7, 2020).

507. Cawood, *The South African Mineral and Petroleum Resources Royalty Act*, *supra* note 484, at 203; *see also* Otto, *Mining Royalties*, *supra* note 263, at 67; Readhead, *Tax Incentives in Mining*, *supra* note 493, at 39.

508. Garnaut, *supra* note 67, at 277; *see also* Otto, *Mining Royalties*, *supra* note 263, at 68.

509. Pablo Heidrich, *Tax Regimes on Mining in Latin America*, Policy Brief, North, South, Ottawa: Institute at 4 (2013); *see also* Otto, *Mining Royalties*, *supra* note 263, at 68-69.

510. Otto, *Mining Royalties*, *supra* note 263, at 68-69.

alleviate the adverse impact of the mining-specific accounting measure, the government should consider if it is better to assess royalties from taxable income as when calculated for income taxes. This solution could be an efficient way to gain leverage on potential tax liabilities and could serve as a tool for assessing and collecting the royalties. Objections to such an approach might arise when acknowledging that the costs of exploration, development and depreciation of the new emerging mining industries require special treatment. Moreover, applying common accounting measures to these industries has the potential of creating concerns regarding the need of ring-fencing protections for risky industries, in which each of the taxpayer's operations are treated independently from all of the taxpayer's other operations for tax purposes. Ring-fencing will also protect the new tax base generated by the new space industry by averting a mining enterprise from deducting exploration or development expenditures from its new project against income of projects that are already generating taxable income by combining all of its mines' profits and losses when calculating its net taxable base and, thereby, postponing government tax revenues. Aggregating income and expenses from all space operations by applying the same accounting measures could lead to the lack of ring-fencing. It can be argued that the absence of ring-fencing could encourage investments into the exploration of more mineral sites and support internalizing costs because costs may be offset against other mining operations. However, this absence may also be discriminatory to newer investors among the ESEs, who have no income against which they can offset expenditures, particularly once the space mining industry matures. Additionally, as much as ring-fencing prevents investors from taking advantage of their affiliated operations, it also helps protect these investors by limiting risk, and encouraging an optimal reallocation of their investments. Hence, ring-fencing would protect certain socially beneficial activities performed by the private sector and maintain this sector's efficiency. However, since the adoption of ring-fencing cannot, by itself, guarantee economic efficiency and can still leave the tax system vulnerable to tax manipulation and loopholes through, for example, the usage of abusive transfer pricing for shifting profits to downstream activities outside the ring-fence, other tax tools should accompany ring-fencing. Therefore, a combination of ring-fencing under an output-based royalty type which provides flexibility and adapts royalty rates in accordance to an agreed-upon measured factor of profitability, as discussed above, should be carefully and more easily structured than under an income- or profit-based royalty system.[511]

Appropriate computational rules should be required for the income- or profit-based royalty regimes, particularly where capital recovery is allowed and a measure of the cost of capital and the rate of interest need to be specified and indexed to the

511. ISA, *Making the Most of Deep Seabed Mineral Resources*, *supra* note 374, at 47; *see also* Otto, *Mining Royalties*, *supra* note 263, at 68-69, 101 and 134; Steven L. Schwarcz, *Ring-Fencing*, 87 Southern California L. Rev. 69, 110, at 69 and 73-74 (2013); Emil M. Sunley and Thomas Baunsgaard, *The Tax Treatment of the Mining Sector: An IMF Perspective*, World Bank, Washington D.C., Background paper prepared for the World Bank workshop on the taxation of the mining sector, at 5 (Apr. 4-5, 2001).

inflation level.[512] All these factors can again exacerbate the complexity of the system and subject the system to potential disputes and litigations.

Despite the flaws of the profit or income-based royalty method discussed above, in order to attract private investors to the new mining industry, governments might at least consider royalty-based approaches solely on the basis of profits.

While production-based taxes may be collected from the developers early on in the project's life, and are easier to collect, these may not be popular since production can take place in nonprofit-making or even loss-making years. Mining productions can take years to become profitable, particularly in times of cash-flow problems, such as short periods of price downturns, particularly if governments wish to ensure that the mines do not close prematurely. Therefore, it can be argued that profit-based taxes should be more desirable in the unprecedented space mining industry, even though it may not yield revenues for many years, particularly since the risks and returns profiles of such an industry is, as yet, unknown.[513]

Additionally, given the likeliness under such a system of risk-shifting from the private investors to the governments, governments could consider higher royalty rates than might be selected if the royalty rate is strictly based on revenues. This higher rate is justified when considering the fact that royalties will begin to be generated and collected only later in the project and may even be absent when prices fluctuate and drop.[514]

Trying to balance the advantages and disadvantages of revenue stability and economic efficiencies in the royalty methods discussed above, some mining regimes may wish to adopt different hybrid systems. Examples of hybrid systems can be seen where a profit-based royalty is subject to a minimum specific-floor or an *ad valorem* royalty, so both the *ad valorem* and the profit-based royalty need to be calculated, but only the higher of the two is payable, or when both are payable, but a credit in the amount of the *ad valorem* royalty is allowed to be offset against the profit-based royalty.[515] These types of hybrid systems aim to ensure minimum royalty revenue, and at the same time, are less disruptive in terms of economic efficiency.

After setting a type and a rate of royalty, a taxpayer should be entitled to offset income for income tax purposes, either by getting a deduction or a tax credit. However, it should be decided whether any excess of royalty over the income tax of a given year may or may not be deducted, as a loss, or credited against income tax in successive years.[516] It should be noted that in the early wording of UNCLOS, before the IA was signed, it was stated that "[s]tates must respect the extra-territorial nature of deep-seabed mining in the international area and should avoid or minimize double taxation

512. Otto, *Mining Royalties*, *supra* note 263, at 66-69.
513. Cawood, *The South African Mineral and Petroleum Resources Royalty Act*, *supra* note 484, at 203; *see also* Otto, *Mining Royalties*, *supra* note 263, at 12 and 112; SPC, *SPC—EU Deep Sea Minerals Project*, *supra* note 405, at 2.
514. Otto, *Mining Royalties*, *supra* note 263, at 101 and 112.
515. *Id.*, at 111; *see also* Mangondo Kismore, *The Economics of Gold Mining Taxation*, PhD diss., University of South Africa, at 33-34 (2006); U.S. Gov't Accountability Off., GAO, 93-109, *Minerals Royalties, Royalties in the Western States and in Major Mineral-Producing Countries* (1993), at 28.
516. Otto, *Mining Royalties*, *supra* note 263, at 112.

on the proceeds of deep-seabed mining in order to ensure optimum revenues for the Authority [ISA]."[517] However, in the final version of UNCLOS, this principle was removed, despite the concern, which exists until the present, that states would eventually impose their own national tax regimes at the expense of the international community.[518] It is unclear whether tax credits or deductions would be provided to offset the ISA royalty payments, and would alleviate the above concerns. Similar concerns should be settled in the context of space mining. However, if deductions are allowed, then a royalty payable of, say, one dollar would reduce corporate taxes payable by 21 cents in a jurisdiction with a 21% corporate income tax rate, such as in the U.S., whereas when tax credits are given, the whole amount of the paid royalty would be saved in taxes. The latter decision may pave a better way to level the international tax playing field.

Additionally, in order to ensure that mining operations continue to develop in space and to mitigate cash-flow problems they may encounter, governments could decide to partially insulate the mines from the market, or to defer royalty payments, or to exempt a mine from royalty liability where the royalty system is not based on profitability or on income. However, these types of discretionary relief powers can be politically abused, and, once these are granted, they are only rarely removed and are unlikely to include sunset provisions. Thus, in the context of royalties derived from the treasures of mankind, these reliefs could be impractical and should not be recommended.[519]

E. ROYALTIES AS INTERNATIONAL PROFIT-SHARING TOOLS IN THE RACE TO TAX THE TREASURES OF MANKIND

For structuring a tax system for space mining, it is important to understand that the royalties that governments impose on mining operations are commonly only a part of, and merely one determinant of, the taxation structure with many context variables to consider. For example, income and withholding taxes also need to be included. Therefore, although mining royalties make mining operations stand out from other types of economic activities, royalty rates and types need to be appraised within the larger context of overall levels of taxation, as does the base against which the royalty rate is applied.[520]

As mining in unique realms, such as outer space, becomes accessible from everywhere on Earth, the global competition between states greatly increases. The competition for private mining investments could be accomplished by higher expected rates of return that the country offers to investor's projects, and lower levels of risks associated with those projects. The ultimate success in these endeavors would depend

517. Secretary-General's Informal Consultations on Outstanding Issues Relating to the Deep Seabed Mining Provisions of the United Nations Convention on the Law of the Sea, INTERNATIONAL SEABED AUTHORITY at 61 (2002).
518. ISA, *Making the Most of Deep Seabed Mineral Resources*, *supra* note 374, at 20-21.
519. Otto, *Mining Royalties*, *supra* note 263, at 113.
520. *Id.*, at 117-18.

less on the absolute attractiveness of each country's investment climate than on its attractiveness relative to other countries.[521]

To really compare across jurisdictions, investors might look at the overall level of taxation or on their effective taxation rates. It can be argued that, in general, taxation powers are inflexible, often due to constitutional constraints. However, while most states may have little or no flexibility regarding certain types of tax rates, such as the income tax rate or the withholding tax rate, the royalty base may be open to adjustments. These adjustments could eventually impact the investor's rates of return on investments (e.g., by allowing a 100% bonus depreciation in the first year of a mining operation or accelerated depreciations on mining that would result in larger deductions early on in the lifecycle of a mining project). Generally, an exception to rate inflexibility is often found in the royalty system, particularly since the latter is unique to the mining sector and, thus, it might be politically easier to adjust and negotiate over time than taxes applying to all sectors.[522]

However, royalties are not the overriding determinant of a country's investment attractiveness. Whereas some countries, with or without royalties, enjoy favorable investment climates, some countries, with and without royalties, do not.[523]

Besides royalties, which constitute one aspect of the mining fiscal regime, a country's investment climate depends on additional important factors, such as political stability, geological potentials, government regulations, and policies that incentivize investments. Different types of royalties, which can be divided into in rem or in personam taxes,[524] in addition to the rest of the tax regime, which encompasses other types of in rem and in personam taxes, are all designed to establish and sustain a viable industry. Typically, in the mining industry, companies compare numerous development options internationally and screen these options to obtain the best balance between risk and reward. The key factor determining investment decisions is the geological potential of a mine site, but this is strongly offset by fiscal and socio-political considerations. Tax rates affecting the profitability of operations are enumerated as a

521. *Id.*, at 185. Land Bryan, *Capturing a Fair Share of Fiscal Benefits in the Extractive Industry*, 18.1 TRANSNATIONAL CORPORATIONS 157, at 168-70 (2010) (hereinafter "Land Bryan, *Capturing a Fair Share of Fiscal Benefits*").

522. Otto, *Mining Royalties, supra* note 263, at 35, 118 and 186; *see also* regarding "Race to the Bottom" in Land Bryan, *Capturing a Fair Share of Fiscal Benefits, supra* note 521, at 169; Otto, *The Taxation of Extractive Industries, supra* note 474, at 9 and 11.

523. Otto, *Mining Royalties, supra* note 263, at 186; *see also* The World Bank, *How Developing Countries Can Get the Most Out of Direct Investment*, International Development Association (IDA), 1-166, at 139 and 140-47 (Oct. 25, 2017).

524. Note that there are two main categories of tax: in rem or in personam. In rem taxes "can be divided into two groups: taxes that affect the variable costs of the project (such as unit-based royalties, ad valorem–based royalties, sales taxes, and excise taxes) and taxes that affect the fixed costs of the project (such as certain types of property taxes, import/export duties, registration fees, land rents, value added tax, some types of stamp duties, and withholding taxes on loan interest and services)." *See* Otto, *Mining Royalties, supra* note 263, at 30-31. In personam taxes are imposed on net revenues, i.e., revenues after deducting allowable costs, such as income tax, capital gains tax, progressive or additional profits tax, excess profit tax, withholding tax on remitted dividends, profit- or income-based royalty. *See also* Laporte Bertrand, *What Do We Know About Mineral Resource Rent Sharing in Africa?, supra* note 383, at 9.

part of the fiscal considerations, whereas the stability of the tax system, which directly impacts the ability to predetermine tax liabilities, is included under the socio-political considerations.[525]

Obviously, in the context of DSM or space mining, the geological potential will be replaced by oceanography and space research potentials. Investors will seek investment opportunities in countries which are able to offer them access to those realms that were previously perceived to be unreachable. Countries, including landlocked countries, developing countries and other countries that lack the knowledge to participate in these races, especially in space, might be limited in the ways that they are able to attract investors from these emerging industries. However, dissimilar to terrestrial mining, as the access to mining minerals outside any jurisdiction evolves globally, the key factors determining investment decisions might mainly be dominated by fiscal and socio-political frameworks, which might give tax considerations an even greater weight. Therefore, by establishing subsidiaries in countries that have access to these industries, investors might be attracted to seek the most convenient forums for establishing their operations in jurisdictions that assure them a better investment climate (e.g., higher profitability, legal and political stability and so on).[526]

To ensure a share of the treasures of mankind and the redistribution of monetary benefits derived from the high seas, the ISA offers to collect value or volume-based royalties from all emerging investors in the DSM industry. Adopting simple systems that are uniform for all minerals is an easy and feasible method. However, the tax base for collecting the royalties needs to be fixed and uniform, as well. By applying these in rem taxes to mining companies, the sovereignty of states to impose their own tax system (including other in rem taxes and in personam taxes[527]) on the same companies, and the states' abilities to compete between themselves by offering a better investment climate and a better overall tax regime, will not be limited, especially if the companies' royalty payments would largely be offset against the expected taxes, either as deductions or as tax credits.[528] As a result, each state's tax regime could be tailored and maintain its attractiveness independent of the royalty payments made to any intergovernmental federation that would be established for the space industry.

Moreover, ensuring the redistribution of mankind's resources to all countries, including any non-spacefaring states, through a uniform collection of royalties transferred to an international body, could help reduce international political pressures to change the resource management and fiscal regimes by ensuring a stable and modest flow of profit-sharing. These pressures might be exacerbated, particularly when mineral commodity prices fluctuate (i.e., prices are too low or too high), or when mining companies are earning supernormal profits, or no profits at all, and are, thereby, paying no corporate income taxes. This mechanism for distribution of benefits from the global "common heritage" might reduce political risks at the international

525. Mitchell, *Taxation and Investment Issues in Mining*, *supra* note 371, at 27-28; *see also* Otto, *Mining Royalties*, *supra* note 263, at 183 and 215.
526. Otto, *Mining Royalties*, *supra* note 263, at 184-86.
527. *Id.*, at 30-34; *see also* Laporte Bertrand, *What Do We Know About Mineral Resource Rent Sharing in Africa?*, *supra* note 383, at 9.
528. Otto, *Mining Royalties*, *supra* note 263, at 187.

level for many investors. Importantly, this mechanism should be settled before the emerging mining industries evolve and the ESEs, which currently seem to be only a small elitist group of entrepreneurs, gain the political and economic power to become strong global lobbyists who could impose their will on governments. The threat that the power and wealth that these mining companies could pose should not be underestimated in order to avoid situations where notions of public and social goods will be replaced by corporate profits. The power and wealth embedded in celestial bodies could drive the space industry away from potentially beneficial scientific collaborations with government scientists and commercial partnerships, and without providing an offsetting benefit to the public, as soon as space resources start being harvested. The private space industry should abide by current domestic and international laws to ensure that any space company that receives federal aid (e.g., federal-owned research and knowledge; governmental loans) or becomes a party to a cooperative research agreement or a federally-owned partnership or contract is obliged to provide its product to the public on reasonable terms after obtaining a reasonable rate of return in order to protect the taxpayer's interests from exorbitant product pricing. Furthermore, it is well-known that the lobbying powers of corporate America have dramatically grown since the 1970s, and there is no reason to believe that this emerging industry will be any different. Just as the pharmaceutical companies and their lobbyists have been accused of using nearly-unlimited funds to buy preferential policies from the U.S. Congress, the political and economic powers of private space companies could become globally unbridled and gain influence on the political and economic world—unless it is regulated at the international level at the time that the space industry is forming. Without adopting mechanisms to secure a reasonable sharing rule and minimal returns from profits generated by the exploitation and exhaustion of space resources, there will be fiscal and political repercussions. Taxpayers may be forced to pay twice for space products and resources, first as taxpayers to support and fund space research and exploration, and then as consumers padding the profits earned by the space mining industry. Royalty payments could resolve this by serving as a reasonable sharing tool. However, in order to prevent the ESEs from rolling back the royalty payments onto the consumers, a reasonable pricing mechanism should also be sought and regulated.[529]

---

529. *Id.*, at 187; *see also* Emel Jody and Matthew T. Huber, *A Risky Business: Mining, Rent and the Neoliberalization of "Risk,"* 39.3 Geoforum 1393-1407, at 1393-94 and 1399 (2008). In this article the history of mineral political economies during the 1990s, particularly in sub-Saharan Africa, is described stating that "International institutions used the trope to compel landowner states to offer highly desirable terms to mining companies looking for production sites in a purportedly highly competitive global investment environment. Risks borne by landowners – in most cases, nation-states – were of less concern and tended not to show up in dialogue or discourse on distribution issues. Thus, financial risks, including political risk, commercial risk, and the special geological risks of mining, clearly overwhelmed the environmental, political, social and economic risks assumed by the landowners (including local communities)." *See also* Le Billon Philippe, *Angola's Political Economy of War: The Role of Oil and Diamonds, 1975–2000*, 100.398 African Affairs 55-80 (Jan 2001); Eric Pianin, *Sanders Charges That Big Pharma "Owns the United States Congress,"* The Fiscal Times (Feb. 8, 2017); Ryan Grim and Aida Chavez, *How the Senate Paved the Way for Coronavirus Profiteering, and How Congress Could Undo It*, The Intercept (Mar. 2, 2020). Also *see*, in general, Naomi Klein, *This Changes*

Recently, countries around the world have begun taking initial steps to preserve the precious resources embedded in the high seas. The ISA, as the international body that governs DSM, agreed, during its annual meeting in August of 2017, to finalize the regulations that would govern commercial deep-sea mining in the international area of seabeds by 2020. By meeting this target, large-scale commercial mining of the deep seabeds can begin in international waters within a few years, assuming that market conditions are favorable.[530]

The ISA is taking the significant step of moving from simply handling bids for mineral exploration and licenses to considering how to license the first real mining operations, and how to share the proceeds in a way that will ensure the development of a sustainable fiscal regime for the DSM industry. Similarly, in the case of space, the chosen proceeds-share mechanism needs to ensure not only that the benefits from space mining go beyond the companies that were engaged in the mining, but also that non-spacefaring countries gain a share of the proceeds and are financially compensated for the loss of the world's common resources—finite resources for all of mankind. However, at the same time, this mechanism also needs to foster commercially viable operations and incentivize the private sector companies who are risking high investments on capital in this industry.[531]

Arguments that have been made about whether the U.S. should ratify UNCLOS and join the international "profit-sharing" mechanism (either through the international "tax" regime or via an international royalty regime) could also be made about the exploitation of minerals in outer space. In light of all of the above, a distribution mechanism through the most administratively efficient and simple form of value or volume-based royalties could be an easy, just, and effective international route for developing a sustainable tax regime that can support the development of the space mining sector.

F. CONCLUSION

Given the extraterritorial and unique nature of space resources as "the province of all mankind" and the uncertainty surrounding the space mining industry, and in light of the associated risks within this industry and the difficulties in assessing the quantity and quality of the minerals in space, among different revenue allocation methods including bonus bids, annual rentals, and royalties, the latter method is the best way of allowing for rents from space minerals to be paid, and for the global community to earn a return on its resources. This royalty policy should be adopted in a manner that simultaneously reduces the risk of either overpayment, which would stall the development of the private space industry, or underpayment, which would be followed by

Everything: Capitalism vs. the Climate (Simon and Schuster Paperbacks 2014); Shane Gunster, *This Changes Everything: Capitalism vs the Climate*, 11.1 ENVIRONMENTAL COMMUNICATION 136-38 (2017).

530. *See DSCC Calls on International Seabed Authority to Be More Transparent as the Race to Explore the Deep Sea Accelerates*, DEEP SEA CONSERVATION COAL. (Aug. 18, 2017).

531. David Shukman, *Deep Sea Mining "Gold Rush" Moves Closer*, SCIENCE & ENVIRONMENT, BBC NEWS (May 18, 2013).

adverse international repercussions. This method of revenue division is not a tax that is imposed in order to finance the cost of governments for the common welfare and is not a return to a factor of production in exchange for specific services provided.[532] Therefore, this policy should also not be imposed on net profits, as it would then be similar to an income tax, where a type of international entity has a power as a sovereign entity to tax. But, in practice, it is as a factor payment, where mankind has the right to earn a return on the commons' minerals. This royalty regime will help secure a just, equitable and efficient division of revenues derived from the utilization of the world's commons and ensures that the mining industry will not exceed the socially desirable amount of extracted resources, since any greater economic surplus returns from these resources will not only be subject to this royalty regime, but even at higher rates. To make it a neutral system and easy to be administered, a volume, instead of value, basis should be recommended. At the international level, it can be harder to implement and administer *ad valorem* royalties that are based on value. These can be subject to dispute, suspicions, and criticism as being manipulated, since value tends to fluctuate not only globally but also throughout the different production stages. For example, the value of minerals can be different at the extraction or quarrying stage than at the smelting or refining stage and can change at various points when a valuable output can be created. A mechanism which tracks these changes in value would be costly and arguably more than a simple type of unit royalty. Therefore, although the unit-based royalty is similar to a fixed interest payment on capitals, regardless of the value of the capital loaned, as it is based merely on one factor—the output—it avoids complexities associated with determining the value, costs, or even profits.[533] However, in order to incentivize the development of a sustainable industry in space, this mechanism should also provide flexibility by allowing it to be updated as the space industry evolves from a start-up phase, where there is uncertainty regarding the technological and financial risks involved with space mining, to a more steady phase of mining operations, when best practices, business and scientific knowledge, and a range of values and pricings for space resources have been developed and have become accessible. This additional flexibility should be fleshed out by allowing the royalty system to adapt a "two-phase" mechanism that supports a transfer from a unit-based royalty to a value-based one in accordance with efficiency and just considerations under the simplest and fairest system. In addition, as the industry matures, the royalty system rates could be adjusted according to a pre-consented measure of profitability (such as a graduated scale of rates based on the level of profits, or on cumulative annual production, or even on cumulative annual sales). Implementation of such an option, which could be formed as a "two-or even multiple-tier" tax rate, would serve, in the long run, as an incentive tool for the growth of the space industry by securing a progressive tax system that balances the social optimum yield that governments could gain with the private costs that companies would be willing to bear.[534]

532. Salvatore Lazzari, *The Federal Royalty and Tax Treatment of the Hardrock Mineral Industry: An Economic Analysis*, CRS Report for Congress (Jun. 13, 2008).
533. *Id.*
534. *See*, in general, Industry Position Paper, ISA Royalty Regime, *supra* note 483, at 5, 11 and 12.

Moreover, the recommended tax basis for imposing the royalties should be based on gross revenues, before deducting all costs of development, and not on a net basis. When adopting a net basis, actual costs can be exploited by firms (which will have more incentives to increase costs) and any attempt to reach a global consensus on best practice costs for this industry can be too complicated and unreasonable, which will merely hinder the space mining industry, especially at such an early stage. In addition, as typically happens when the tax basis is based on net revenues, the tax rate is set at a higher rate. Although many tax authorities are encouraged to adopt taxes based on net revenues for the goal of avoiding various efficiency effects, the tax rate is typically set very high since the tax base after deducting all costs of development approximates economic rents. These high rates may sharply reduce the payoff to entrepreneurial efforts designed to control the overall efficiency of the use of resources.[535] In the case of space mining, high royalty rates may disincentivize the development of the emerging space industry, as these could result in inefficient exploitation and decrease in production, and are likely to be susceptible to global political pressures to provide royalty relief for the industry. These relief measures would likely be granted on account of the valuable resources of the international community and, thus, should be avoided.

535. Heaps, *supra* note at 34, at 424-25.

CHAPTER 5

Conclusion

Access to extraterritorial resources, both in deep space and the seabeds, has driven an enormous amount of commercial interest and opened up a new horizon for the extractive industries.[536] Due to the "common" and stateless nature of the "fruits" of these industries, where there are high expectations for generating significant economic benefits and profits, the development of these emerging industries greatly depends on the cooperation and consent between states on how to regulate and mitigate potential concerns and pressures over what legal framework should be adopted to protect the interests and rights of the extraction corporations and their respective countries (also known as "host countries," or in the context of DSM "sponsoring states" and "launching states" in the context of space). This global cooperation should be built at an early stage, before the harvest of the world's shared commons starts, in order to secure a "rule of right" rather than a "rule of might" for the sake of a promising future for the new space economy.[537] Without establishing a global consensus around "the rule of right" at the beginning of the emerging extractive industries that could be backed by powers of might when needed, the future of the new space economy would always be at risk.

536. Hannah Lily et al., *Deep Sea Mining: Regulating an Emerging Industry* (Jul. 25, 2017); *see also* Sarah Scoles, *Luxembourg's Bid to Become the Silicon Valley of Space Mining*, SCIENCE WIRED (Oct. 1, 2017).
537. The distinction between "the rule of right" and "the rule of might" has been initially mentioned in 1924 in Sun Yat-sen's speech on pan-Asianism, who is known as the Father of Modern China. Sun Yat-sen asserted in his speech that "European civilization is nothing but the rule of Might. The rule of might has always been looked down upon by the Orient. There is another kind of civilization superior to the rule of Might. The fundamental characteristics of this civilization are benevolence, justice and morality: This civilization makes people respect, not fear, it." *See* Sun Yat-sen, CHINA AND JAPAN: NATURAL FRIENDS, UNNATURAL ENEMIES (China United Press 1941) currently in the Library of Congress in Washington, D.C., USA. Nevertheless, once a new civilization is developed in space this distinction might take other directions and venues as "the rule of might" may become associated with other sides, not necessarily with the European or the West Worlds.

The vast are the opportunities embedded in the DSM, the vaster are the opportunities that could be found in space mining, and the vastest are the opportunities for making profits that the mankind could find in the latter realm. As technological and economic constraints for participating in the space mining industry will be surmounted globally, this mining industry is likely to expand, and the different policy choices made by each state on how to license, regulate, and tax space mining endeavors might eventually lead to the "flag of convenience" and "forum and treaty shopping" phenomena. This will largely occur as a result of the fact that the ESEs will seek the tax and regulatory regimes that are the most beneficial to them and that will allow them the most leeway to minimize taxes and other costs, which, in turn, will harm local economies.[538]

In the case of space mining, the severity of these phenomena might be exacerbated as the legal and economic nexus to Earth becomes less robust. For example, when water mined from asteroids is used for refueling satellites during routine service by a company incorporated and headquartered in a space station colony, which has legal entitlement as a sovereign territory, the profit-sharing between this potentially-rich company and any jurisdictions on Earth would likely be deemed dubious and questionable (even given the TCJA regime with the BEAT and GILTI taxes that potentially could partially secure tax revenues to the U.S.). This scenario, composed of two different commercial activities, e.g., space mining and rendering services, both of which do not necessarily need to be conducted by the same entity, illustrates how the stateless nature of space income and potential double—or even total—nontaxation results could become paramountly relevant in commercial space activities. According to my analysis, only the mining portion should be taxed under an international royalty tax mechanism as the best choice among other equally precarious ones. The severity of this situation might even become further amplified when considering the immense profits and endless funds that will be in the hands of the private space mining industry and could end up being entirely untaxed. All of this, in spite of the fact that these extractions are from resources that belong to everyone and are possible in large part due to costly R&D done on Earth, primarily are made for government space programs bankrolled by taxpayers.

In order to avoid harmful tax competitions or any other detrimental safety or license regulatory regimes derived by competitions between jurisdictions (e.g., by applying low standards of employment, insurance and operating conditions, or preventing a complete erosion of the tax base, as illustrated in the case above), it is better to resolve the legal and fiscal commercial frameworks of the space industry at the international level. The resolution should be set in a way that will ensure states' minimum equitable profit-sharing for using and exhausting the world's "common" resources.

Establishing an "International Mining Royalty" regime in space to split profits globally will provide a cooperative and collaborative environment for the space industry without undermining the sovereignty of states to apply either their own tax

538. Herzfeld, *New Analysis, supra* note 470.

systems or their own regulatory and legal frameworks. Additionally, this will not undermine any state's interests in becoming an attractive investment location "for the sake of some supposedly higher or nobler cause."[539] Of course, this needs to be done according to agreed-upon proportionalities between states, such as a scale based on GDP, and after allowing for allotting a fixed percentage of the royalties for financing the potential costs of negative externalities associated with space activities, such as removing debris, as recorded by an international body (e.g., the U.N. or the IMF[540]). Furthermore, in the case of space, this regime would not slow any distributive justice (in fact, it could be the opposite) or add costs (which could, in fact, be the opposite, mainly since space resources aimed prominently to be consumed in space and not on Earth, thus, may not impact similar products consumed on Earth, but rather offer a healthy competition for space resources in space and even on Earth), including any political participation costs (but it would more likely include rewards, mainly to the developing countries), as arguably can happen where multilateral cooperation efforts and pressures may lead to distortion of economic efficiencies and inequality by negating tax competition in the global economy, and, thereby, promoting power imbalances among countries in favor of the countries which enjoy stronger economic and political powers.[541]

Since the success of a regulatory regime lies in its ability to induce compliance, this regime would provide the private space sector with its most important need, which is the required legal and fiscal stability and certainty to decide how to invest and restructure its domestic, global and universal mining operations. It would also ensure, for the sake of private investors, an international legal framework for an indisputable and free cross-border trade of space resources and products, which might otherwise be banned under an international code of conduct for commercial space activities that define the rules of the road for global trade in space resources for promoting and supporting a sustainable space economy, both in Space and on Earth. An effective regulatory regime, therefore, should both incentivize compliance based on greater

539. *Id.*; *see also* Hatch Statement at Finance Hearing on OECD BEPS Reports Senate Committee on Finance (Statement of U.S. Senator Orrin Hatch, Chairman, Hatch Statement at Finance Hearing on OECD BEPS Reports). On Dec., 1, 2015, during the opening statement at an hearing on OECD base erosion and profit-shifting project, the Senate Finance Committee Chair Orrin G. Hatch, R-Utah said that "while international efforts to align tax systems are worth exploring, we [the U.S.] shouldn't be negotiating agreements that undermine our [its] own interests for the sake of some supposedly higher or nobler cause. The interests of the United States—[its] our own economy, [its] our own workers, and [its] our own job creators—should be [the U.S.] our sole focus … [and] how various policies and proposals will or will not serve [the U.S.'s] our nation's interests and advance these important goals."

540. Note that the International Monetary Fund has a strong record in the field of management of natural resource wealth and taxation of natural resources and established a multi-donor topical trust fund (TTF) to help countries in overcoming the resource curse and strengthen management of their natural resource wealth. *See* International Monetary Fund, Managing Natural Resource Wealth (MNRW-TTF), Topical Trust Fund, Program Document, (2010), pp. iii and 19; Carla Grasso, *IMF Fund Helping Countries Manage Their Natural Resources Receives US$7.1 Million from Switzerland*, IMF (Sept. 13, 2016); IMF, *Fiscal Transparency Initiative: Integration of Natural Resource Management Issues* (January 2019).

541. Herzfeld, *New Analysis, supra* note 470.

public-private cooperation and global harmonization and set sanctions against non-compliance, through trade sanctions or even bans on knowledge exchange with noncompliant companies that would tend to undermine the viability of any participant in the space industry.

In fact, promoting and adapting the royalty regime would help in settling potential tensions and concerns created by the fragile nature of the world's common resources and their associated ownership rights. This regime would be consistent with international obligations, which govern both the ocean and space arenas, and the notions embedded within it, such as "the common heritage of mankind" (in the case of the oceans)[542] and "the province of all mankind" (in the case of space).[543]

Given the "gold rush effect" that accelerates the pace of space exploration, especially when rights can be acquired on "first-come first-served" basis, the taxation of the revenues generated by the mining industry under an international royalty mechanism will better correlate with notions of mankind's treasures that are enshrined under the international space law regime in a way that will lure the development of the space mining industry and will provide a stable legal framework under any chosen optimal resource management regime.

Royalties at a low rate on a gross basis, which are also easier to administer, will minimize the effect of tax on the efficiency of space resource production/development and on the pace of resource use and exploration relative to some competitive norms. These gross royalties should be based on gross volume/output, unlike royalties based on value, in order to not discriminate against high-cost resource deposits. By continuing to be easy to administer, these types of royalties will secure an attractive regime for the emerging space mining industry, particularly in its nascent stage, and at the same time help control and achieve optimal production levels of mining operations, either of low-quality grades or high-cost resources.

This royalty regime, when accompanied with a relief period—such as the royalty mechanism articulated under UNCLOS—ensures a sustainable industry along with a globally fair and efficient distribution mechanism of the proceeds from mining the world's shared resources, as is appropriate when the world's "common" resources are being exhausted and when dealing with an international jurisdiction over economic resources. A royalty mechanism based on the simplest royalty type, which is floored at a minimum percentage and capped at a maximum percentage, and which only applies after a relief period of a fixed number of years of extraction, could help foster and support the development of the private commercial space mining industry.

This mechanism could also help shape a stable and sustainable tax system for any jurisdiction on Earth or beyond that is interested in joining the space race, and could achieve economic efficiency despite the difficulties of calculating optimal tax revenues for the emerging space industry, especially since the tax base is based, to a large extent,

542. UNCLOS, *supra* note 5, under its Preamble. Part XI of the Ocean. UNCLOS also sets the concept of the "common heritage of mankind" to govern the exploitation of minerals on the deep seabed of the ocean. *See* Part XI, Arts. 136 and 137 of the UNCLOS.
543. Outer Space Treaty, *supra* note 17. Under Art. I of the Outer Space Treaty it is stated that *"[t]he exploration and use of outer space ... shall be the province of all mankind."*

on economic theory, untested market conditions (mainly since the economic incentives to develop space mining depend largely on the evolution of a consumer's market in space), and numerous technical considerations, e.g., space research and other technological capabilities, all affecting the economic feasibility of the space industry as well as its potential after-tax profits.

Furthermore, in the case of space, the international royalty mechanism might also best align with the collaborative and multinational cooperative environment typically found in today's second space race era, which is reflected, for example, through the co-foundation of the ISS and the continued endeavors to enhance integrated science research on it among fifteen nations for the advancement of STEM developments.[544]

This space race is quite different from the first, which was merely a bilateral race between the U.S. and the former Soviet Union, in which these countries competed on military and spacefaring capabilities. In today's second space era, more nations (roughly seventy-five, included among them Australia, Canada, China, France, Germany, India, Italy, Israel, Japan) and government-sponsored space exploration players are collaborating as they all share the human desire to render the impossible possible for both science and commercial exploration. Furthermore, today's competitive space race is mainly found within the private sector, between companies, such as SpaceX and Blue Origin that are competing with Boeing to send the first crewed rocket to Mars.[545]

Whereas space exploration relies heavily upon, and is driven by, a cooperative and collaborative environment, the adoption of the International Space Mining Royalty regime would correlate with the new space landscape and spirit. This regime can form a rule for share that will benefit governments, the private sector and the entirety of mankind. The trade-off between the collection of royalties and the costs of transactions, as well as exchange and wealth distribution pressures, will ensure that the most efficient management regime can be established alongside a stable and attractive investment environment for the sake of future exploration and exploitation of the world's commons without risking the high investments that the long journey into our future requires. In light of the high financial prospects of mankind's treasures in outer space, the adoption of this regime is a small price that must be paid by the private space industry for a greater evolution of the space economy and the entirety of humanity.

---

544. Christian Davenport, *The Trump Administration Wants to Turn the International Space Station into a Commercially Run Venture, NASA Document Shows*, WASH. POST (Feb. 11, 2018).
545. Eva Botkin-Kowacki et al., *Racing to Space, Together*, THE CHRISTIAN SCIENCE MONITOR (Jan. 29, 2018). *See also* Doug Mohney, *SpaceX and Blue Origin Talk Seriously Going to Mars*, TECH ZONE 360 (Sept. 29, 2016); Michael Sheetz, *How Elon Musk's Rocket Company SpaceX Beat Boeing to Become a $28 Billion Aerospace Juggernaut*, CNBC (May 22, 2018); Jackie Wattles, *Boeing Will Redo Bungled Test Flight of Its Starliner Spacecraft*, CNN BUSINESS (Apr. 6, 2020); Stuart Clark, *Nasa Picks Bezos's Blue Origin and Musk's SpaceX to Build New Lunar Landers*, THE GUARDIAN (Apr. 30, 2020); Kenneth Chang, *How NASA's Astronauts Became SpaceX's Customers*, The N.Y. TIMES (May 26, 2020); Srishti Deoras, *SpaceX Vs Blue Origin: Who Wins The Space Race*, AIM (Jul. 4, 2020).

Index

D

E

F

G

H

I

L

M

N

O

SERIES ON INTERNATIONAL TAXATION

1. Alberto Xavier, *The Taxation of Foreign Investment in Brazil*, 1980 (ISBN 90-200-0582-0).
2. Hugh J. Ault & Albert J. Rädler, *The German Corporation Tax Law with 1980 Amendments*, 1981 (ISBN 90-200-0642-8).
3. Paul R. McDaniel & Hugh J. Ault, *Introduction to United States International Taxation*, 1981 (ISBN 90-6544-004-6).
4. Albert J. Rädler, *German Transfer Pricing/Prix de Transfer en Allemagne*, 1984 (ISBN 90-6544-143-3).
5. Paul R. McDaniel & Stanley S. Surrey, *International Aspects of Tax Expenditures:* A *Comparative Study*, 1985 (ISBN 90-654-4163-8).
6. Kees van Raad, *Nondiscrimination in International Tax Law*, 1986 (ISBN 90-6544-266-9).
7. Sijbren Cnossen (ed.), *Tax Coordination in the European Community*, 1987 (ISBN 90-6544-272-3).
8. Ben Terra, *Sales Taxation. The Case of Value Added Tax in the European Community*, 1989 (ISBN 90-6544-381-9).
9. Rutsel S.J. Martha, *The Jurisdiction to Tax in International Law: Theory and Practice of Legislative Fiscal Jurisdiction*, 1989 (ISBN 90-654-4416-5).
10. Paul R. McDaniel & Hugh J. Ault, *Introduction to United States International Taxation* (3rd revised edition), 1989 (ISBN 90-6544-423-8).
11. Manuel Pires, *International Juridicial Double Taxation of Income*, 1989 (ISBN 90-6544-426-2).
12. A.H.M. Daniels, *Issues in International Partnership Taxation*, 1991 (ISBN 90-654-4577-3).
13. Arvid A. Skaar, *Permanent Establishment: Erosion of a Tax Treaty Principle*, 1992 (ISBN 90-6544-594-3).
14. Cyrille David & Geerten M.M. Michielse (eds), *Tax Treatment of Financial Instruments*, 1996 (ISBN 90-654-4666-4).
15. Herbert H. Alpert & Kees van Raad (eds), *Essays on International Taxation*, 1993 (ISBN 90-654-4781-4).
16. Wolfgang Gassner, Michael Lang & Eduard Lechner (eds), *Tax Treaties and EC Law*, 1997 (ISBN 90-411-0680-4).
17. Glória Teixeira, *Taxing Corporate Profits in the EU*, 1997 (ISBN 90-411-0703-7).
18. Michael Lang et al. (eds), *Multilateral Tax Treaties*, 1998 (ISBN 90-411-0704-5).
19. Stef van Weeghel, *The Improper Use of Tax Treaties*, 1998 (ISBN 90-411-0737-1).

20. Klaus Vogel (ed.), *Interpretation of Tax Law and Treaties and Transfer Pricing in Japan and Germany*, 1998 (ISBN 90-411-9655-2).
21. Bertil Wiman (ed.), *International Studies in Taxation: Law and Economics; Liber Amicorum Leif Mutén*, 1999 (ISBN 90-411-9692-7).
22. Alfonso J. Martín Jiménez, *Towards Corporate Tax Harmonization in the European Community*, 1999 (ISBN 90-411-9690-0).
23. Ramon J. Jeffery, *The Impact of State Sovereignty on Global Trade and International Taxation*, 1999 (ISBN 90-411-9703-6).
24. A.J. Easson, *Taxation of Foreign Direct Investment*, 1999 (ISBN 90-411-9741-9).
25. Marjaana Helminen, *The Dividend Concept in International Tax Law: Dividend Payments Between Corporate Entities*, 1999 (ISBN 90-411-9765-6).
26. Paul Kirchhof, Moris Lehner, Kees van Raad, Arndt Raupach & Michael-Rodi (eds), *International and Comparative Taxation: Essays in Honour of Klaus Vogel*, 2002 (ISBN 90-411-9841-5).
27. Krister Andersson, Peter Melz & Christer Silfverberg (eds), *Liber Amicorum Sven-Olof Lodin*, 2001 (ISBN 90-411-9850-4).
28. Juan Martín Jovanovich, *Customs Valuation and Transfer Pricing: Is It Possible to Harmonize Customs and Tax Rules?*, Second Edition, 2018 (ISBN 978-90-411-6134-5).
29. Stefano Simontacchi, *Taxation of Capital Gains under the OECD Model Convention: With Special Regard to Immovable Property*, 2007 (ISBN 978-90-411-2549-1).
30. Michael Lang, Josef Schuch, & Claus Staringer (eds), *Tax Treaty Law and EC Law*, 2007 (ISBN 978-90-411-2629-0).
31. Duncan Bentley, *Taxpayers' Rights: Theory Origin and Implementation*, 2007 (ISBN 978-90-411-2650-4).
32. Sergio André Rocha, *Interpretation of Double Taxation Conventions: General Theory and Brazilian Perspective*, 2008 (ISBN 978-90-411-2822-5).
33. Robert F. van Brederode, *Systems of General Sales Taxation: Theory, Policy and Practice*, 2009 (ISBN 978-90-411-2832-4).
34. John G. Head & Richard Krever (eds), *Tax Reform in the 21st Century: A Volume in Memory of Richard Musgrave*, 2009 (ISBN 978-90-411-2829-4).
35. Jens Wittendorff, *Transfer Pricing and the Arm's Length Principle in International Tax Law*, 2010 (ISBN 978-90-411-3270-3).
36. Marjaana Helminen, *The International Tax Law Concept of Dividend*, Second Edition, 2017 (ISBN 978-90-411-8394-1).
37. Robert F. van Brederode (ed.), *Immovable Property under VAT: A Comparative Global Analysis*, 2011 (ISBN 978-90-411-3126-3).
38. Dennis Weber & Stef van Weeghel, *The 2010 OECD Updates: Model Tax Convention & Transfer Pricing Guidelines - A Critical Review*, 2011 (ISBN 978-90-411-3812-5).
39. Yariv Brauner & Martin James McMahon, Jr. (eds), *The Proper Tax Base: Structural Fairness from an International and Comparative Perspective— Essays in Honour of Paul McDaniel*, 2012 (ISBN 978-90-411-3286-4).
40. Robert F. van Brederode (ed.), *Science, Technology and Taxation*, 2012 (ISBN 978-90-411-3125-6).

41. Oskar Henkow, *The VAT/GST Treatment of Public Bodies*, 2013 (ISBN 978-90-411-4663-2).
42. Jean Schaffner, *How Fixed Is a Permanent Establishment?*, 2013 (ISBN 978-90-411-4662-5).
43. Miguel Correia, *Taxation of Corporate Groups*, 2013 (ISBN 978-90-411-4841-4).
44. Veronika Daurer, *Tax Treaties and Developing Countries*, 2014 (ISBN 978-90-411-4982-4).
45. Claire Micheau, *State Aid, Subsidy and Tax Incentives under EU and WTO Law*, 2014 (ISBN 978-90-411-4555-0).
46. Robert F. van Brederode & Richard Krever (eds), *Legal Interpretation of Tax Law*, 2014 (ISBN 978-90-411-4945-9).
47. Radhakishan Rawal, *Taxation of Cross-border Services*, 2014 (ISBN 978-90-411-4947-3).
48. João Dácio Rolim, *Proportionality and Fair Taxation*, 2014 (ISBN 978-90-411-5838-3).
49. Paulo Rosenblatt, *General Anti-avoidance Rules for Major Developing Countries*, 2015 (ISBN 978-90-411-5839-0).
50. Gaspar Lopes Dias V.S., *Tax Arbitrage through Cross-Border Financial Engineering*, 2015 (ISBN 978-90-411-5875-8).
51. Geerten M.M. Michielse & Victor Thuronyi (eds), *Tax Design Issues Worldwide*, 2015 (ISBN 978-90-411-5610-5).
52. Oktavia Weidmann, *Taxation of Derivatives*, 2015 (ISBN 978-90-411-5977-9).
53. Chris Evans, Richard Krever & Peter Mellor (eds), *Tax Simplification*, 2015 (ISBN 978-90-411-5976-2).
54. Reuven Avi-Yonah & Joel Slemrod (eds), *Taxation and Migration*, 2015 (ISBN 978-90-411-6136-9).
55. Alexander Bosman, *Other Income under Tax Treaties: An Analysis of Article 21 of the OECD Model Convention*, 2015 (ISBN 978-90-411-6610-4).
56. John Abrahamson, *International Taxation of Manufacturing and Distribution*, 2016 (ISBN 978-90-411-6664-7).
57. Frederik Boulogne, *Shortcomings in the EU Merger Directive*, 2016 (ISBN 978-90-411-6713-2).
58. Angelika Meindl-Ringler, *Beneficial Ownership in International Tax Law*, 2016 (ISBN 978-90-411-6833-7).
59. Andreas Waltrich, *Cross-Border Taxation of Permanent Establishments: An International Comparison*, 2016 (ISBN 978-90-411-6832-0).
60. Sergio André Rocha & Allison Christians (eds), *Tax Sovereignty in the BEPS Era*, 2017 (ISBN 978-90-411-6707-1).
61. Peter Antony Wilson, *BRICS and International Tax Law*, 2018 (ISBN 978-90-411-9435-0).
62. Louise Otis, Brigitte Alepin & Blanca Moreno-Dodson (eds), *Winning the Tax Wars: Tax Competition and Cooperation*, 2018 (ISBN 978-90-411-9460-2).
63. Marta Castelon, *International Taxation of Income from Services under Double Taxation Conventions: Development, Practice and Policy*, 2018 (ISBN 978-90-411-9594-4).

64. D.M. Broekhuijsen, *A Multilateral Tax Treaty: Designing an Instrument to Modernise International Tax Law*, 2018 (ISBN 978-90-411-9872-3).
65. John Abrahamson, *International Taxation of Energy Production and Distribution*, 2018 (ISBN 978-90-411-9101-4).
66. Leopoldo Parada, *Double Non-taxation and the Use of Hybrid Entities: An Alternative Approach in the New Era of BEPS*, 2018 (ISBN 978-90-411-9991-1).
67. Richard Snoeij, *International Tax Aspects of Sovereign Wealth Investors: A Source State Perspective*, 2018 (ISBN 978-90-411-9431-2).
68. Aleksandra Bal, *Taxation, Virtual Currency and Blockchain*, 2019 (ISBN 978-94-035-0103-1).
69. Werner Haslehner, Georg Kofler, Katerina Pantazatou & Alexander Rust (eds), *Tax and the Digital Economy: Challenges and Proposals for Reform*, 2019 (ISBN 978-94-035-0361-5).
70. Eva Escribano, *Jurisdiction to Tax Corporate Income Pursuant to the Presumptive Benefit Principle: A Critical Analysis of Structural Paradigms Underlying Corporate Income Taxation and Proposals for Reform*, 2019 (ISBN 978-94-035-0640-1).
71. Jérôme Monsenego & Jan Bjuvberg (eds), *International Taxation in a Changing Landscape: Liber Amicorum in Honour of Bertil Wiman*, 2019 (ISBN 978-90-411-9234-9).
72. Kasper Dziurdz´, *Non-discrimination in Tax Treaty Law and World Trade Law: The Impact of Formal, Substantive and Subjective Approaches*, 2019 (ISBN 978-94-035-0904-4).
73. Félix Daniel Martínez Laguna, *Hybrid Financial Instruments, Double Nontaxation and Linking Rules*, 2019 (ISBN 978-94-035-1074-3).
74. Jan Gooijer, *Tax Treaty Residence of Entities*, 2019 (ISBN 978-94-035-1301-0).
75. John Abrahamson, *International Taxation of Banking*, 2020 (ISBN 978-94-035-1094-1).
76. Richard Krever & François Vaillancourt (eds), *The Allocation of Multinational Business Income: Reassessing the Formulary Apportionment Option*, 2020 (ISBN 978-94-035-0614-2).
77. Ajit Kumar Singh, *Exploring the Nexus Doctrine in International Tax Law*, 2021 (ISBN 978-94-035-3363-6).
78. Galya Savir, *Regulation and Tax in Space*, 2021 (ISBN 978-94-035-3393-3).

www.ingramcontent.com/pod-product-compliance
Lightning Source LLC
Chambersburg PA
CBHW071245230926
51849CB00001B/238
9789403533933